Queen Elizabeth I's Governess

Queen Elizabeth I's Governess

The Real Kat Ashley

ROSEMARY GRIGGS

PEN & SWORD HISTORY

AN IMPRINT OF PEN & SWORD BOOKS LTD.
YORKSHIRE – PHILADELPHIA

First published in Great Britain in 2026 by
PEN AND SWORD HISTORY
An imprint of
Pen & Sword Books Ltd
Yorkshire – Philadelphia

Print ISBN 978 1 03614 237 7
ePUB ISBN 978 1 03614 239 1
ePDF ISBN 978 1 03614 241 4

A CIP catalogue record for this book is available from the British Library.

Typeset in Times New Roman 10.5/13 by
SJmagic DESIGN SERVICES, India.
Printed and bound in the UK by CPI Group (UK) Ltd.

The Publisher's authorised representative in the EU for product safety is Authorised Rep Compliance Ltd., Ground Floor, 71 Lower Baggot Street, Dublin D02 P593, Ireland.
www.arccompliance.com

For a complete list of Pen & Sword titles please contact
PEN & SWORD BOOKS LIMITED
George House, Units 12 & 13, Beevor Street, Off Pontefract Road,
Barnsley, South Yorkshire, S71 1HN, England
E-mail: enquiries@pen-and-sword.co.uk
Website: www.pen-and-sword.co.uk

or

PEN AND SWORD BOOKS
1950 Lawrence Rd, Havertown, PA 19083, USA
E-mail: uspen-and-sword@casematepublishers.com
Website: www.penandswordbooks.com

MIX
Paper | Supporting responsible forestry
FSC www.fsc.org FSC® C013604

Contents

List of Illustrations

Author's Note

I have devoted many years to researching one Devon family – the Champernownes. Many generations of this well-connected family have been fiercely proud of their family history. They have left behind a fascinating cache of records and papers for me to study. As early as 1542, Sir Philip Champernowne engaged in learned discussions with the antiquary John Leland, who recorded their conversations in the notes of his itinerary in the west of England.[1] In the early seventeenth century, Sir Richard Champernowne of Modbury had a heraldic scroll drawn up to support an ultimately unsuccessful claim to adopt the arms of the Blount family.[2] In the eighteenth century when the head of the family, Rawlin Champernowne, left no male heirs to preserve the family name and right to bear arms, they sought King George III's permission for letters patent for 'Grant of Arms and name change' so that Rawlin's nephew, Arthur Harrington, could inherit and continue the family name.

I am especially grateful to the Champernowne scholars of the late nineteenth and early twentieth century who went to great lengths to discover their family history. Their notebooks detailing the sources they found, the letters they exchanged with archivists and historians, together with a compilation of family records produced in 1914 by James Frederick Williams, a Champernowne cousin, have been invaluable.[3] They also recorded the family traditions and stories handed down, to be told and retold over hundreds of years.

In the early 1950s, Miss C.E. Champernowne investigated further and produced a comprehensive typewritten account of the family history from their origins in France to the late eighteenth century.[4] Working without the aid of modern-day search-engines and online catalogues, she corresponded with archivists and historians and studied original documents, often transcribing by hand. Like me, Miss Champernowne paid particular attention to the sixteenth century Champernownes, for that is when the family reached the pinnacle of their achievements on the national stage. Her work, and that of her forebears, has served as a signpost for me, helping me to find many useful sources. I have tracked down and interrogated her source documents in archives and have followed up on many additional 'leads' from my own wider research, using modern day search methods.

This detailed research, together with wide reading about the Tudor and Elizabethan period, underpins my historical fiction novels in the 'Daughters of Devon' series.

When I started planning a novel about Katherine Champernowne, governess to the young Elizabeth I, and later the wife of John Astley, I found that the character emerging from my investigations was not the woman historians and popular culture have usually described. I had uncovered additional evidence from the historical record and a story that differed from the accepted narrative.

Determined to set aside assumptions, I cast my net wider than the usual focus on Elizabeth Tudor, delving into the recorded deeds of family members and associates. I questioned historians' statements about Katherine's character and actions, asking, 'What is the source?' 'How do we know this?' 'Is there evidence to support this statement?' I set aside preconceptions and went back to original documents in my search for the woman known to many people as 'Kat Ashley'. A highlight of my research was visiting Hatfield, where she lived for many years. There I examined original papers in the Cecil collection. Samuel Haynes transcribed them in 1740, but it meant a lot to me to study the documents themselves. Seeing Katherine Astley's signature for the first time was a powerful moment.

Another exciting moment came at Lambeth Palace Archives, where I discovered family trees compiled by someone who knew her, confirming her identity. I also found a largely overlooked record of her burial in a parish register.

Before I could weave a fictional account of her life I knew I must set my research findings on the record and challenge some long-held and oft-repeated ideas about this intriguing woman. This book, my first non-fiction work, is the result. I hope it will encourage an informed debate about a remarkable woman.

In a letter written soon after her marriage to his friend John Astley, the scholar Roger Ascham, addresses Elizabeth's governess as 'Gentle Mrs Astley'. While it was merely a standard form of address in Elizabethan England, that a man of Ascham's standing would write to her in such terms suggested to me another side to the woman so many people know as 'Kat'.

Before going any further, a word about names.

A long-standing suggestion that Elizabeth used the 'pet' name 'Kat' when addressing her faithful servant and confidante has been called into question by recent scholars.[5] Elizabeth wrote her name as 'Kat' in a letter to Edward Seymour, Protector Somerset, in 1549. Historian Elizabeth Norton has suggested that this may have been an abbreviation.[6] Yet this short form, written in Elizabeth's own hand, led to the widely held belief that the young Elizabeth called her governess, later her Lady Mistress, 'Kat' as a sign of affection. Perhaps she did. However, with only the written record to work from, it is difficult to establish such details with certainty. I use the name 'Kate' in this book.

It should come as no surprise that we find different spellings of Kate's married name in the historical record. Early modern spelling was extremely variable, and even within families, the spelling of surnames had not settled. For example, in my research into the Raleigh family, I discovered documents signed in 1559 and 1579 by Walter Raleigh senior and his two sons Carew and Walter, later Sir Walter. These three well-educated men each spelled their name differently on the same document.[7] Sir Walter, a prolific letter writer, continued to use many variants during his lifetime. William Stebbing, an early biographer, claims to have found around seventy variations of Raleigh's name.[8]

In her letter to Edward Seymour in March 1549, Elizabeth spells the name 'Aschiley'.[9] Kate herself also uses that spelling. However, Kate's husband John always uses the form 'Astley', which became the accepted spelling of his surname for future generations. I will adopt John's preferred spelling throughout, except in direct quotations.

Many variations of the Champernowne name also occur in the record. Unless quoting verbatim I will use the modern form, Champernowne, throughout.

There were relatively few given names in circulation in the sixteenth century. There are a lot of Katherines in this narrative. At one point we find three women, all named Katherine Champernowne, all living at the same time. Successive generations also had a tendency to repeat given names. For example, we will also meet three men named George Carew. I have added a clarification where appropriate, and varied spellings to distinguish individuals named Katherine.

Unravelling the tangled web of connections between the Champernownes and other high-profile families is a complex task. I have provided simplified family trees and pen pictures of key individuals in Kate's world, drawn from the documentary evidence I have discovered.

Henry VIII's younger daughter was declared illegitimate in 1536, to be called the Lady Elizabeth. She was reinstated in the succession in 1543, but it is not clear exactly when she began to adopt the title 'Princess' once more. I will refer to her as 'Elizabeth' before her accession, and Elizabeth, 'the queen' or 'Queen Elizabeth' after.

When I quote monetary values, I have employed the latest National Archives Currency Convertor, which provides approximate 2017 equivalents. Equivalent values will have changed, and likely increased, since 2017.

In Tudor times the New Year did not officially begin until Lady Day, 25 March, not on 1 January, which was celebrated and was the start of church year. I have used the Gregorian calendar, under which the number of the year changes at 1 January, when quoting dates.

RG
2026

Acknowledgements

There are many people I would like to thank for their help in bringing my dream project on the life of Katherine Astley to completion.

First and foremost a huge thank you to my husband David. Without his unfailing support I could never have finished this book. He has listened patiently to my sixteenth-century ramblings for years – I've even caught him listening to history podcasts himself recently. David accompanies me to my many speaking events, is my adviser on all things technical – he's a whiz with computers and PA systems – he's my accountant, my chauffeur and he's my lady's maid when I'm dressing in my Elizabethan finery. He's also a brilliant cook and reminds me to eat when I'm lost in their world.

Thanks also to the rest of my long-suffering family and friends. Your encouragement as I embark on a writing career at this rather late stage in my life means a lot to me.

I would especially like to acknowledge all the people at the various archive collections I have visited or consulted, including Hatfield House, Lambeth Bridge Palace Library, The National Archives, South West Heritage Trust (SWHT), Tavistock Subscription Library, The Fitzwilliam Museum, and the Devon Rural Archive. Their assistance has been invaluable in helping me locate and interpret numerous documents and references. Special thanks go to the staff at SWHT who helped me to decipher some tricky texts.

I am enormously grateful to Pen and Sword Books for the opportunity to bring Kate into the light, and for the wonderful cover design. Special thanks go to Amy, who has guided me through the production process, and to Karyn, my editor, for her help in polishing the text. Thanks also to all the Pen and Sword authors who have been generous in offering encouragement and advice as I navigated the writing process. I should also mention the National Trust staff at Seaton Delaval Hall who allowed me to examine some fascinating items in their collection. They also helped arranged access for my photographer, who has captured such a striking image of the portrait of Kate. I am also grateful to Lord Hastings and to all the other people and institutions who have given their permission for me to reproduce pictures, photos and images from their collections.

Introduction

On 17 July 1565, Queen Elizabeth I sat at the bedside of her Chief Gentlewoman of the Privy Chamber. Perhaps they spoke of old times at Hunsdon or Hatfield. Perhaps they prayed together for Kate's recovery. If so, it was to no avail, for Kate Astley died the following day.

Devastated and overwhelmed by the loss of her devoted companion, Elizabeth shut herself away at Richmond Palace. She retreated to the same rooms where, some thirty-eight years later, she would await her own death. Elizabeth would see no one. All state business ceased. She refused to grant audiences for several days, saying she was 'greatly grieved by the death of the lady who brought her up'.

On 23 July, a disgruntled Baron Zwetkovich, envoy to the Holy Roman Emperor Maximilian II, wrote to the emperor:

> Some few days ago a lady of the name of Ashley died here. The Queen visited her before her death, for she it was who had the upbringing of the Queen. Her decease grieved the Queen so much that she did not command me to appear until 22 July.

Diego Guzmán de Silva, the Spanish ambassador, reported on the same day that: 'Her Majesty went to see her the day before, and I am told she is greatly grieved'. He added, in cipher, 'And what a heretic she was.'[1]

Appointed as a waiting gentlewoman to King Henry VIII's younger daughter in 1536, Kate had shown love and kindness to the 3-year-old child, left motherless after Anne Boleyn's downfall. Over the three decades that followed, the two women forged a bond that remained unbreakable, even through enforced separations and perilous times when their lives were under threat. In 1549, when Kate was in the Tower of London accused of high treason, Elizabeth stood up for her. Taking a significant risk, she wrote to Edward Seymour, Duke of Somerset, at that time the most powerful man in England. In an eloquent letter in her beautiful Italianate (Italic) script, she defended her own good name and asked Somerset to treat Kate kindly. She cited St Gregory's words, writing:

> For Saint Gregory sayeth that we are more bound to them that bringeth us up well than to our parents, for our parents do what is natural for them, that is bringeth us into the world, but our bringers up are the cause that make us live well within it.[2]

When Elizabeth came to the throne, one of her first actions was to promote the woman who had been her teacher, mentor, confidante and closest friend. She appointed Kate Chief Gentlewoman of the Privy Chamber, the most prestigious position a non-titled woman could hold at the court of a female monarch. In her new role Kate could control who had access to the queen and she continued to exercise considerable influence until her death.

Yet, we know little about the powerful woman who helped shape young Elizabeth's character. Only one image of Kate survives, the portrait by an unknown artist reproduced on the jacket of this book and at Plate 1 with the kind permission of Lord Hastings. It shows a woman with an honest, open face, homely rather than beautiful. Liquid dark eyes stare steadfastly forward. A hint of a smile hovers on her lips, as though something has amused her. Yet she does not appear unduly frivolous. Dressed in sombre black as befits a woman of Protestant leanings, she wears no jewels. Loose and untied laces of the simple ruffled collar of her shift show beneath her dark gown. Beside her is a painted skull, a memento mori, a symbol often used in sixteenth-century art to signify mortality, vanity and the transient nature of life. The early years of the intriguing woman in the portrait remain shrouded in mystery. Doubts even persist about her identity and parentage. Although her role changed over time, many people know Kate simply as Elizabeth's governess.

The Oxford English Dictionary (OED) defines a governess as 'a woman employed to live in a household and teach children, especially in the past'. That definition calls to mind a character often featured in Victorian novels – someone like Jane Eyre; an impoverished woman forced to support herself through teaching. In the nineteenth century, a governess often occupied a powerless position 'between stairs', neither a servant nor a member of the family. It wasn't until the early eighteenth century that people started calling a woman paid to educate children at home a governess.[3] The role in Tudor royal nurseries held much greater significance.

The term 'governess' comes from the French word '*governesse*', meaning a female protector or tutelary deity. That in turn comes from the use of the title 'tutelary deity' within Ancient Greece and Rome for a guardian, patron or protector for a specific place or individual. The responsibilities assigned to a Tudor royal governess encompassed all of those roles, and more.

Tudor monarchs established a separate household for their children soon after they were born. Headed by a Lady Mistress, and initially functioning as a nursery, these establishments expanded and changed as the child grew to provide the education a young prince or princess needed to equip them for their future role. The Lady Mistress was usually a married woman of high standing and the position carried significant status. A 'governess' served under the Lady Mistress and was responsible for the first steps in the child's education.

Confusingly, sometimes historians use the terms 'Lady Mistress' and 'governess' interchangeably. For example, writing in the nineteenth century, Agnes Strickland refers to Lady Bryan as being appointed as Elizabeth's governess, but called the 'Lady Mistress'. She writes:

> The Lady Margaret Bryan, whose husband, Sir Thomas Bryan, was a kinsman of Queen Anne Boleyn, was preferred to the office of governess in ordinary to Elizabeth, as she had formerly been to the Princess Mary: she was called the lady mistress.[4]

In the household set up to care for young Elizabeth it seems the two functions were fulfilled by different individuals, although there must have been significant overlap in their exact duties. Lady Margaret Bryan was appointed Lady Mistress following Elizabeth's birth in 1533, and had overall responsibility for Anne Boleyn's daughter's care and upbringing as a royal princess.

In 1536, following the Anne's dramatic downfall, Kate Champernowne was one of six gentlewomen appointed to serve Elizabeth, although not specifically to teach her. When Margaret Bryan moved to head Prince Edward's nursery in 1537, Lady Troy took her place in Elizabeth's nursery, and soon after Kate took charge of Elizabeth's education.

So, some time after her first appointment as a serving gentlewoman, the formidably well-educated Kate, on the recommendation of Thomas Cromwell and, with the approval of the king himself, became Elizabeth's governess. She took on responsibilities that went far beyond academic education, also acting as a guardian, protector and mentor. While Lady Troy remained in post for some time, Kate later replaced her as Lady Mistress, again on King Henry's insistence,[5] giving her even wider influence.

The king had entrusted Elizabeth's early education to Kate's hands, and reports suggest she did an excellent job, instilling in the young princess a lifelong love of learning. Most importantly, she won the confidence, love and lasting trust of the little girl whose position after her mother's death was precarious. Elizabeth would later comment that Kate took 'great labour and pain in bringing me up in learning and honesty'.[6]

Despite that, historical fiction and on-screen portrayals often depict 'Kat Ashley' as a rather foolish, gossiping, middle-aged nanny figure. A sort of Tudor Mary Poppins who failed in her duty to protect her young charge from the predatory attentions of an older man, Admiral Thomas Seymour. Yet Elizabeth was a highly intelligent, gifted child who became an astute and determined woman. In later life, she did not suffer fools gladly. As Bea Howell pointed out in 1954,[7] it seems highly unlikely that she would have tolerated or grown so close to the silly, misguided 'Kat' of fiction.

Over many years, historians have mentioned Kate in learned biographies of Queen Elizabeth. Focusing on the 'Thomas Seymour affair' they have concluded Kate lacked judgement. In 1547, not long after Henry VIII died, Thomas Seymour, uncle of the young King Edward VI, married the dowager queen, Catherine Parr. Kate was one of those who accompanied Elizabeth when she went to live with the newly married couple at Chelsea. Elizabeth got on well with her stepmother, who encouraged her in her studies. All was well until her new stepfather began to pay too much attention to the 14-year-old princess. Eventually, Elizabeth was whisked away amid damaging rumours, though how far the gossip actually spread at the time may be open to question.

Catherine Parr died in September 1548 shortly after giving birth to a daughter, and Thomas Seymour hoped to advance his political ambitions by marrying Elizabeth. He had long been jealous of his brother, Edward, the Lord Protector, and was even accused of attempting to kidnap the king. On 17 January 1549, Thomas Seymour was arrested on suspicion plotting to usurp the throne. Elizabeth's possible involvement in his plans came under intense scrutiny. If evidence surfaced that she had consented to marry him without the council's approval, she too could be accused of treason.

On 21 January 1549, Kate was arrested and taken to the Tower of London, along with Elizabeth's cofferer, Thomas Parry. Her description of Seymour's inappropriate behaviour in her 'confession', extracted under extreme duress, has led to suggestions that she failed in her 'duty of care' to the 14-year-old Elizabeth. Taken alongside Parry's recollections of a fireside conversation, Kate's own words have set her in negative light.

Many studies of Elizabeth's early years home in on Kate's personality. Writing in the nineteenth century, against the background of the societal norms of her time, Agnes Strickland praises Lady Bryan, saying: 'Much of the future greatness of this princess may reasonably be attributed to the judicious training of Lady Bryan.'[8] She is somewhat dismissive of Kate, however, writing: 'Elizabeth, through the imprudence of Mrs. Ashley and others in her household, was involved in much trouble on this account.'[9]

Other writers have concluded that Kate had less good sense than her teenage charge. For example, in 1952, Neale writes: 'Kate Ashley, who was married to a kinsman of her mistress, was a well meaning, affectionate, but not very sensible woman.'[10] He goes on to describe her as 'misguided and matchmaking', and when describing her conversation with Thomas Parry says: 'Parry came back to have a heart to heart with Mistress Ashley and to probe Elizabeth's mind, He found the woman a babbler, and the girl a cautious, clever, person, moving with that circumspection her elders ought to have been showing.'

In the 1960s W.K. Jordan describes her as: 'Katherine Ashley, a foolish and romantic woman quite enthralled by Seymour's blandishments.'[11]

In 1976, Dulcie M. Ashdown, writing about appointments following Elizabeth's accession, includes the following paragraph in her book *Ladies in Waiting*:

> There were rich rewards to mete out to those who had proved themselves loyal to her in her trials. First, there was Catherine Ashley, long her governess for all her weak confession of Elizabeth's youthful indiscretions, with Thomas Seymour, had borne patiently the rages and tempests of the Princess's frustrations and, apart, from that one lapse, had never swerved in her devotion.[12]

Faint praise indeed!

In the 1930s Dame Edith Sitwell calls Kate 'a babbling brook' who, she says, like Lady Bryan, had 'much of the nature of Juliet's nurse'.[13]

Shakespeare's nurse is a secondary mother figure for Juliet in *Romeo and Juliet*. A talkative character who constantly makes interjections and interrupts herself, she makes bawdy remarks and brings a hint of comedy into the tragedy of star-crossed lovers. 'Nursie' who attends Queen Elizabeth I in the BBC series *Blackadder* echoes Shakespeare's character, and may reflect a view of Kate.[14] However, the association of Kate and Lady Bryan with Juliet's nurse misunderstands the role of a royal governess. This association may also have influenced opinions that Kate stood 'in place of a mother to Elizabeth'. The relationship was likely rather different from that of a mother and daughter.

Also writing in the 1970s, Alison Plowden reinforced the idea that Kate was a gossip, saying she 'could not resist' passing on gossip about Admiral Seymour. After hearing that Thomas Seymour was a heavy man after his wife's death, Plowden says: 'Mrs Ashley was, of course, all agog.'[15]

In a twenty-first century context, Thomas Seymour's actions seem to fit a pattern we might call 'grooming'. By this assessment, Kate seems even more negligent in failing to put a stop to it. Some authors suggest that she herself had fallen under Seymour's spell, or that, as a somewhat frustrated middle-aged woman, she took some sort of vicarious pleasure from imagining her young charge in a romantic entanglement with the dashing admiral.[16]

We can contrast all of those rather negative assessments with what Edmund Bohun wrote about Kate in 1693: 'Her Tutoress was the Lady Champernowne, a Person of Great Worth, who formed this great Wit (Elizabeth) from Her Infancy and Improved her Native Modesty with Wise Counsel and a Liberal Sage Advice.'[17]

Social attitudes at the time of writing may have shaped assumptions about Kate's character. Nineteenth-century values were as different from those of Kate's time as they are from those of the twentieth and twenty-first centuries. However, negative assessments persist, while the broader context of Kate's situation within the turbulent political climate of her era, and her close ties to other significant figures during dangerous times for the young Elizabeth, are often overlooked. For many writers, the events of those two years overshadow every other aspect of the relationship between these two remarkable women – a relationship that lasted for nearly thirty years.

In her 1953 account of the family history, Miss Champernowne suggested that many writers, including Strickland, Dame Edith and Mumby, had 'not known who Kate was, or in what relationship she stood to those surrounding the Princess, and so have missed interesting points and perhaps given a false impression'.[18]

Over the years, different ideas about Kate's parentage have emerged. The foghorn of the internet, with its profusion of online genealogy sites and social media, continues to share and amplify them, leading to misconceptions. This confusion over her identity has obscured some important relationships.

Lambeth Palace Library holds a remarkable collection of documents known as the Carew Manuscripts.[19] Sir George Carew (1555–1629) collected them during his period in Ireland as President of Munster, intending to write the history of the island from the reign of Henry II to that of Queen Elizabeth. He died before he could complete the project, but his papers, compiled between 1586 and 1595, with a few additions in 1615, remain to offer significant insights for persistent researchers. Ten years old at the time of Kate's death, Sir George, later the first Earl of Totnes, may well have met her, for she was a relative. George's father, also named George, was Kate's uncle.

Within the collection is a substantial bound volume comprising a series of hand-written genealogies of the families of Devon, including Carew's own family, and also of Irish families. Sir George Carew owned this book. From the handwriting, the archive catalogue description places the Astley (or Ashley) family tree among the entries made in Sir George's own hand, or in the hands of secretaries or others known to be closely associated with him. Mid-way down the page is the name of John Astley, Master of the Jewel House. John's first wife's name appears to the left of his. The entry reads clearly: 'Catharina, da. of Sir Philip Champernon in county Devon'.[20]

The Astley family tree among the Carew Manuscripts, drawn up less than fifty years after Kate's death by someone who knew her, provides clear evidence she was the daughter of Sir Philip Champernowne. It dispels any lingering doubts about Kate Astley's parentage. The Champernowne family historians had none. Among the papers held in the Devon Archives at South West Heritage Trust is a notebook which includes a reference taken from *The English Baronetage*, published in 1741 naming Kate as Sir Philip Champernowne's daughter.[21] Miss Champernowne confirmed Kate as Sir Philip's daughter and also as the sister of Joan Champernowne/Denny and of the 'other' Katherine, mother of Sir Walter Raleigh. Several historians have reached the same conclusion in recent years.[22]

Armed with certainty about her parentage we can place Kate within a highly influential circle. Far from being minor gentry confined to rural Devon, her father, brother, sisters, cousins and uncles all served at King Henry VIII's court. Both before and after her appointment to Elizabeth's household, Kate mingled with many of the king's closest friends and advisers, including humanist thinkers and champions of religious reform. Continuing confusion about Kate's true identity has obscured links to key figures in times of shifting political and religious allegiances.

The first part of this book therefore covers Kate's family background. While perhaps not widely recognised outside the West Country, the Champernownes had achieved court positions by the sixteenth century. Their lives intertwined with the fortunes of prominent figures, including the Marquess of Exeter, a cousin of King Henry VIII. Kate's people were close to those at the heart of power.

Placing her in her circle, and examining the evidence from the historical record anew, allows us to reconsider Kate's whole career from her appointment in 1536 until her death on that July day in 1565. Since many assumptions stem from the time of the 'Thomas Seymour affair', it must take up what is perhaps a disproportionately long section in Kate's story.

To fully understand her relationship with Elizabeth, we need to get to know Kate better. To do so, we also need to know more about those closely associated with her, to 'join up the dots' between connected lives. Turning the spotlight away from Elizabeth, it's time to set aside preconceptions and bring the real Kate Astley out from the shadow of her mistress.

Who's Who in Kate's World

The Inner Circle

The Champernownes

***Sir Philip** (1479–1545) Kate's father*

Sir Philip Champernowne; married Katherine Carew before 1503; six daughters and two sons. Squire of the body to Henry VIII in 1524; Sheriff of Devon in 1529; Justice of the Peace, Deputy Warden of the Stannaries, and a major West Country landowner.

***Joan** (Johane or Jane) **'the elder'** Kate's sister*

Joan the elder married Robert Gamage of Coity, in Wales before 1531; two sons and five daughters. May have served as maid of honour to Catherine of Aragon. Joan was grandmother of the heiress Barbara Gamage who married Sir Robert Sydney, later Earl of Leicester.

***Elizabeth** (d.1574) Kate's sister*

Elizabeth married first William Cole of The Slade, Cornwood, Devon; one son, Philip, b.1539. Married second, John Pollard, a high ranking clergyman, Archdeacon of Cornwall and of Barnstable, no children.

***Joan 'the younger'** (c.1513–1553) Kate's sister*

Joan the younger married Sir Anthony Denny in 1538; five sons and four daughters. May have been maid of honour to Catherine of Aragon and Anne Boleyn. Served Anne of Cleves, possibly Katheryn Howard, and definitely Catherine Parr, who shared her interest in learning and religious reform.

***John** (c.1517–1541) Kate's brother*

John served at court and is listed as a squire in 1540. He married Catherine Blount, daughter of Lord Mountjoy, and sister of Gertrude Blount, Marchioness of Exeter. In 1568 their only son, ***Henry of Modbury,*** (1538–1570) led a troop of English soldiers in support of the Huguenots in France. After John's death Catherine married Sir Maurice Berkley.

Katherine 'the younger' *(c.1519–1594) Kate's sister*
Married first Otho (Otes) Gilbert of Compton and Greenway; one, possibly two daughters and three sons who survived childhood – Sir John, Sir Humphrey and Adrian Gilbert. Married second Walter Raleigh of Fardell; one daughter, Margaret, and two sons, Carew and Sir Walter.

Frances *(c.1521 aft.1574) Kate's sister*
Married Roger Budockside,[1] of St Budeaux, Devon. Three sons, seven daughters, but several children died in infancy. Her second daughter, Winnifred, married Sir Thomas Gorges, great uncle of Sir Ferdinando Gorges, who married Winnifred's granddaughter.

Sir Arthur *(1524–1578) Kate's brother*
Sir Arthur married Mary Norreys, widow of his cousin George Carew; five sons and one daughter. Under Elizabeth he became Vice Admiral of the Fleet of the West, and, a staunch Protestant, he supported the Huguenots in France. The first of the family at Dartington Hall in Devon. Arthur's daughter, Elizabeth, married Edward Seymour of Berry Pomeroy, grandson of Protector Seymour.

The Carews
Sir Edmund *(c.1464–1513) Kate's Grandfather*
Soldier and diplomat. Married Katherine Huddesfield (1478/1479–aft.1528); four sons and four daughters.

Katherine Carew *(d. aft.1545) Kate's mother*
Katherine was the eldest the daughter of Sir Edmund Carew, and Katherine Huddesfield (c.1462– aft.1528). May have served Gertrude Blount, Marchioness of Exeter. In his will, Sir Philip recognised Katherine for her 'most obedient duty and gentleness'.

George Carew Priest, *George the elder (1497/1498–1583) Kate's uncle*
Third son of Sir Edmund Carew, and Katherine Huddesfield. Educated at Broadgates Hall, Oxford; Archdeacon of Totnes 1534–1549, Canon of Exeter 1535, Precentor of Exeter 1549 and Archdeacon of Exeter 1556–1569. Dean of the Chapel Royal 1558–1583, and adviser to Elizabeth on religious affairs. Married Anne Harvey, daughter of Sir Nicholas Harvey; two sons, Sir Peter, the younger, (1552–1580) and Sir George, Earl of Totnes, (1555–1629) and two daughters.

Sir Gawen Carew *(c.1503–1585) Kate's Uncle*
Fourth and youngest son of Sir Edmund Carew, and Katherine Huddesfield. Courtier and soldier. Married first Anne Brandon, sister of Charles, Duke of

Suffolk, and widow of Sir John Shilston, (d. bef.1540). Married second Mary Wotton, (*c.*1499–bef.1558) widow of Sir Henry Guildford and third Elizabeth Norwich (*c.*1530–1594) MP for Devon 1542, 1545, 1547 and 1563; Sheriff of Devon 1547; Master of Henchmen 1558–1565; MP for Plympton Erle 1559; Justice of the Peace and Deputy Lieutenant of Cornwall and Devon 1569. No children from any of his three marriages.

Sir George Carew *(c.1502–1545) Kate's Cousin*
Eldest son and heir of Sir William Carew of Mohun's Ottery. Married first Thomasine Pollard (d.1539). Married second, Mary Norreys, daughter of Henry Norreys, one of those executed with Anne Boleyn. No children form either marriage. MP for Devon, Sheriff of Devon 1536/1537. Captain of Ruysbank Castle, Calais, in 1539. Captain of the *Mary Rose* and died when she went down.

Sir Peter Carew *(c.1505/1510–1582) Kate's cousin*
Courtier, soldier and adventurer. Married in 1547 Margaret Talboys, daughter of Sir William Skipwith of Lincolnshire and widow of George Talboys (2nd Baron Talboys of Kyme). No children. Gentleman of the Privy Chamber to King Henry VIII. MP for Tavistock, 1545, Dartmouth 1547 and for Devon 1553–1559. Sheriff of Devon 1547.

Others of the inner circle
Sir Anthony Denny *(1501–1549) Kate's brother-in-law*
The second son of Sir Edmund Denny. Educated St Paul's School and St John's College, Cambridge, a member of 'the Cambridge Set'. Married Joan Champernowne in 1538. Five sons and four daughters. Public servant and administrator. Gentleman of the Privy Chamber from 1539. Groom of the Stool, 1546–1547, trusted adviser of King Henry VIII. Privy Councillor under Edward VI working closely with Edward Seymour.

John Astley *(c.1507–1596) Kate's husband*
John was a younger son of Sir Thomas Astley of Hill Morton and Melton Constable, and distantly related to Elizabeth I, through the Boleyns. Married first Katherine Champernowne (no children), second, Margaret Lenton, alias Grey, illegitimate daughter of Lord Thomas Grey; three sons and three daughters. Gentleman Waiter to Edward VI before joining the household of Elizabeth. Master of the Jewel House, 1558–1559. An honorary member of 'the Cambridge Set'.

The 'Cambridge Set'

***Roger Ascham** (c.1515–1568)*
Yorkshire born scholar educated at St John's College and one of John Cheke's students. Tutor to Elizabeth 1548 and 1550. Latin secretary to Mary I and Elizabeth I. Close friend of John Astley.

***Sir John Cheke** (1514–1557)*
Classical scholar from the Isle of Wight. Educated at St John's College, Cambridge where he became the first Regius Professor of Greek at Cambridge. Married Mary, a poet and courtier, daughter of Richard Hill (formerly Sergeant of the Wine Cellar to Henry VIII). Tutor to Edward VI and Elizabeth. MP and briefly Secretary of State for King Edward VI. His sister Mary married William Cecil.

***Sir Thomas Smith** (1513–1577)*
Classical scholar, parliamentarian and diplomat from Saffron Walden, Essex. Educated at Queen's College, Cambridge. Friend of John Cheke and William Cecil. Served on diplomatic mission to Brussels under Edward VI, knighted 1548. Lost his offices under Mary I, but was prominent under Elizabeth as a Member of Parliament and Privy Councillor, and ambassador to France.

***William Grindal** (d.1548)*
William Grindal is thought to have come from Cumberland as a poor scholar to St John's College and was friend, pupil and protégé of Roger Ascham. He was Elizabeth's tutor, teaching her Latin and Greek, before dying prematurely of the plague in 1548.

***William Cecil, Lord Burghley** (1520–1598)*
Lincolnshire-born William Cecil was educated at King's School Grantham, Stamford School and St John's College, Cambridge, where he was taught by Sir John Cheke, who became his brother-in-law. Cecil was distantly related to both Blanche Parry and Sir Thomas Parry. Cecil managed Elizabeth's estates from 1550, and became her closest adviser, and, in 1558, her Secretary of State. In 1571 he was ennobled as Baron Burghley.

***Matthew Parker** (1504–1575)*
Norwich-born churchman who studied at St Benet's College (now Corpus Christi), Cambridge. Ordained as a priest in 1527. Popular preacher and chaplain to Anne Boleyn. Married Margaret Harlestone in June 1547, (before

clerical marriages were allowed), and had five children. Parker was deprived under Mary I, but became Archbishop of Canterbury in 1559.

Thomas Cranmer *(1489–1556)*
Nottinghamshire-born theologian and leader of the Reformation. Educated Jesus College, Cambridge, ordained by 1520 and Doctor of Divinity in 1525. Archbishop of Canterbury from 1532 until 1555. Married first Joan who died in childbirth. Second, secretly married Margarete Osiander, niece of a prominent German reformer, in Nuremberg in 1532. Played an important role in annulment of Henry VIII's marriage to Anne Boleyn. Under Edward VI he significantly advanced Protestantism, introducing the English Bible and the Book of Common Prayer. Supported Lady Jane Grey, and was convicted of treason, and burnt at the stake in Oxford in 1556.

The Courtenay Connection

Henry Courtenay, Marquess of Exeter *(1498–1538) Kate's father's second cousin*
Eldest son of William Courtenay, Earl of Devon and Katherine Plantagenet, daughter of King Edward IV. Close friend of the young Henry VIII. First wife, Elizabeth Grey, died soon after they married. In 1519, he married Gertrude, daughter of William Blount, Lord Mountjoy, a maid of honour to Catherine of Aragon; two sons, Henry who died young and Edward, (*c.*1527–1556). Created Marquess of Exeter, admitted to the Order of the Garter in 1525. Largest landowner in the west of England. Accused of involvement in a plot and executed in 1539.

Gertrude Blount Marchioness of Exeter *(c.1504–1558)*
Gertrude was the daughter of William Blount, Baron Mountjoy, and his wife Elizabeth Saye. Married Henry Courtenay in 1519. Two sons, Henry who died young and Edward (*c.*1527–1556). Gertrude and her husband were staunchly Catholic and supported Queen Catherine of Aragon. Godmother to Elizabeth I and Edward VI. Imprisoned 1539, released and retired from court. Returned in 1553 and became one of Queen Mary's most trusted ladies. After Mary married Philip of Spain in preference to Edward Courtenay, she retired from court once more and died in1558.

Edward Courtenay *(c. 1527–1556)*
Son of the Marquess and Marchioness of Exeter, Henry and Gertrude Courtenay. Imprisoned in 1539 and remained in the Tower. Released and created Earl of

Devon in 1553. Potential suitor to both Mary and Elizabeth. Implicated in plots, exiled and died in Venice.

Elizabeth's Household

Elizabeth Tudor *(1533–1603)*
Daughter of Henry VIII and Anne Boleyn, Elizabeth was declared illegitimate after her mother's downfall, but reinstated in the succession in 1544. In a perilous position during the reign of her sister Mary. After Mary's death in 1558 she became queen and ruled for forty-five years.

Thomas Parry *(c.1515–1560)*
Welsh-born Thomas Parry had a position under Thomas Cromwell, then joined Elizabeth's household as her cofferer. Married Anne, widow of Sir Adrian Fortescue; two sons and two daughters. Questioned during the Thomas Seymour affair. Knighted on Elizabeth's accession, and Privy Councillor until his death in 1560.

Lady Bryan *(c.1468–1551/1552)*
Lady Bryan, maternal aunt of Anne Boleyn and Katheryn Howard, headed the nurseries of King Henry VIII's children. Born Margaret Bourchier, she married three times, to Sir John Sandys, Sir Thomas Bryan, and David Zouche. 'Lady Mistress' for Mary, possibly for Henry Fitzroy, and for Elizabeth until in 1537 when she moved to care for Edward. With her second husband she had two children who survived to adulthood: Sir Francis Bryan, a prominent courtier, and Elizabeth Bryan who married Nicholas Carew. Through her daughter, Elizabeth, she was the great-grandmother of Elizabeth Throckmorton, wife of Sir Walter Raleigh. Her son, Sir Francis Bryan, was a diplomat, soldier, sailor, and writer, with a reputation as a rake and a libertine.

Lady Troy *(d. c.1557)*
Blanche Milborne, Lady Herbert of Troy married, first to James Whitney, then to Sir William Herbert of Troy Parva, the illegitimate son of William Herbert, Earl of Pembroke; five children from two marriages. Aunt of Blanche Parry. Nominally Elizabeth's Lady Mistress on the birth of Edward, and continued in post for some years before retiring and receiving a pension until she died.

Blanche Parry *(1507/1508–1590)*
Blanche, was born at Newcourt, Bacton, Herefordshire, on the Welsh borders. Unmarried. Lady Troy's niece. Rocked baby Elizabeth in her cradle. Chief Gentlewoman of the Privy Chamber 1565–1590.

***Mary Hill** (c. 1532–1616)*
A poet and courtier, daughter of Richard Hill (formerly Sergeant of the Wine Cellar to Henry VIII). Married first, Sir John Cheke, then, Henry MacWilliam, (d.1586). Gentlewoman to Elizabeth 1540–c.1547.

***Frances Newton, later Baroness Cobham** (aft.1530–1592)*
Daughter of Margaret Poyntz and Sir John Newton, a Somerset gentleman. Frances's grandmother, Elizabeth Huddesfield, and Kate's grandmother, Katherine Huddesfield, were half-sisters. Appointed chamberer before Elizabeth's accession. Married, as his second wife, William Brooke, 10th Baron Cobham (1527–6 March 1597) in February 1560; four sons, three daughters. As Baroness Cobham Frances continued to serve in the Privy Chamber until her death, and became very close to the queen.

***Dorothy Broadbelt** (d.1577)*
Dorothy had joined Elizabeth's household as cofferer by 1543. She married John Abingdon, Clerk of the Kitchen in 1567 and served as a Gentlewoman of the Bedchamber from 1553 until her death.

The Wider Circle

***Thomas Cromwell** (c.1485–1540)*
Statesman and lawyer who rose from humble origins to become chief minister to Henry VIII from 1534 to 1540, when he was beheaded on orders of the king. Driving force of the English Reformation, oversaw the dissolution of the monasteries and strengthened royal government.

The Seymour Brothers

Edward (1500–1552)
The eldest brother of Jane Seymour. Soldier and politician. Created Earl of Hertford, 1537. Lord Protector of the Realm and Governor of the King's Person, 1547–1552. Created Duke of Somerset in 1547. Fell from power and in 1552 was executed for treason.

Thomas (*c.*1508–1549)
A charismatic courtier and soldier. Created Baron Seymour of Sudeley and Lord High Admiral in 1547, a member of Edward VI's Privy Council. Married the king's widow, Catherine Parr, 1547; one daughter, Mary, who died young. His inappropriate attentions to the teenage Elizabeth during

his marriage and designs on marrying her after Catherine Parr's death, together with other suspicious activities led to his arrest and execution in February 1549.

***John Dudley** (1504–1553)*
Son of an executed minister, Dudley rose to prominence as a soldier and statesman, serving as vice admiral and Lord High Admiral from 1537 until 1547. Created Earl of Warwick and later 1st Duke of Northumberland, he effectively ruled England from 1550 until 1553, after Somerset's downfall, Dudley unsuccessfully tried to install Jane Grey, whom he had married to one of his sons, on the English throne, and was executed for treason after Mary's accession.

***Robert Dudley** (1532–1588)*
Statesman and soldier, and Elizabeth's companion and lifelong suitor. Son of John Dudley. Married Amy Robsart, 1550. (Amy died in suspicious circumstances in 1560.) Imprisoned in the Tower, following the failure of his father's attempt to install Jane Grey. Released October 1554. Master of the Horse from 1558 until his death, and Privy Councillor from April 1559. Created Earl of Leicester in 1564. He secretly married the widowed Lettice Knollys in 1578.

In Addition

Kate's life unfolded against the backdrop of the Tudor Court. Born during the later years of Henry VII (1457–1509), King of England between 1585 and 1509, she knew every subsequent Tudor monarch:

Henry VIII (1491–1547)	King of England, 1509–1547.
Edward VI (1537–1553)	King of England, 1547–1553.
Jane Grey (*c*.1536/1537–1554)	Declared Queen of England for nine days in 1553.
Mary I (1516–1558)	Queen of England, 1553–1558.
Elizabeth I (1533–24 March 1603)	Queen of England, 1558–1603.

And all of the wives of Henry VIII:

Catherine of Aragon (1485–1536)	Crowned queen 1509, mother of Mary I, marriage annulled, 1533.
Anne Boleyn (*c*.1501/1507–1536)	Crowned queen 1533, executed 1536.

Jane Seymour (*c*.1508–1537)	Married Henry VIII 1536, mother of Edward VI.
Anne of Cleves (*c*.1515/1516–1557)	Married Henry VIII January 1540, marriage annulled July 1540.
Katheryn Howard (*c*.1523–1542)	Married Henry VIII July 1540, executed February 1542.
Catherine Parr (*c*.1512–1548)	Married Henry VIII July 1543; married Thomas Seymour by April/May 1547.

And:

King Philip II of Spain (1527–1598)	Queen Mary's consort from July 1554 until 1558.

Family Trees

The Courtenay Connection

Sir Hugh Courtenay, 2nd or 10th Earl of Devon
(died 1377)

Both Philip Courtenay and Edward Courtenay descend from Sir Hugh through several generations.

Sir Philip Courtenay
(of Molland)

Margaret *m.* Sir John Champernowne

Sir Philip Champernowne

Elizabeth *m.* Edward Courtenay *

William Courtenay
m
Katherine of York
(daughter of Edward IV)

Edward
(died young)

Henry
Marquess of Exeter
(1st cousin of Henry VIII)
(died 1539)
m.
Gertrude Blount
Marchioness of Exeter

Margaret
m.
Henry Somerset

Henry
(died young)

Edward, Earl of Devon, died 1556
(possible suitor to both Mary I and Elizabeth I)

Notes *The senior line of the Courtenay family, previously Earls of Devon, was extinguished during the Wars of the Roses. Henry VII created Edward Courtenay Earl of Devon in 1485.

The Champernownes

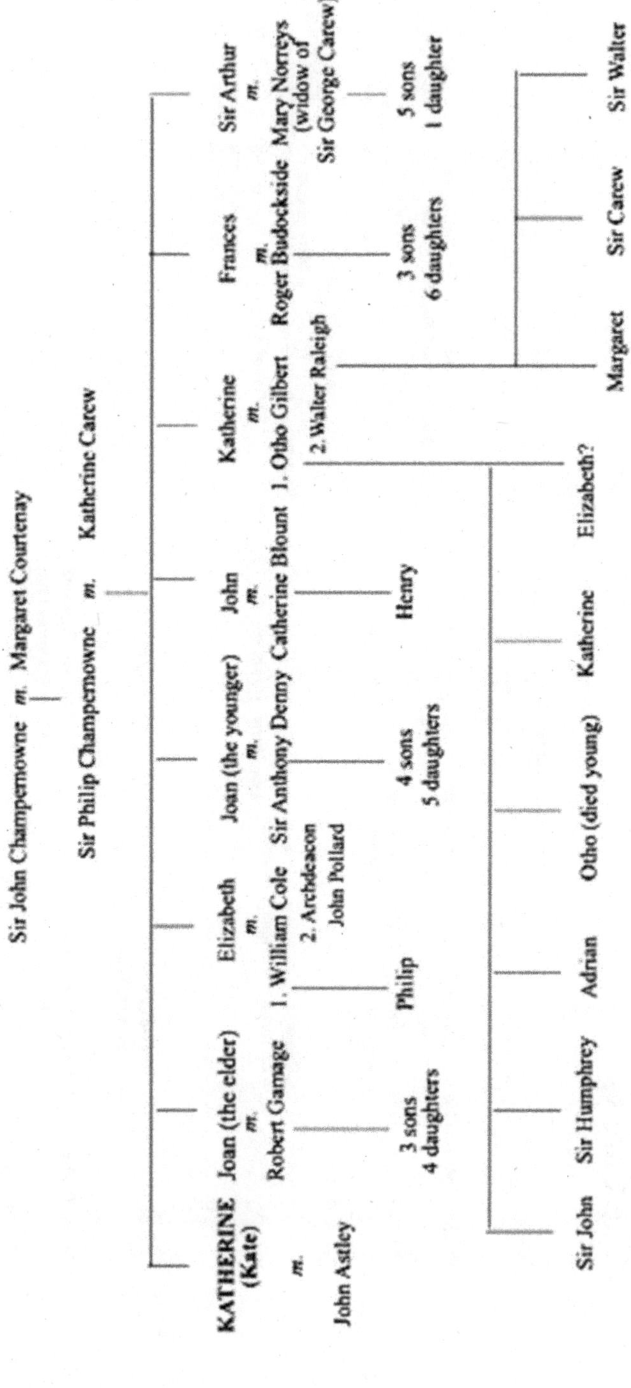

The Carews

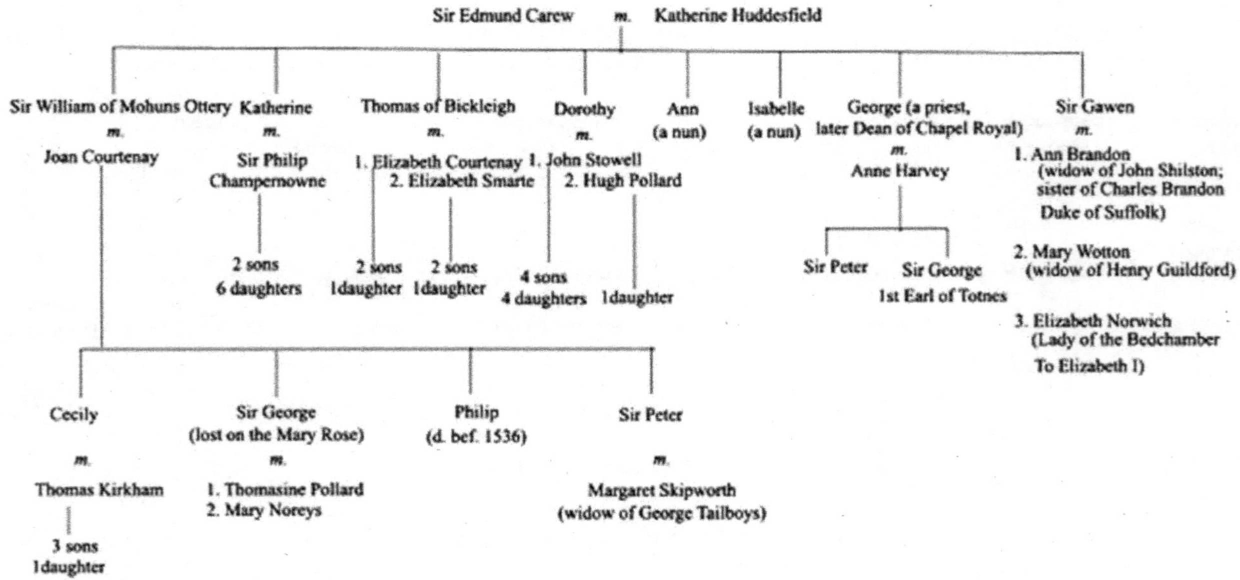
Sir Edmund Carew m. Katherine Huddesfield
Sir William of Mohuns Ottery m. Joan Courtenay
Katherine m. Sir Philip Champernowne
2 sons 6 daughters
Thomas of Bickleigh m. 1. Elizabeth Courtenay 2. Elizabeth Smarte
2 sons 1daughter
2 sons 1daughter
Dorothy m. 1. John Stowell 2. Hugh Pollard
4 sons 4 daughters
1daughter
Ann (a nun)
Isabelle (a nun)
George (a priest, later Dean of Chapel Royal) m. Anne Harvey
Sir Peter
Sir George 1st Earl of Totnes
Sir Gawen m.
1. Ann Brandon (widow of John Shilston; sister of Charles Brandon Duke of Suffolk)
2. Mary Wotton (widow of Henry Guildford)
3. Elizabeth Norwich (Lady of the Bedchamber To Elizabeth I)
Cecily m. Thomas Kirkham
3 sons 1daughter
Sir George (lost on the Mary Rose) m. 1. Thomasine Pollard 2. Mary Noreys
Philip (d. bef. 1536)
Sir Peter m. Margaret Skipworth (widow of George Tailboys)

PART I

BACKGROUND

Chapter 1

The Champernownes

Courtenay and Carew Connections

By the time Sir John Champernowne, Kate's grandfather, died in 1503, her family was among the most influential in western England. They had become major landholders, and their relationship by marriage to the powerful Courtenays provided access to the royal court. Despite this, the name is not widely recognised outside of the west of England.

Originally from Normandy, the Champernownes first settled in Devon in the twelfth century during the reign of King Henry II. Over many generations, they built their wealth through successive marriages, forming alliances with powerful families in Devon and beyond. When Kate was born in the early years of the sixteenth century, the family had built connections to almost all of Devon and Cornwall's foremost families. Their Devon holdings were extensive, from Chulmleigh in the north to Dartmouth in the south. In addition, their influence had spread beyond the West Country, into Wiltshire, Leicestershire and Oxfordshire. After the dissolution, they added the priories of Polsloe, St Germains, Plympton and part of Totnes Priory to their expanding property portfolio. They held many acres of fertile farmland ideal for sheep farming, extensive moorland with centuries-old tin mines, and a warehouse in Plymouth to support their shipping operations.

Kate's ancestors can be traced back to Normandy, long before Duke William brought his army to defeat Harold Godwinson and seize the English crown. In the year 902, the 'knight's tenure of the Manor of Cambernon' belonged to the family of Jourdain de Cambernon (Jourdain de Campo Arnulphi, or Jordon I) and their relations, the family of d'Isigny.[1]

Today, the village of Cambernon, inland from Coutances and about 14 miles from Saint-Lô, sits among green fields and country lanes in a landscape rather like Devon. A magnificent chateau once overlooked the village, high on a mound, its western and northern sides surrounded by water, the south and east by forest. Until recently, people called the area behind the Notre-Dame en l'Assomption church 'La Motte'. The chateau encompassed part of the current churchyard, the church initially serving as a chapel.

In the late nineteenth century Reverend Richard Champernowne visited the area with his daughter. He discovered stonework incorporated into farm buildings which he speculated might have come from a more elaborate, later house. He reported that he 'climbed up the little turret staircase, almost impassable from generations of rooks' nests, and coming out at quite a height had surveyed the surroundings'.[2]

The Second World War left Cambernon heavily damaged, and the church and churchyard have since been rebuilt. Only a slight rise beyond the churchyard wall now hints at the grand chateau that once stood there.

Over time, the name 'de Cambernon' became Chambernon, and eventually, through many other variant spellings, Champernowne. A heraldic scroll drawn up for Richard Champernowne of Modbury in 1605 starts with Thomas de Cambernon, who fought with Duke William at the Battle of Hastings. William rewarded his victorious knights with land, as he quelled rebellions and established order. William de Cambernon seems to have returned to Normandy, but by the early twelfth century a second Jordan de Campo Arnulphi, possibly William's grandson, held lands in both Cambernon and in North Devon.

Kate's branch of the family settled in the market town of Modbury in the early fourteenth century. Set among the rolling hills of Devon's South Hams, Modbury grew to become a bustling community, ranged around a crossroads. Kate's childhood home in Devon stood at the top of a steep hill beside a small Benedictine priory and St George's Church. Beyond stonework in many Modbury gardens, nothing remains of their fortified manor house, known as the Court House, Modbury Manor, or Modbury Castle. After the mansion suffered severe damage during the Civil War, the family moved away and sold the dilapidated buildings for the value of the stone.

The first of the family to be connected with Modbury was Richard, the younger son of Henry de Chambernon of Ilfracombe (died before 1296) and his wife, Dionysia de English. Richard established a pattern that would serve succeeding generations well: he married an heiress. Left with no inheritance of his own, he married Joan de Okeston, heiress to the extensive Valletort estates. A family story suggests that through Joan, the Champernownes descend from Richard, Earl of Cornwall (1209–1272), who was King John's younger son and also known as the King of the Romans. Joan or her mother, another Joan, was supposed to have been a mistress of Richard, Earl of Cornwall. If that is so, Joan was almost certainly but one among many mistresses. Other families share similar tales about Richard, Earl of Cornwall, and Kate probably doesn't have a legitimate claim to such noble ancestry.[3]

Over the years the Champernownes garnered estates through judicious marriages. One of the most significant was when Thomas Champernowne (*c.*1314–aft.1387) married Eleanor de Rohant, daughter of Sir Roger de Rohant, at Dodbrooke, Devon, in 1344.[4] Eleanor's inheritance expanded the Champernowne properties and influence beyond Devon into Oxfordshire, Leicestershire and Northamptonshire. It was Eleanor who brought the manor at Aston Rowant, near Thame in Oxfordshire, into the family. Kate spent some of her childhood there.

The Champernownes had links through marriage to both of the two families vying for power in the south-west during the fifteenth century: the Bonvilles and the Courtenays. A long-running feud resulted in open warfare in December 1555. Kate's great-grandfather William (1438–1464) was too young to fight in the battle at Clyst Heath near Exeter between William Bonville, his great-uncle, and Thomas Courtenay, Earl of Devon. Earl Thomas died in 1458, and his successors supported the Lancastrian side. Three Courtenay brothers died within a decade during the 'Wars of the Roses'. For a time Bonville remained outwardly loyal to Henry VI, but in 1560 he nailed his colours to the Yorkist mast, as did Kate's great-grandfather.

John Champernowne (1458–1503)

Kate's great-grandfather, William, fought alongside his great-uncle, William Bonville, at the second battle of St Albans. Bonville was captured and beheaded, but William Champernowne survived and returned to Devon, where he died suddenly on 7 October 1464, aged only 22. His will, made the day before his death and proved on 24 November,[5] mentions his brother Thomas, his wife Elizabeth and his son and heir John, then aged only 6.

William's widow, Elizabeth, married Charles Dynham, brother of Lord Dynham, a prominent Yorkist. Six years old when his father died in 1464, and standing to inherit a considerable estate, John Champernowne was a valuable commodity in the market for wardship. Unfortunately, the record, does not tell us who benefited. He may have remained a royal ward, or been brought up by his mother Elizabeth and the influential Dynhams.[6] Alternatively, Sir Philip Courtenay of Molland, (*c.*1430–1489) may have gained his wardship with a view to marrying him to his daughter, Margaret.

In 1478, John and Margaret were married in the second Courtenay/Champernowne marriage in the direct line.[7] John was 20 years old, his bride a couple of years younger. Their marriage was the most significant in all the family history. It not only brought the Champernownes close to the most powerful family in Devon, but also, eventually through them, to the Crown.

Around 1474, Margaret's sister Elizabeth had married Edward Courtenay, mending a rift between different branches of the Courtenay family. Edward and Elizabeth Courtenay's son, William, was born in 1475. Four years later,

Margaret gave birth to Kate's father, Philip, her only child.[8] Being close in age, it is likely that Philip Champernowne and William Courtenay spent time together in their youth.

Edward IV died suddenly on 9 April 1483, and the coronation of the young Prince Edward, planned for June, never took place. Instead, the prince's uncle seized the throne and was crowned King Richard III on 6 July 1483.

Miss Champernowne suggests that John Champernowne was High Sheriff of Devon in 1483, but this is not confirmed.[9]

John's brother-in-law, Edward Courtenay, was a staunch supporter of Henry Tudor. Attainted by Richard III and banished, Courtenay joined the Tudor faction in France. During his time there he acted as a courier between France and England, and sought patronage of Henry's mother, Margaret Beaufort. Courtenay returned to fight at Henry's side at the Battle of Bosworth. Some sources suggest that 27-year-old John Champernowne also fought for Henry Tudor at Bosworth.[10]

On 26 October 1485, the new king, Henry VII, rewarded Edward Courtenay by creating him Earl of Devon. The title had been vacant since 1471 following the extinction of the ancient line of Edward's cousins, who had either died in battle or had been executed.[11] Edward Courtenay became an influential courtier and effectively ruled over most of Devon on behalf of the Crown.

On 25 November 1487, at the coronation of Elizabeth of York, King Henry VII invested Edward Courtenay's 12-year-old son, William, into the Order of the Bath. In 1494 Edward was inducted into the Order of the Garter, a prestigious honour granted to few men. But an even higher honour awaited. In late summer or early autumn 1495, his son William married 16-year-old Katherine Plantagenet, daughter of Edward IV. John Champernowne's nephew was now married to the sister of the Queen of England, Elizabeth of York. The queen paid for the wedding clothes for the groom, and John and his son Philip may have attended the wedding. Later, Katherine Courtenay served her sister as her principal lady.

In 1497, John Champernowne likely fought alongside Courtenay and his son, and other West Country lords to prevent the Yorkist pretender Perkin Warbeck from entering Exeter.[12] In 1501 John and his son, Philip, may have joined the citizens of Plymouth who thronged the streets to greet Catherine of Aragon when she arrived unexpectedly on 2 October 1501.[13] Travelling from Spain with her entourage to marry Henry VII's eldest son, Prince Arthur, storms blew her ship off course from the intended destination of Southampton. Lord Willoughby de Broke,[14] Lord Steward of the King's Household, rushed down from Southampton to Exeter and organised escorts of local gentry and nobles for her journey from Plymouth, before another formal reception when she reached Exeter.

John Champernowne was one of twenty-six knights of the sword created on 14 November 1501. Knights of the sword, sometimes referred to as 'carpet' knights were those who obtained their honours 'with unhacked rapier and on carpet consideration'. This was a gift from their sovereign during peacetime, rather than an honour bestowed on the field of battle, or by victory at a tournament.

Sadly, he did not live long to enjoy his new status. Kate's grandfather died on 30 April 1503, his cause of death unknown, although records show a virulent outbreak of plague at around the same time.[15]

By the time of his death, John Champernowne may have had a position at court.[16]

Miss Champernowne quotes from Prince, who wrote in the seventeenth century: 'Champernowne of Modbury was in 1502 the possessor of 27 manors.'[17]

Of those, it seems Aston Rowant was his favourite because it was convenient to the court. However, he preferred to be buried at Modbury. In a recessed alcove in the south aisle of Modbury church is an effigy of the recumbent knight with a collar and sword belt studded with roses; a Yorkist badge. Although identified as Sir John, it seems odd that the tomb advertised Yorkist sympathies, after he had been successful under Henry VII. Alternatively, the effigy may represent his Yorkist father William, or it may be a reference to the Courtenay connection. Hamilton Rogers[18] notes that it bears a striking resemblance to the effigy of Sir Philip Courtenay of Loughtor (d.16 December 1463) at Plympton. He says:

> At Modbury the knight has on a small collar of roses, and the sword belt is studded with a similar ornament. This was probably the badge of the House of York; a collar of roses and suns alternately was often worn by the adherents of York in contradistinction to the collar of S.S., which was adopted by the Lancastrians. Should this be the case, the presence of this decoration would date him after the accession of Edward the IV, which took place in 1461.

This suggests the effigy more likely represents William Champernowne, Kate's great-grandfather who died in 1463, rather than her grandfather, John.[19]

Philip Champernowne (1578–August 1545) Kate's Father

Records of Philip's early life are scarce. His father was a wealthy man and could afford to engage the best tutors to provide Philip with an education designed to fit him for life both as a courtier and as a major landholder. He may have left home to continue his education elsewhere, possibly in the Courtenay household, sharing his lessons with his cousin William Courtenay. Wherever he was educated, Philip grew up to be a sensitive, cultured and well-read man, able to command respect among his peers and scholars of the day.

Courtenay Connections

Accompanying his father at court, among other noblemen, or in the company of his cousin, William Courtenay, Philip may have met William Blount, Lord Mountjoy.[20] Blount was born in the same year as Philip and studied under the humanist scholar Erasmus. The two men had a lot in common, both coming from noble families steeped in the ideas of chivalry and military service, and sharing an avid interest in the 'new learning'. Blount became the young Prince Henry's companion in his studies. William Courtenay's son Henry was first cousin to Prince Henry, who, after his brother Arthur's untimely death in 1502, became heir to the throne.

John Champernowne and his son Philip benefited enormously from the Courtenay connection. (See family tree at page xxviii) However, their close relationship with Courtenay had its downside. Henry VII was always fearful of a challenge to the Tudor dynasty he hoped to establish. Although the principal threat faded in 1599 with the death of Perkin Warbeck and the young Earl of Warwick, anyone with Yorkist blood could still come under suspicion of plotting to overthrow the Lancastrian king, Henry Tudor. Even men like William Courtenay, who, like his father before him, had demonstrated his loyalty to the house of Tudor over many years.

In 1502 William Courtenay was accused of treason, suspected of corresponding with his cousin, Edmund de la Pole (d.1513). When Edmund's father died in 1492, Henry VII refused to grant him the title of Duke of Suffolk, which his father had held. This was likely because Edmund's brother, the Earl of Lincoln, had been a key figure in the 1487 uprising that was crushed at the Battle of Stoke. Instead, Edmund was given the lesser title of earl, which fuelled his resentment and eventually led him to flee the country. In 1501 Edmund de la Pole was at his Aunt Margaret's court in Burgundy, where he called himself the 'White Rose'. By 1502 he had been declared an outlaw, thought to be plotting to take the throne. William was one of a group of men accused of conspiring with him.

It is doubtful William Courtenay was involved in any plot, but he had dined with his cousin before he left England. William was attainted and imprisoned in the Tower of London, leaving his wife and children destitute. Elizabeth of York may have had prior warning of William's arrest for she sent his children, Edward, Henry and Margaret (her nephews and niece), to be cared for by Lady

Margaret Cotton at the royal house at Havering, Essex. Queen Elizabeth's Privy Purse records reveal that she covered the funeral expenses after young Edward died in the summer or early autumn of 1502.[21] The queen continued to fund the children's care and clothing until her death in February 1503. Katherine Plantagenet Courtenay was the chief mourner at her sister's funeral before leaving for Devon to live with her father-in-law, taking the children with her.

Although there's no evidence the Champernowne family suffered because of the Courtenays' problems, Philip might later recall that having relatives close to the monarchy wasn't always advantageous.

Carew and Poyntz Connections

Kate's father married well, forging another important alliance – this time with the Carew family. His bride, Katherine Carew, was the daughter of Sir Edmund, Baron Carew,[22] a diplomat and soldier who Henry VII knighted on the battlefield at Bosworth in 1485. Sir Edmund was only 6 years old when his own father died, and became a ward of Edward IV. Eventually he inherited manors worth over £60 per annum (over £41,000 today). Edmund's marriage to Katherine, daughter and joint heiress of Sir William Huddesfield, Attorney General for both Edward IV and Henry VII, brought further lands. Through Katherine Huddesfield's sister, the Champernowne's also forged an important connection to the powerful Poyntz family.

Katherine Huddesfield's mother was Jennet Bosome,[23] William had another daughter, Elizabeth, with his second wife, Katherine Courtenay.[24] In 1499 Elizabeth Huddesfield married Anthony Poyntz, son of Robert Poyntz of Iron Acton in Gloucestershire. Like Edmund Carew, Robert Poyntz had been a ward of Edward IV and served at his court. Robert married Margaret, illegitimate daughter of Anthony Woodville, Lord Rivers, who was the brother of Edward IV's queen. However, after Richard III took the throne, Robert became a strong supporter of Henry Tudor and was knighted on the battlefield at Bosworth. He entertained King Henry VII at his manor of Acton Court on two occasions, in 1586, and again ten years later.[25]

A touching inscription in a beautifully illuminated late fourteenth-century Book of Hours, shows that Katherine Huddesfield and her sister Elizabeth were close. In a handwritten note in the margin Elizabeth asks her sister to pray for her.[26]

A copy of Edmund Carew and Katherine Huddesfield's pre-nuptial settlement dated 26 December 1478 survives.[27] Their eldest son, William, was born in 1483, verified by his father's IPM. Kate's mother, Katherine Carew, was their eldest daughter.[28] William and the second son, Thomas of Bickleigh, both married girls from the wider Courtenay family. Daughter Dorothy married first John Stowell and then Sir Hugh Pollard, forging a link with another of Devon's major landowning dynasties. Two other girls, Anne and Isabelle, became nuns. Katherine Carew's younger brothers, George and Gawen, were born around 1498 and 1503 respectively. See family tree at page xxx.

Philip and Katherine were already married and living at Aston Rowant by 1503, when John Champernowne died.[29] Before his death, he conveyed the manor of Aston Rowant to Walter Courtenay, Sir William Huddesfield and others, 'for the use of Katherine, daughter of Sir Edmund Carew and wife of Philip Champernowne'.

By 1503, Katherine Carew was of childbearing age. It's even possible she'd already given birth.

Chapter 2

Kate's Early Life

The Inner Circle and the Courtenays 1503–1530

Historians suggest tentative birthdates of 1502 or 1505 for Kate, either just after or shortly before Sir John Champernowne's death. This means she was very close in age to her two Carew uncles, George and Gawen. She also had two cousins, Sir William Carew's sons, the elder, confusingly also named George, born around 1505 and Peter only a few years younger. The lives of these five children, linked by kinship, intertwined over the years.

Philip and his wife were living at Aston Rowant when John Champernowne died.[1] So, although her family hailed from Devon, Kate may have been born at her grandfather's beloved Oxfordshire manor.

Nestled on the edge of the Chiltern Hills, near the M40, Aston Rowant is now a peaceful village with charming thatched cottages and a village green. Parts of St Peter and St Paul's church date back to the twelfth century, long before Kate's ancestor Thomas Champernowne gained the manor when he married Eleanor de Rohant. Kate's baptism may even have taken place at the fifteenth-century font, still in use in the church today.

Kate and her siblings likely divided their early childhood years between Aston Rowant and Devon. Many people passed through Aston, which lay on the main road between London and Oxford, and travellers often carried with them diseases such as the plague. The country air of Modbury probably seemed safer during the summer months. However, if Philip had a position or business at court, then Aston was perfect.

Unfortunately, no one recorded Kate's baptism date. It was not until 1538 that Thomas Cromwell backed the innovation of routinely recording baptisms, marriages and burials in parish registers. Prior to that time, priests occasionally kept their own records of the foremost families in their parish, but unfortunately none have survived from Aston Rowant, or Modbury in Devon, which is another possible birthplace.[2]

Kate's early life remains a mystery. Her name does not appear in the known record until 1536. This lack of evidence for her early years does not imply that she was from an obscure, unimportant background. It was not unusual for women of her time, even those from elite families, to leave a light impression on the historical record. For example, the birthdate and childhood of Henry VIII's third wife, Jane Seymour, are similarly unknown.[3]

However, Kate is unusual in that, as the eldest daughter of a flourishing, well-connected family, she remained unmarried for so long. She was the eldest of six girls and two boys born over a period of some twenty years.[4] All five of Kate's sisters made good marriages, some when they were apparently quite young. Kate's life took a different course – her career would be devoted to the service of a royal princess.

Brothers and sisters

That Philip Champernowne and his wife had two daughters named Katherine and two named Joan has added to confusion about Kate's identity. Vivian, the nineteenth-century compiler of the Heralds' Visitations in Devon, who is not always a reliable source, compounded this by omitting Joan the elder and Kate from the Champernowne family tree.[5] The handwritten family trees in the Carew Manuscripts record both 'Catharina married to John Astley' and 'Katherine married to Walter Raleigh' as Philip Champernowne's daughters, as well as 'Joan, married to Robert Gamage of Coity', and 'Joan married to Anthony Denny'.[6]

Giving a second child the same name as a living sibling seems strange in the twenty-first century. However, during the middle-ages and well into the sixteenth century, it was not unusual. This confusing practice lingered into the eighteenth century, before gradually transferring to using the same name as that of an earlier child who did not survive. The family might use birth order to distinguish between same-name siblings, or a 'pet' name. For example, Duffy's study based on the records of the Devon parish of Morebath, cites three unmarried brothers sharing the same name in 1534, identified as John major, John minor, and John minimus.[7] Sometimes children baptised with the same name were born to different mothers, as with the sons of Protector Edward Seymour. However, this is not always the case. For example, in his will made in 1570 Christopher Chudleigh (Chidley) of Ashton in Devon mentions bequests to four daughters: 'Besse the elder, Besse the younger, Marye and Anne, £200 (roughly £48,000) when they reach the age of 21 years.'[8] Christopher was married only once, to Christian Stretchley.[9]

Relatively few given names were in use in the early sixteenth century. Parents often named their children after a benefactor or godparent, or a member of the royal family, resulting in recurring names.

The order in which Kate's siblings arrived is uncertain, although we can confirm Arthur as the youngest, born in 1524.[10] Unfortunately, John's exact date of birth and position within the family remain unconfirmed. He died before his father so we have no details of his age in a will or Inquisition Post Mortem. Some years likely separated the births of the first and second Katherine and the first and second Joan. The older girls may have left home well before their younger namesakes arrived. Katherine, the wife first of Otho Gilbert and then Walter Raleigh, must have been younger than Kate since she was still giving birth in the 1550s. When Elizabeth Cole (alias Pollard), another of Kate's sisters, wrote her will in 1567, she confirmed the order of birth for her surviving sisters.[11] Elizabeth left her best gown of silk to the elder sister, Katherine Raleigh, while she bequeathed to the younger sister, Frances, the best gown of cloth. The family tree at page xxix. shows a tentative order or birth for the family.

No record survives of any marriage negotiations for Kate. Yet dynastic marriages formed the basis of a career for most high-status women of Kate's time.[12] Girls from elite backgrounds expected nothing more. Their parents brought them up and educated them to present an attractive prospect in the marriage market. They were expected to marry whoever their parents or advisers selected.[13]

However, attitudes to women's education were shifting. Women often had to step in and manage large households and estates when their husbands were elsewhere, so they also needed a grounding in household management, accounts and a smattering of the law. To gain this, girls might join their brothers for lessons with tutors engaged by the family. The growing interest in humanist thinking led to the addition of Classics and languages to the girls' curriculum, alongside their brothers. Music, dancing, good manners and etiquette, needlework for the girls and martial sports for the boys completed a demanding education for high-status children.

Philip Champernowne was clearly in favour of giving his girls a broader education with all the benefits of the new interest in Classical, humanist education. Joan 'the younger' later gained recognition at court for her book learning. David Starkey refers to her as 'something of a bluestocking'.[14]

Initially, like most children of the elite and gentry, Philip's daughters learned their letters from their mother at home, but later they may have joined lessons with tutors Philip appointed to educate his sons.

Two Carew aunts, Ann and Isabelle (Elizabeth), became nuns and their names appear in the records of Polsloe Priory at the time of the priory's dissolution.[15] However, it is most unlikely that the nuns of Polsloe could tutor Kate or Joan to the standard they attained. Nor is it likely that Kate herself became a nun, only leaving the cloistered life in 1536 to take up her position caring for Elizabeth

Tudor. Before the Reformation it was not unusual for younger daughters from a large family to be placed in a convent, as were the younger Carew girls. Marrying daughters off was a costly business, and the smaller dowry required by convents might be attractive for a man who had many daughters to settle. However, it was usually younger daughters who entered convents. As the eldest, Kate would have been expected to make a dynastic marriage.

Historians agree Kate was proficient in several languages. It is tempting to wonder if, like Anne Boleyn and Anne Brandon (daughter of Charles Brandon and Anne Browne), Kate travelled to Mechelen to the court of Margaret of Austria in the Netherlands, or even to the French court, and gained her impeccable education there. Or to consider whether she might have accompanied Mary Tudor to her marriage to the King of France. Having spent time at a foreign court might explain Kates's reported facility with languages. Sadly, no evidence has yet emerged to support these theories.

Nor is there any evidence to suggest Kate gained her language skills while serving the king's daughter Mary. In October 1523 Catherine of Aragon received detailed advice on her daughter's education from Juan Luis Vives, a Spanish-born scholar recommended by Thomas More, whose own daughters were among the first women recognised as having a broad humanist education. Vives recommended Mary should work on her Latin in the company of other girls her own age.[16] Kate was a few years older, so perhaps missed this opportunity.

A promising line of enquiry suggested Kate might have had a connection with Cardinal Wolsey in her youth, but this could not be proven.[17]

Despite exhaustive searches, we still know nothing of Kate's education, beyond that it was wide-ranging. Nor do we know where she spent her early years. However, the record yields more information concerning her close family.

Relationships mattered in Tudor England and a flexible concept of 'cousinship' meant connections spread across many families. By untangling some of the threads that link individuals we can offer plausible explanations of how Kate may have spent her early years and gained her formidable education. Following the fortunes of Kate's 'inner circle' also provides useful insights into why, in 1536, Thomas Cromwell chose her to play such an important role in the king's younger daughter's formative years.

The Inner Circle

Philip Champernowne does not seem to have taken an active part in Devon affairs during the first two decades of the sixteenth century. He is also mentioned in a few routine matters concerned with the management of the Champernowne estates. For example, he recommended Walter Southcott as rector of Bridford on 10 January 1508.[18] Philip's father had installed the two previous incumbents in 1473 and 1498. The pardon roll of 1509 mentions Philip, but provides no explanation. In 1505 and again in 1514, he was involved in legal action to reclaim deeds of properties in Devon in the possession of his mother, who had remarried John West.[19] However, there is no mention of Philip as a Justice of the Peace or in any other official role in Devon before 1522, when his name appears on the sheriff roll.[20] It is therefore reasonable to assume that Philip Champernowne held a position at court for some years before 1523, when he was a 'squire of the body' to the king.[21] Alternatively, he may have served Katherine, Countess of Devon, or her son, in some capacity.

Philip's prospects may have improved when, on his accession in 1509, Henry VIII released William Courtenay from imprisonment. Katherine of York had a hand in young Prince Henry's early upbringing, and the new king was fond of his Aunt Katherine. She had offered him comfort after his mother's death, a severe blow to the 11-year-old heir to the throne so soon after the unexpected loss of his brother, Arthur.[22]

Immediately after his father's death, Henry VIII invited his aunt back to court, where she attended Henry VII's funeral. The king covered the costs of his aunt's return to court, where she served his sister, Mary. One of his first state acts was to pardon William Courtenay. With his rights as sword bearer restored, William took part in the jousts following Henry and Catherine of Aragon's joint coronation in June 1509. With their close connection to the Courtenays, Philip Champernowne and his wife may well have attended the coronation celebrations, though Kate was probably too young. Edward, Earl of Devon (brother-in-law to Kate's grandfather), died in May 1509, so did not witness his son's return to favour.

On New Year's Day 1510, Queen Catherine gave birth to a son named Henry, and given the title Duke of Cornwall. Katherine of York stood godmother and William Courtenay was prominent in the celebratory jousts on 11 and 12 February. Not long after, the infant prince died, just 52 days old. The king did not appear to blame the nurse appointed to care for the child, Elizabeth Poyntz, to whom he granted a pension of £20 per year (more than £13,000 today). Ideas differ as to the nurse's identity. Some tentative suggestions point to her being the first wife of Anthony Poyntz of Iron Acton. If so, she was half-sister to Kate's grandmother, and therefore Kate's great-aunt. However, Alison Weir identifies her as the unmarried daughter of Sir Robert Poyntz (*c.*1450–1520), Sir Anthony's sister.[23]

Whichever of the Poyntz women held the position in the prince's nursery, the family being in the service of Catherine of Aragon opens the possibility that they found a place for Kate at court. Elizabeth Poyntz's granddaughter

Frances Newton, later Baroness Cobham, joined Elizabeth's post-accession court, and became close to the queen.[24] Kate may have had a hand in Frances's appointment, having maintained contact with her Poyntz relatives. That might indicate that Kate had been close to them in her youth.

William Courtenay's time in prison had taken a toll on his health, and in the summer of 1511 he died of pleurisy. His 15-year-old son Henry became the Earl of Devon, eventually having all of his father's and grandfather's rights restored. Katherine of York retired from court life, taking a vow of chastity. Using the title 'the excellent Princess Katherine, Countess of Devon, daughter, sister and aunt of Kings', she established a near royal court based at Tiverton Castle and Colcombe Castle near Colyton.[25] Girls from good West Country families attended her, and it is possible that Kate and her sisters spent some time with the countess.

Patronage mattered at the Henrican court. It worked both ways; for the individual, it was a mechanism for gaining power and influence, through the monarch's favour and support; for the patron and for the king it was a vital political instrument used to reward loyalists, build alliances, and strengthen the monarchy. In the 1520s, Henry Courtenay, the king's cousin, was in prime position to secure places at court for Philip and his family. In return, he called on them to support him.

The first mention of Philip at court is, ironically, when he left his post. In April 1523, King Henry granted the lease of the manor of Curry Mallet, in Somerset to 'Philip Champernon, squire for the body'.[26]

The Crown also undertook to repair the lodge and granted timber for repairing the 'palace' in the park there. This sounds like a parting gift in thanks for years of loyal service. After this date, Philip's name appears much more regularly in connection with Devon. We don't know how much time Philip spent at the royal manor in Somerset where he was 'keeper of the park', nor whether any of his children went there. He was still keeper there in 1537 when a 'valor' of the lands making up the jointure and dowry of Jane Seymour and listing the names and fees of officers of each place includes Sir Philip as keeper of the park at Curry Mallet.

Leland also records in his itinerary: 'Thence to Curry Mallet, wher is park longing to Chapernoun of Devonshire.'[27]

With their intimate and frequent access to the king, the squires of the body had considerable influence, and were often knights. Other well-known figures who served the king in this intimate role include George Boleyn, Edward Seymour, Francis Bryan and William Parr, uncle to Henry's last queen. The king appointed Francis Bryan as squire of the body in 1522; therefore, Bryan was likely in office at the same time as Philip. A few years later, a young man named Anthony Denny accompanied Sir Francis on diplomatic missions overseas. Anthony was destined to play an important part in the future lives of Kate and her sister, Joan 'the younger'.

Usually six squires of the body, a barber and a page, attended the king in his bedchamber each morning. They helped him dress in his undergarments before he went into the Privy Chamber where the Gentlemen of the Privy Chamber attended him while he finished dressing. At mealtimes, two squires sat at his feet while the king ate, and at least two others served his food. Another gave him a drink in a cup provided by the Chief Butler. Others presented the ewer and basin for the king to rinse his hands. At other times, the squires waited in case they were needed for other tasks, such as carrying his cloak. They also helped the king undress and prepare for bed. During the night, the squires of the body on duty had complete control of the king's household, taking the place of the Lord Chamberlain and Vice Chamberlain and Gentlemen Ushers who held sway during the day. The duty squire had to approve all dispatches delivered to the king. As a high-ranking official, Philip mingled with the likes of Cardinal Wolsey and other high-profile figures.

The record does not tell us when Philip took up this appointment, but he retired from court in 1523, possibly because the king and Courtenay wanted a 'safe pair of hands' to manage affairs in Devon. Philip became more active in Devon from 1522, when his name appears in the sheriff roll, but he was not selected. In 1523 and 1524, Philip was one of those appointed to collect the lay subsidy in Devon – effectively, he was a tax collector for the king.[28]

Carew cousins and uncles

If links to the Courtenays secured Philip's advancement at court, the Carew connection through Philip's marriage with Sir Edmund Carew's daughter proved to be a more mixed blessing. Sir Edmund Carew was a staunch supporter of Henry Tudor and joined him in France before being knighted at the Battle of Bosworth for his valour. He continued to serve the new king, Henry VII, and was one of a party who met the commissioners from France who came to treat for peace in 1492. Sir Edmund also played an important part in relieving Exeter in 1597, when the city was under siege by the pretender known as Perkin Warbeck. However, to finance his military and diplomatic ventures in support of both Henry VII and later Henry VIII, Sir Edmund borrowed enormous sums of money. Rhys ap Thomas already held a mortgage on Carew Castle in Wales, the family's ancestral home. Burdened by debt, the family could not keep up the payments and had to give up the castle. Several other long-held family manors also fell into other hands. By 1513, when he and his brother John set off for Henry's war in France, his debts had multiplied and included a substantial sum owed to the Crown.[29] Sir Edmund also owed a large sum to John Gilbert of Compton and Greenway in Devon, whose nephew and heir married Kate's sister, Katherine the younger.[30]

Both Sir Edmund and his brother lost their lives in Henry VIII's French campaign, John at sea, while Sir Edmund, who had charge of the ordnance, died on 24 June 1513, during the Siege of Thérouanne.

Hall's Chronicle records Sir Edmund's death in vivid detail:

> as certain captianes wer in counsail, in the lorde Herbertes tent, sodainly out of the toune was shot a gonne, the pellet whereof slewe a noble captain called the Baron Carew, sitting there in counsail, whiche sodain adventure dismaied muche the asemblie. But the Lorde Herberte valiauntly comforted them, saiying: this is the chaunce of warre, if it had hit me I must be content, a noble harte in warre is never feared of death.[31]

Sir Edmund's untimely demise must be one of the few Tudor deaths, apart from executions, for which we have eye-witness accounts. It was all very well for Lord Herbert to dismiss it as 'the chance of war', but Sir Edmund's death left his heirs with a financial headache that troubled them for many years. The debts racked up by Sir Edmund hung like a millstone around the necks of his sons and grandsons. Philip Champernowne soon became embroiled in the struggle to manage his wife's family's debts. Even before Sir Edmund's death as early as 1510, we find Philip named as guarantor for his father-in-law's debts, along with his brother-in-law, Thomas Carew of Bickleigh.[32] William Carew, Kate's uncle, agreed with Wolsey, Bishop of Winchester, to repay by yearly instalments. In 1517 a payment was due 'Martinmas next' under the heading 'Loan money'.[33] William was still making repayments in 1530.[34] In December 1552, William's son Sir Peter Carew and his wealthy wife Lady Margaret discharged some remaining debts.[35, 36]

William Carew was Sheriff of Devon in 1513, but is not referred to as 'Sir William' until 1522, presumably because until then he could not afford the knight's fee.

Marriages closely linked the Carews and Courtenays, including William's marriage to Joan, daughter of Sir William Courtenay of Powderham. William's brother, Thomas, also married a Courtenay, following a romantic elopement with the young heiress of Bickleigh Castle. To make matters worse, Elizabeth Courtenay was an orphan, placed in William's care by her grandfather. Thinking it best to absent himself for a while, Thomas joined the forces of Thomas Howard, Earl of Surrey (later 2nd Duke of Norfolk), who led the English forces to victory at the Battle of Flodden against the invading Scottish army led by King James IV. Thomas Carew acquitted himself well in King Henry's war against the Scots, but was captured. He returned to Devon following the payment of his ransom.

After his father's death, William assumed responsibility for his two youngest brothers, 15-year-old George and 10-year-old Gawen. They both feature often in Kate's story.

George studied at Broadgates Hall, Oxford, later Pembroke College, graduating in 1522.[37] After leaving Broadgates he may have spent some time overseas 'to cure a heart ache', before eventually entering the church.[38] It's possible the 'heart ache' was because of the death of a young wife.

William Carew arranged for his younger brothers, and his eldest son George, to be placed in the household of Henry Courtenay.[39] The only surviving set of Courtenay's household accounts for the year 1525, mentions George and Gawen Carew among the men receiving crane covered cloth (a greyish white or bluish white) for their livery.[40]

As if his financial worries were not enough, William's three sons seemed intent on living an adventurous life. In 1519, George, his eldest son, attended Middle Temple – an appropriate education for someone of his status. According to John Hooker, Exeter recorder and writer, his younger brother Peter attended the grammar school in Exeter, but not finding schoolwork to his liking, wandered in the city, missing his lessons.[41] Peter's desperate father sent him to the renowned St Paul's grammar school in London, but to no avail. Eventually, William dispatched young Peter to France to serve as a page for a friend. The boy vanished and his family thought he was dead. Peter, a reckless but charming adventurer by all accounts, reappeared a few years later. He regaled everyone with stories of his travels, including an account of the Battle of Pavia, and became a favourite of the king.

Meanwhile, Europe was in turmoil and William's eldest son, George, was also finding his studies irksome. He embarked on a foolish expedition in 1526, taking a Breton ship from Dartmouth. With his companion Edward Rogers, who also received livery in the Courtenay household in 1525, and without the permission of either King Henry or Thomas Wolsey, he offered his services to the captive French king's mother. She declined his offer, leading to his arrest in Paris along with a servant. Although the king pardoned George upon his safe return to England, the servant languished in a Calais prison for eighteen months. The escapade caused unnecessary worry and cost to his hard-pressed father.[42]

William's middle son, Philip, set off in search of glory in Malta, where he joined the Order of St John of Jerusalem in July 1528. Later that year he was arrested in connection with the death of another knight, Sir Thomas Hall, but escaped. In his absence, the court declared him guilty of murder and expelled him from the order. What became of him is unknown, but he was dead by the time his father made his will in 1536.

Courtenay connections – Henry and Gertrude Courtenay, Marquess and Marchioness of Exeter

During the early years of his reign, the athletic young king, Henry VIII, surrounded himself with men who shared his passion for sport. He and Henry Courtenay had grown up together, and Courtenay was one of his closest companions, with apartments in the royal household. They played shuffleboard and indoor tennis together and Courtenay joined in the jousting and winter sports at Greenwich Palace. There was even a snowball fight.[43]

Henry Courtenay's first marriage was brief. Soon after the wedding in 1515, Elizabeth Grey, former ward of Charles Brandon, subsequently Courtenay's mother's ward, died. Courtenay's second wife was Gertrude Blount, daughter of William Blount, Lord Mountjoy, and a maid of honour to Catherine of Aragon. The couple married in 1519 and were prominent at the Field of the Cloth of Gold in June 1520, a grand meeting between King Henry VIII and King Francis I of France. Philip Champernowne is not listed among the squires of the body who attended King Henry at the meeting with the French king. However, he and his wife may have attended in the Courtenay entourage. Several members of the Poyntz family are listed, including Anthony, who was accompanied by a daughter, suggesting that Kate's great aunt, Elizabeth Huddesfield, died before 1520.[44]

At this time, Henry Courtenay's star was in the ascendancy. King Henry made him a Gentleman of the Privy Chamber, and after Edward Stafford's execution on 9 June 1521, Courtenay eventually took his place as a member of the Order of the Garter and on the Privy Council. Claims that Stafford, Henry VIII's cousin once removed, heeded prophecies of the king's death, harboured ambitions to seize the throne, and intended to kill the king, formed the basis of treason accusations against him. His downfall stemmed from rash statements and the implication that his right to the throne surpassed even Henry VIII's. As a scion of the house of York, with a similarly strong claim to the throne, Henry Courtenay might have done well to heed Stafford's example. However, for now, his position seemed secure and he continued to gain significant honours from the king.

Tin miners in Devon and Cornwall had their own set of laws, and the Stannary Courts administered justice and settled disputes. In May 1523, Courtenay became Warden of the Stannary Courts, a powerful position in the south-west. Courtenay's power in Devon was further enhanced when, at the same time as his appointment to the Stannary Court, he also became the King's Steward in the Duchy of Cornwall. This coincided with Philip Champernowne's leaving court and acting on Courtenay's and the king's behalf in Devon.

In April 1525, Courtenay became Constable of Windsor Castle and, in June of that year, Henry VIII bestowed the title of Marquess of Exeter upon his cousin. On the same day, the king created his 6-year-old illegitimate son, Henry Fitzroy, Duke of Richmond and Somerset. By promoting Bessie Blount's son on the same day as he elevated Courtenay, the king was perhaps underlining that there was more than one potential heir to the throne. Fitzroy received a princely education, and the king likely at times considered him a serious contender.

Courtenay's elevation in rank came with the grant of several manors, including Dartington in Devon, Restormel in Cornwall, and the Manor of the Rose at St Laurence in Pountney, Southwark, former home of Edward Stafford, Duke of Buckingham. The Manor of the Rose, which many years before had belonged to John Holland, Duke of Exeter, the builder of Dartington Hall, was near to the Brandon family mansion. It became the Courtenay's London home. They also had a home at Kew, and, in addition, the king later granted West Horsley Place in Surrey for their use.

New furniture was installed at Hatfield, for their stay in November 1525. The Courtenays were again at Hatfield in 1528 when they both caught the sweating sickness.[45]

Gertrude and Henry were the 'power couple' of their time. The household accounts for 1525 detail the Courtenays' lavish lifestyle. They also mention provision for the young lord, showing the couple had a son. It's thought that Edward Courtenay, later to be a suitor to Kate's charge, Elizabeth, was born in 1526 or 1527, so this reference is to an earlier child, Henry, who died in infancy.[46]

Unfortunately, the accounts do not name the gentlewomen who received 24 yards of tawny cambric for their gowns. We cannot, therefore, know for certain whether Philip Champernowne's wife or daughters were among the women waiting on Gertrude Courtenay. However, as we have seen, the accounts name George and Gawen Carew, among those who received crane-coloured cloth (a greyish white colour) for their livery. There are entries recording visits to the West Country, clothing, gifts, payments to servants and foodstuffs including cherries, strawberries and cream, and we also find details of several occasions when Henry Courtenay visited shrines and religious sites.[47] Henry Courtenay was deeply religious and a supporter of the Pope and the Catholic Church. It is interesting to note that the Carews, who were later associated with religious reform, were at this time serving in one of the most staunchly Catholic households in the country.

In 1527, the links between the Courtenays, Carews and Champernownes were on public display at the magnificent funeral of Katherine, Countess of

Devon. Lady Joan Carew, William's wife, was the chief mourner. Six tall yeomen carried the coffin, draped in cloth of silver, in a solemn procession from Tiverton Castle to the nearby church of St Peter. Behind them came four men: Sir Thomas Dennys, Sir John Basset (whose second wife was Honor, later Lady Lisle), Sir William Carew and Philip Champernowne. Kate's cousin, George Carew, carried a banner.[48] Neither Henry, Marquess of Exeter, nor the marchioness attended. This does not show any lack of respect; close relatives of deceased royalty rarely attended funerals, and Courtenay's attendance was probably required at court. Kate's father was in the company of men of the highest rank Devon could muster to give full reverence to Princess Katherine, daughter, sister and aunt of kings.[49]

His mother's death brought the Marquess of Exeter an additional thirty-four Devon manors, twelve in Cornwall, and another sixteen between Dorset and Hampshire. With his vast landholdings and descent from the house of York, according to John Bowle, some people were even beginning to see Henry Courtenay as a potential successor to, or even supplanter of, the king.[50] Perhaps because of his closeness to the king during their youth, Courtenay and his wife failed to see the danger signals, nor remember the fate of Edward Stafford.

Sir Philip in Devon

In the following year, 1528, Kate's father is mentioned for the first time as 'Philip Champernowne, knight', confirming his knighthood and high status in Devon and beyond. Although his public profile was high, Sir Philip's finances were under severe pressure. He had shouldered a portion of his father-in-law's debt and he had six daughters in need of dowries, at least one of whom was serving at court. Although maids of honour and the queen's ladies often received a retainer, they were not necessarily paid for their services. They needed a wardrobe of fine clothes, and although sometimes the court provided clothing, this wasn't always the case.

It may also have been around this time when, if the stories handed down are to be believed, Sir Philip took his musicians and singers to court to entertain the king. There are several versions of the story of the Modbury singers. The one still being repeated in Devon public houses when the Reverend Sabine Baring-Gould was collecting songs and folklore in the late nineteenth century tells how the king failed to cover the costs of Sir Philip's musicians at court. In his *Book of the West*, Baring-Gould records:

> Modbury, a little market town, was a great seat of the Champernowne family. It has always been a musical centre. In the

> reign of Henry VIII. Sir Philip Champernowne, of Modbury, went up to Windsor, taking with him his company of musicians on rote and tabor and psaltery and dulcimer, and all kinds of music, and they performed before King Henry, to that huge monarch's huge content. So pleased was he with their 'consort of fine musicke', that he bade Sir Philip remain with his company at Windsor, to play to him whenever the evil spirit was on him; but forgot to say that this was to be at royal charges. The entertaining of his band of musicians at court by Sir Philip during many months proved so great an expense that when he returned to Modbury he was a wiser and a much poorer man, and had to sell a manor or two to meet his liabilities.[51]

Baring-Gould says that Sir Philip's grandson, Henry, refused a request by Queen Elizabeth that he bring his musicians to court. Other versions attribute this refusal to Sir Richard Champernowne of Modbury in the 1590s. That the Champernownes loved music is in no doubt. The composer Anthony Holborne dedicated his best known work, a collection of sixty-five dances, published in 1599, to Sir Richard of Modbury. It is the largest collection of English music to survive from this period. In his dedication, Holborne stresses how much he values Sir Richard's patronage.[52]

In the 1590s Richard was involved in a dispute with Robert Cecil, who wanted to 'poach' one of Champernowne's finest singers, and this may have added to the confusing stories of the Modbury musicians. Since people still spoke about it in the late nineteenth century, it is likely it was in Sir Philip's time that the musicians played at court, leaving him severely out of pocket. Sir Philip passed on his interest in music to his grandson, Carew Raleigh, who, according to Aubrey, had 'a delicate clear voice' and could accompany himself 'skilfully on the olpharion'.[53]

By 1528, however, since he was no longer attending court regularly, Philip parted with the prestigious manor at Aston Rowant, the upkeep of which must have been a drain on his resources. In 1528 he transferred the manor to Henry Courtenay, perhaps in lieu of debts Philip had built up with his illustrious relative.[54] Alternatively it may have been part of a larger land settlement.[55]

Courtenay immediately exchanged the manor with Sir Thomas Unton of Wadley in Berkshire for land in Surrey. Miss Champernowne quotes a reference in the Rutland Papers which appears to refer to Aston Rowant in 1541 as 'Mr. Chambourne's house', suggesting the family still used the property. Either people continued to refer to Aston Rowant as the Champernowne's house long after the family departed, or the rather vague reference is to another property entirely.[56]

It must have been a wrench to part with his father's favourite manor, which Sir John had designated for the use of Katherine, daughter of Sir Edmund Carew, and Philip. No trace remains of the house Kate knew, which was built in 1352. Brewer referred to a later house on the same site as 'one of the remarkable seats in the county' with a park and gardens and a 2.5 acre lake.[57] It eventually burned down in the mid-twentieth century.

Brothers and sisters at court

Kate's brother John served at court in some capacity, and he was popular with the king. Richard Carew of Antony records in his *Survey of Cornwall*, published in 1603, that 'John Champernowne, son and heir apparent to Sir Philip of Devon in Henry the Eighth's time followed the court, and though his quaint conceits of which much might be spoken, won some good grace with the King'.

Kate and her sisters may also have served at court. Catherine of Aragon had thirty maids of honour, unmarried, well-born girls, often appointed on the recommendation of the queen's ladies, or relations or friends at court.[58] However, not all of their names are recorded. Kate's absence from the known lists does not necessarily exclude a court role.

The usual age for appointment as a maid of honour was around 16. The girls had to be of impeccable backgrounds with no hint of scandal. They must have well-developed skills in needlework, singing, music and card games. They must also be beautiful in order to enhance the appearance of the queen's entourage. If the portrait of Joan Champernowne 'the younger' (Plate 2) is an accurate likeness, then Kate's sister definitely qualified. Perhaps Kate's more 'homely' features (Plate 1) made it more difficult for her to secure a place.

Some sources suggest that Joan 'the younger' served as maid of honour to Catherine of Aragon, as well as being among Anne of Cleves's and Catherine Parr's ladies. According to Anthony Martienssen, Joan Champernowne became a maid of honour to Catherine of Aragon in 1529.[59] Aged only 13, he maintains, she joined a young Catherine Parr and Joan Guildford. Frustratingly, Martienssen gives no sources. The three women certainly became friends when Joan Champernowne and Joan Guildford both served Catherine Parr when she became queen in 1543, and shared her interest in the reformed religion. Joan (Jane) Guildford (1508/1509–1555), who married John Dudley in 1525, may have been at court in the 1520s. Anne Stanhope (bef.1512–1587), later wife of Edward Seymour, was at court in 1529.[60] It is plausible that Joan 'the younger' joined the court, aged around 13, in 1529. However, it is also possible it was Joan 'the elder' who served as maid of honour to Catherine of Aragon. Joan 'the elder' married Robert Gamage of Coity before 1531.[61] Robert's sister, Margaret, was a maid of honour to Anne Boleyn and Katheryn Howard. She married William Howard who was created Baron Howard of Effingham in 1554. It's tempting to conclude that Joan the elder served alongside Margaret Gamage in the late 1520s.

By the end of the 1520s, while some of his children remained at court, Kate's father was playing an important part in West Country affairs. His allegiance was firmly with his patron, Henry Courtenay, and his outwardly expressed religious beliefs relatively conservative. The careers of Kate's Carew uncles were also at this time entwined with the fortunes of the Courtenays.

The 'King's Great Matter' – the annulment of his marriage to Catherine of Aragon – soon tested allegiances to the limit.

Chapter 3

Shifting Loyalties

The Inner Circle
1530–1533

The King's Great Matter

By the early 1530s it was public knowledge that Henry VIII was actively pursuing an annulment of his marriage to Catherine of Aragon, and that he wanted to replace her with Anne Boleyn. Gertrude, Marchioness of Exeter, was deeply shocked by this development. She was fiercely loyal to Catherine of Aragon and her daughter, Mary, having served as a maid of honour, and after her marriage as one of Queen Catherine's ladies. Gertrude's father, Lord Mountjoy, was chamberlain of Catherine's household. As matters progressed, he found balancing his loyalty to his king and to Catherine severely testing.

Catherine of Aragon was popular in the west of England. Many people remembered the young Spanish princess riding by as she made her way from Plymouth through Devon and Somerset on her way to meet her future husband, Prince Arthur. Sir Philip Champernowne, like Lord Mountjoy and many others, must have struggled with divided loyalties. He was perhaps relieved he was no longer often at court. However, Sir Philip's wife may have been one of Gertrude Courtenay's ladies and therefore nearer to the centre of events. Kate's whereabouts at this time are uncertain.

Wolsey had failed to progress the 'King's Great Matter' by negotiating a way for him to set Catherine of Aragon aside. After the cardinal's demise, now advised by Thomas Cromwell, who joined the Privy Council late in 1530, the king pressed ahead with plans to break from the Catholic Church. Anne Boleyn had introduced King Henry to Tyndale's *Obedience of the Christian Man* which maintained that popes had no authority over kings. Anne was also keen on the idea of an English Language Bible. These ideas were anathema to the Marchioness of Exeter.

Encouraged by Anne, the king began introducing laws to pave the way to his making himself Head of the Church in England, replacing the Pope. He could then appoint a new Archbishop of Canterbury with the power to annul his marriage to the popular Queen Catherine of Aragon, freeing him to marry Anne Boleyn. The king was not only in love with Anne but also hoped she would bear him the legitimate heir Catherine had failed to provide. He was prepared to take radical measures to secure Anne as his lawful wife. In addition, and perhaps even more importantly, the idea of being independent from the Pope, being God's chosen representative with sole authority over the church in England, had great appeal.

Gertrude Courtenay disapproved of what she saw as Anne's scandalous relationship with King Henry. She blamed Anne for upsetting the rightful order of things. King Henry seeking to annul his marriage to Catherine of Aragon must have been profoundly upsetting for all the women of England; if a king could set aside a wife who did not provide an heir, any man might do the same.

These shocking developments came at the time Kate would, in the usual course of events, have expected her parents to be negotiating a marriage for her. Yet there is no evidence that they did so. While women who served at court often married a little later than those who remained in the country, Kate was by now in her twenties. If she was to marry and have children, the clock was ticking. Did the events of the early 1530s influence Kate's own views on marriage? Did she pass any of these ideas on to young Elizabeth? As a well-educated woman, did Kate make a stand for her own independence and refuse suitors? Were no offers forthcoming? Or have records of negotiations not survived? We simply do not know.

Gertrude and her husband detested Anne Boleyn's religious views and especially opposed an English Bible. In the summer of 1531 reports that Courtenay was assembling the people of Cornwall reached the king's ears. Courtenay's servants were interrogated because some of them had said that the marquess was 'heir apparent and in case the king should die or marry Anne Boleyn, then he should be king'. Others were heard saying, 'our master will wear the garland at the last', suggesting they hoped to see him crowned king. The king removed Courtenay from the Privy Council for a while, but later reinstated him. Catherine of Aragon reportedly suspected Anne Boleyn was behind the rumours to spite Courtenay for his continuing support of her and her daughter Mary. It later transpired that the allegations had arisen after Courtenay intervened in a dispute on behalf of his father-in-law, Lord Mountjoy.[1] William Kendall, an unpopular man in the marquess's employ, whipped up rumours by recruiting men in the West Country.[2] Courtenay survived this episode, and was even awarded damages, but it roused the king's suspicions.[3]

In the circumstances, it was perhaps unwise of Gertrude to continue to send gifts and messages to Catherine of Aragon after the king sent her away from court.[4] By doing so, Gertrude was advertising her continuing support for Catherine and her daughter Mary. This likely made the king doubt the Courtenays' loyalty even more.

Sir Philip Champernowne had benefited from his cousin's influential family. However, Gertrude's ongoing opposition to Anne Boleyn and religious reforms suggested that his connections to the marquess might become less advantageous.

Meanwhile, Kate's uncle, Gawen Carew, was forging ties with another key player at Henry's court. His marriage on 28 January 1531 to Anne, sister of Charles Brandon, Duke of Suffolk and Henry VIII's brother-in-law, had the potential to enhance Gawen's position significantly.[5] Brandon, second husband of King Henry's sister Mary, was one of the few close companions of Henry VIII's youth who survived unscathed through all the vagaries of the quixotic king. Despite some disagreements, they remained friends until Brandon's death in 1545. The king paid for his burial near the south door of the choir in St George's Chapel at Windsor.[6]

Anne Brandon's first husband, John Shilston of Wood, in Devon, had been a protégé of the Duke of Suffolk, having fought alongside him in France. With Brandon's support, Shilston became MP for Southwark just before his death. Shilston and Anne probably lived at the Brandon mansion there. Sir John Shilston made his will on 10 December 1528 and died soon after.[7] Gawen was the Duke of Suffolk's new protégé, and a month after Shilston's death he married Anne. That made Mary, the former Queen of France, Gawen's sister-in-law. Unfortunately, Brandon's recommendation in 1532 that Gawen be the next Sheriff of Devon, was unsuccessful. Gawen's career at court advanced relatively slowly, perhaps because he was apt to 'get into trouble'.[8]

The Brandons were not fans of Anne Boleyn, and in 1531, the king banished Charles Brandon from court after he accused Anne of having had a relationship with Thomas Wyatt. Mary, the king's sister, also spoke out publicly against her brother's marriage on 23 April 1532.[9] However, King Henry did not fall out entirely with his sister, and Brandon was soon back at court.

Sir Philip Champernowne mentioned Gawen Carew in an interesting letter written from Exeter on 28 July 1532. Misidentification because of people sharing names has perhaps caused the significance of this communication to be underestimated. Sir Philip addresses his letter to Sir George Carew, beginning 'Brother George'. George Carew the younger, son of Sir William Carew and ill-fated admiral of *Mary Rose* fame, did not receive his knighthood until the summer of 1536.[10] Nor would Sir Philip have addressed him as 'Brother'. It was, however, not unusual for the honorific 'Sir' to be used when addressing a priest, although this was more usual for non-graduate priests.[11] It is most likely that Sir Philip's brother-in-law George Carew the elder, the priest, was the intended recipient, not his nephew of the same name.

We can sense his concern as Sir Philip writes about information concerning a 'foolish friar', who 'spake and wrote slanderous words' against the king, which had been brought to his attention:

> Brother Sir George Carew, credit this bearer in a great matter concerning my duty to the King; and if you cannot speak with my lord Marquis, show this letter, which was sent me to my lord of Norfolk, Mr. Cromwell, or Mr. Controller, with such presumptions as the bearer will explain. Although the letter is dated the morrow of St. John's Day, it did not come to my hands before 28 July.[12]

St John's day was celebrated on 24 June, so there had been a considerable delay. Sir Philip explained he could not bring the letter to George as fast as the bearer, suggesting it contained urgent news. He goes on, also mentioning his other brother-in-law, Gawen Carew, and 'wishes he had mentioned it to some, so that the king had knowledge of it. By Gawyn's letter he seems to have stricken out the man's name that made the report, because he would not endanger him. Thinks, from the second line, it is one of Plymouth.'

This was clearly a dangerous matter, since he mentions the name of the informant being struck out to protect him. Frustratingly, Sir Philip does not specify exactly what information the letter he encloses contained. The reference to a 'foolish friar' might indicate a connection with the 'Nun of Kent' affair, with which Lady Champernowne's name would later be linked. Sir Philip suggests George should report the matter to Cromwell, or one of several other key figures, naming the Duke of Norfolk first. This may indicate that in the summer of 1532 Sir Philip did not yet see Cromwell as necessarily the chief among the king's advisers.[13]

This episode underlines the difficult task of people like Sir Philip in serving the king amid swirling undercurrents with different courtiers and advisers striving for the king's ear.

The full details of the matter that prompted Sir Philip to write with such urgency remain unknown. Sir Philip continued to play a key role in West Country affairs. Appointed Vice Warden of the Stannary Courts in 1532, he often presided in Courtenay's stead, as he did at the open air meeting of the court of the Stannary Council held at Crockern Tor, on Dartmoor a year later.[14]

Meanwhile, the king's moves to separate from the Church of Rome were gathering pace. In the spring of 1532, parliament brought in an act restricting the amount of money (annates) sent from England to the Pope in Rome. It was among a series of measures that gradually reduced the Pope's authority over the English Church; these measures were not popular with devout Catholics.

This act was the final straw for one of the fiercest critics, Sir Thomas More, who resigned as Lord Chancellor on 16 May of that year. Despite his opposition to the king's relentless search for a way to clear the path for his marriage to Anne Boleyn, More had accepted the position of Lord Chancellor. He had trusted Henry's promise to keep him out of the matter. But moves to give the king such power over the English church were a step too far.

Yet Henry persisted, and planned a trip to France in the hope he could gain the French king's support for his radical plans to break with the papacy. Before setting off, on 1 September 1532, he created Anne Boleyn Marquess of Pembroke, making her the most prestigious non-royal woman in the realm.

On their way to Dover, the king and Anne paused in Canterbury where they met a woman named Elizabeth Barton, also known as the Nun of Kent. She made dire predictions of the consequences should King Henry persist in a marriage to Anne. Barton had quite a following by the time she accosted the king. In 1525, when she was a servant in the household of a land agent to the Archbishop of Canterbury, she fell ill. As she lay in agony, she had visions and made prophecies. Her fame spread and, now a professed nun, Cardinal Wolsey met her. She seems to have impressed Wolsey and on his recommendation, the king met with her. At first her prophecies were not damaging, and King Henry allowed her to continue. Over several years Barton met influential figures, including Sir Thomas More, who she impressed with her fervent religious beliefs and her warnings against heresy. Bishop John Fisher also held the nun in high regard and praised her work. She met and corresponded with Fisher, seeking his counsel and support. However, Barton's prophesies about the king became more and more pointed. In 1532, in Canterbury, she went so far as to say:

> She had knowledge by revelation from God that God was highly displeased with our said Sovereign Lord [Henry VIII] … and in case he desisted not from his proceedings in the said divorce and separation but pursued the same and married again, that then within one month after such marriage he should no longer be king of this realm, and in the reputation of Almighty God should not be king one day nor one hour, and that he should die a villain's death.[15]

Notwithstanding the nun's predictions, the king and Anne travelled on to France with a large retinue of nobility and bishops. Henry Fitzroy, Duke of Richmond, and, according to *Hall's Chronicle*,[16] the Marquess of Exeter were among those who faced a rough autumnal channel crossing. Reports of the visit do not specifically mention whether Gertrude and her ladies or George and Gawen Carew or Kate's brother John, also went to France. It is possible they were among the entourage, which numbered over 2,000. Kate's cousin, Peter Carew, certainly joined the party and attended the meeting with Francis I in Calais. Although he was merely a 'henchman' in the king's service at this time, Peter had become fluent in French during his exploits in Europe. He had a reputation as a wit, and was fond of manly pursuits like jousting, and soon became a favourite with Henry VIII.

On his return to England, King Henry married Anne, in secret on St Erkenwald's Day, which was celebrated in 14 November.[17] Another ceremony, likely on 25 January, at Whitehall Palace confirmed the marriage. The king had courted Anne for seven years. His previous marriage to Catherine of Aragon had not been formally annulled. Anne was already pregnant.

On 30 March 1533, Cambridge-educated Thomas Cranmer replaced William Wareham, the 82-year-old staunchly conservative Archbishop of Canterbury who had died the previous summer. Cambridge was emerging as a 'hotbed of religious reform'. Long before they became more widely known, in a back room of The White Horse Inn in Cambridge, a group of Cambridge scholars, including Matthew Parker, had discussed Luther's early writings. Cranmer initially opposed Luther's ideas, perhaps because he recognised a need for caution in view of the king's early antipathy.[18] By 1533, however, Cranmer had become an advocate of religious reform, and while overseas he had married a German woman. Although his marriage was probably an open secret at court, the king either remained unaware or turned a blind eye.

On 23 May 1533 Cranmer gave his opinion that Catherine and Henry had never been lawfully married. This paved the way for Anne to be crowned in a lavish ceremony on 1 June. The king insisted that Gertrude, Marchioness of Exeter, attend.[19] It is likely that Sir Philip Champernowne's wife and some of his daughters were also among nearly sixty female attendants; Joan, perhaps as maid of honour to the new queen, and the others attending the marchioness.[20]

It is likely that Kate's brother John and Kate's Carew uncles and cousins were also there to see Anne crowned in Westminster Abbey. Anne Boleyn and her predecessor were the only ones among Henry's six wives actually crowned queen. It was a huge triumph for the Boleyn faction, but reports suggest the people of London were less enthusiastic. The Imperial Ambassador Eustace Chapuys, who was hostile towards Anne, reported that the procession had been 'a cold, meagre and uncomfortable thing, to the great dissatisfaction, not only of the common people, but also of the rest'.[21]

Henry Courtenay did not attend; the excuse he gave for his absence is unknown – perhaps ill health. The king's sister also missed the coronation. She and her daughter Frances were ill at the Suffolk's country seat of Westhorpe Hall. Mary Tudor died on 23 June 1533, shortly after Anne's coronation.

Brandon married his ward, the 14-year-old Katherine Willoughby, barely two months after Mary's death. She had been betrothed to his eldest surviving son, but he was too young to marry. The new Duchess of Suffolk was the daughter and heiress of the wealthy Lord Willoughby de Eresby and Maria de Salinas, a Spanish lady who served Queen Catherine of Aragon.

Trouble was brewing for Gertrude, and the Champernownes and Carews did not escape scrutiny. Shortly after the coronation, the king ordered Thomas Cromwell to lead an investigation into Elizabeth Barton, the Nun of Kent. Cromwell had Barton arrested, along with several of her contacts and supporters, including the monks, Edward Bocking and John Dering. Later, Cromwell's officers also arrested other priests and friars associated with her and her prophecies, including Henry Gold, Hugh Rich and Richard Risby. These arrests must have caused alarm in the Courtenay household. Different sources give different dates, but all agree that Gertrude, Marchioness of Exeter, consulted Elizabeth Barton on more than one occasion. Sir Philip's wife had also seen the nun's revelations, which were now deemed treasonous.[22]

As summer slipped towards autumn in 1533, Anne Boleyn's position must have seemed unassailable. Crowned queen, and thought to be carrying the king's longed-for heir, Anne was sympathetic to the humanist reformers who criticised corruption and wealth of the monasteries. However, unlike Cromwell, who saw monastic wealth as a vast reserve to replenish and enlarge the royal coffers, Anne thought it should support charitable activities. Both Cromwell and Anne championed the printing of the Bible in English, also favoured by Cambridge scholars.

People like Sir Philip and the Carews had to tread a fine line, keeping the conservatively minded Courtenays happy while still serving the king. Thomas Cromwell was emerging as the power behind the throne, but Anne's influence was strong. Kate's family later espoused the cause of religious reform, although it is debatable whether a pragmatic wish to support the winning side outweighed deeply held religious conviction in their decisions.

Chapter 4

From Royal Princess to Motherless Child

The Inner Circle: 1533–1536

On 7 September 1533, Queen Anne Boleyn gave birth to a daughter named Elizabeth, a special child who gave Kate her overarching purpose in life.

Although disappointed that Anne Boleyn's first child was a girl, Henry went on hoping the marriage would bring him his longed-for son and heir. Although he cancelled some of the planned celebrations, the jousts and feasting, he organised a grand christening in the Church of the Observant Friars in Greenwich, giving Elizabeth the full status of a royal princess. However, unlike her sister Mary, the king did not give Elizabeth the title 'Princess of Wales'. Henry reserved Prince of Wales for the son he was sure would follow.

The king insisted that the Marchioness of Exeter, known to be a supporter of Catherine of Aragon, play a prominent part in the grand ceremony of baptism on 10 September. Archbishop Cranmer presided and served as godfather to the infant Elizabeth, while Gertrude was one of the godmothers. Her husband made no excuses this time and carried the taper of virgin wax.

An intriguing note among the notebooks in which the early twentieth-century Champernownes recorded their family history research suggests that Sir Philip Champernowne's wife held the infant Princess Elizabeth at her christening.[1] However, no supporting evidence has emerged. It is likely simply another example of confused identity.[2] The only reference that might support Kate caring for Elizabeth before 1536 comes in 1559, when in a frustrated outburst Kate refers to strangling the princess in her cradle.[3]

Shortly after the birth, the king established a separate household for Elizabeth at Hatfield in Hertfordshire (Plate 6). He stripped his elder daughter of her royal status and dismissed Mary's own personal staff.[4] Known as 'the Lady Mary', she would now serve her sister. This demotion was a significant blow to Mary's pride, and she refused to acknowledge Elizabeth as a princess.

The arrangements Henry and Anne made in the autumn of 1533 for their daughter's care at Hatfield House did not, so far as is known, include Kate Champernowne. There were places, however, for some of Anne Boleyn's relatives. Sir John Shelton and his wife Anne, Lady Shelton, Anne Boleyn's paternal aunt, and her sister Lady Clere had oversight of the household that now included both king's daughters. But it was Lady Bryan, as Lady Mistress, who was in charge of Elizabeth's nursery, not the Sheltons. Lady Bryan slept in the infant princess's bedchamber, to be on hand at all times. In contrast, Elizabeth saw her parents rarely in her first years.

Margaret Bryan's mother remarried after her first husband's death, and her second husband was Thomas Howard. This made Margaret Bryan half-sister to Elizabeth Howard, Anne Boleyn's mother, and also connected her to the powerful Howard family. She had been Lady Mistress (or governess) to Princess Mary, born in February 1516. In 1519, Catherine of Aragon appointed Margaret Pole, Countess of Salisbury, the princess's godmother, to have oversight of Mary's household. Kate and her sisters may have known Lady Bryan when she served in Mary's nursery and schoolroom.

On 7 July 1519 Henry VIII had rewarded Lady Bryan with her own title, Baroness Bryan, and a pension which included 'one tun of Gascon wine yearly, out of the wine received for the King's use'.[5] It is not entirely clear if she continued to serve Princess Mary after that date. Some sources suggest that Lady Bryan became governess to Henry's illegitimate son, Henry Fitzroy.

Besides serving in the royal nurseries, Lady Bryan also had hands-on experience from bringing up three children of her own. Her daughter Elizabeth married the courtier Sir Nicholas Carew, a distant relative of the Devon Carews. Elizabeth was also related to Anne Boleyn through a shared great-grandfather, Lord Hoo. Margaret Bryan's son, Sir Francis Bryan, was one of the group of Gentlemen of the Privy Chamber known for intemperate behaviour in the early years of Henry's reign. He remained close to the king.[6]

Lady Bryan was 65 years old when she came out of retirement to head Elizabeth's nursery. Agnes Strickland describes her as 'sensible and conscientious governess.'[7] A team of nurses, rockers, laundry maids and other attendants, including Lady Troy supported her. She is described as a 'wise lady of dignity'[8] in an elegy written by a contemporary Welsh bard.

Blanche Milborne, Lady Herbert of Troy, brought plenty of experience to her role. She had been married twice and had five children of her own.[9] Blanche married James Whitney in 1494. Following his death in 1500, which left her with three small children, she became the wife of William Herbert of Troy, with whom she had two more children. Lady Troy served both Catherine of Aragon and Anne Boleyn, and like her niece Blanche Parry, she was probably fluent in the Welsh language. Lady Troy was involved in the selection of a wet nurse.[10] Blanche Parry also joined the nursery, and rocked baby Elizabeth in her cradle.[11]

After her first birthday, Elizabeth's nursery moved to Enfield, her father's childhood home. This relocation was part of a larger pattern of movement between various residences. Elizabeth also spent a good deal of time at Hunsdon, also in Hertfordshire.

In those first years Elizabeth had the full status of a royal princess with every comfort and luxury.[12] Anne Boleyn's daughter's position seemed secure and, when she was barely a year old, there was even talk of a betrothal to Charles de Valois, the Duke of Angoulême, the French king's youngest son, although it never came to fruition. The French king refused to recognise Anne as Henry's lawful wife, and the negotiations fell through.

The Nun of Kent

Not long after Elizabeth's birth, the investigation of the Nun of Kent and her associates drew the Champernownes and Carews into danger. Under interrogation, Elizabeth Barton apparently confessed that she had fabricated her revelations. She admitted that monks, especially Edward Bocking, her spiritual guide, had encouraged and supported her prophecies. The information we have about her confessions comes from Thomas Cromwell and his agents. Their investigations revealed Barton had met the Archbishop of Canterbury, Bishop John Fisher, Thomas More and many monks at Canterbury, including Observant Franciscan Friars from Greenwich and Richmond and the nuns and priests of the Bridgettine Priory of Syon.

It also emerged that the Marchioness of Exeter went in disguise to consult the nun at Canterbury, and she later sent two of her women to the abbess at Syon Abbey to invite Barton to West Horsley Place, the Courtenays' favourite residence. One of Gertrude's women is later named as Constance Baynton.

Gertrude Courtenay was a close friend of Agnes Jordan, Abbess of Syon.[13] Elizabeth Barton visited Syon on a number of occasions. Gertrude's name appeared high on the list of all those to whom Barton's associates had shown the nun's revelations, among those Hugh Richmond showed them to were 'John Carewe and his brother; Mrs. Katharine Champer, his brother's wife, and somewhat to his brother.'[14]

Although the names are confused (a later version substitutes George for John), these must be brothers George and Gawen Carew, Philip Champernowne, and his wife. In the sixteenth century, people commonly used 'brother' when referring to brothers-in-law.[15] The 'foolish friar' Sir Philip mentioned in his 1532 letter, may be Father Rich. It is not clear why or when Kate's mother, uncles and possibly Sir Philip, saw the revelations. One explanation might be that Sir Philip's wife was one of Gertrude's ladies, perhaps even the second woman Gertrude sent to Syon Abbey.

Convicted of treason, Elizabeth Barton met a terrible death by hanging on 20 April 1534, along with five of her closest associates. Those who had seen the nun's revelations faced threats of attainder, potentially having all their lands and assets seized by the Crown. The Marchioness of Exeter only escaped this fate when she wrote a grovelling letter to the king, excusing her actions as the frailty of a silly woman.[16] The Carews and Champernownes also survived unscathed, but this close brush with danger must have been a 'wake up call' for them.

An Act of Succession, passed at the end of March 1534, declared the king's marriage to Catherine of Aragon null and void, effectively rendering his daughter Mary illegitimate. If Henry and Anne had a son, he would inherit the throne. If they had no son, their daughters would be eligible to inherit.

Everyone had to take an Oath of Succession affirming the legality of Henry and Anne's marriage, and also an Oath of Supremacy. Passed in 1534, soon after the Act of Succession, the Act of Supremacy declared King Henry VIII as the Supreme Head of the Church of England, severing all ties with the pope and the Roman Catholic Church. All of Kate's family swore the oaths, as did the Marquess and Marchioness of Exeter, despite their continuing loyalty to Catherine of Aragon and her daughter, and their Catholic leanings. However, Fisher and More could not bring themselves to sign. The king ordered them to the Tower of London, imprisoned for their refusal to sign the Act of Succession.

The Fortunes of the Inner Circle

On 28 April 1534, John Veysey the Bishop of Exeter, installed Kate's uncle, George Carew, as Archdeacon of Totnes. This was a prestigious post for a young man only just embarking on his ecclesiastical career, and George's connection with the Marquess of Exeter may have helped secure the appointment.

Other family members continued to advance their careers at court, bringing them into close contact with proponents of religious reform. If Joan the younger was already at court, she may have heard discussions and begun to move towards reform. We don't know where Kate was at this time, but these two highly intelligent sisters surely discussed the new ideas. While their father likely remained circumspect in expressing his views because of his allegiance to the Courtenays, the younger generation could quietly explore and embrace new ideas.

Joan may also have met members of the Cambridge Set, including her future husband Anthony Denny. Educated at St Paul's School and St John's College,

Cambridge, Denny was universally popular, with a flair for administration; the ideal public servant.[17, 18] He had honed his diplomatic skills in the service of Lady Bryan's son, Sir Francis, and by the early 1530s had a position in the Privy Chamber. In 1534, however, marriage was far from Anthony Denny's mind. He was working his way up, intent on earning the king's trust.

In 1534, Peter Carew became a Gentleman of the Privy Chamber, serving alongside Denny and Edward Seymour, who was a squire of the body to the king. Around 1530, Seymour's brother, Thomas, perhaps struggling to follow his intellectually gifted brother at court, carried messages for Sir Francis Bryan, whom Denny had accompanied on earlier diplomatic missions.[19]

Lord William Howard took Peter to Scotland with him on a mission the following February, during which James V received the Order of the Garter. They also took a gift of 'great horses' for the Scottish king. According to Hooker, Peter 'behaved himself in such good order in the court there, the Scots persuaded themselves, by reason of his ripenes in the French tongue, and his behaviour after the French manner, that he had been some French lord'.[20]

Gawen Carew and Kate's brother John remained in unspecified positions at court. Sir Philip kept his head down, concentrating on affairs in Devon.

The Henrican court was a 'small world' where alliances, friendships and rivalries thrived as young men vied to gain the king's favour. Anthony Denny, the Seymour brothers and Peter Carew, (Plate 7) all featured in Kate's story. They knew each other well.

The Inner Circle — Conservatives or reformers?

While reformed thinking was making some headway at court, many of the ordinary people of rural Devon preferred the old familiar ways. Following one show of resistance, in February 1536, Sir Philip was one of those who sat in judgement on a group of Exeter women accused of causing a riot and attacking workers sent to dismantle the church at St Nicholas' Priory. As one of the smaller religious houses, St Nicholas' was in the first wave of Cromwell's reforms. The changes had not gone down well locally, since the priory had always provided for the poor of the city. The Marquess of Exeter found it hard to believe the rioters had indeed been women. Sir Philip and his colleagues refrained from harsh punishments. However, the women could not save the church and it was dismantled; the stone was sold and used to mend the Exe Bridge that led into the city.[21]

Senior members of the Carew family held differing views on religion. When Hugh Latimer visited Exeter in 1534 to preach Henry VIII's reforming ideas he met with hostility and was termed a 'heretick knave'.[22] One of those who called him out was Thomas Carew, suggesting he was in the Catholic camp. However, Thomas's brother, Sir William, appeared to take the opposite stance when he became involved in allegations of heresy against a shoemaker of Axminster named John Gammon. Gammon's neighbours and fellow tradespeople eventually took the case to The Star Chamber, the only case of heresy to be heard there.[23] Richard Drake, steward of the hundred of Axminster, tried, seemingly without success, to convince Sir William of Gammon's guilt. Several legal cases followed, and those pursuing the case against Gammon said that Sir William sided with a Protestant heretic.

Meanwhile, Gertrude Courtenay was in regular contact with the Spanish ambassador, Eustace Chapuys. Cromwell had a network of informants, and he likely used Gertrude as he gathered intelligence. In November 1534, Gertrude had a secret meeting with Chapuys to tell him that Catherine and her daughter were under threat. Cromwell may have orchestrated this hoping to persuade them to sign the Oath of Supremacy. In December 1534 the Treason Act made refusal to sign the oath punishable by death. Just before he set out with Anne on their summer progress in June 1535, King Henry sent both Bishop Fisher and Thomas More, his erstwhile favoured adviser, to the executioner's block for refusing to sign.

At that time Anne Boleyn's position seemed secure as the royal party visited the West Country, staying at Acton Court, Sudeley Castle and Wulf Hall, the Seymour's Wiltshire home. It may have been during this visit that the king first noticed Jane Seymour.

Cromwell's position was growing ever stronger, as he pushed ahead with parliamentary acts that continued the separation for Rome. On 21 January 1535, in addition to his other offices as Clerk of the Hanaper, Chancellor of the Exchequer, Principal Secretary and Master of the Rolls, Cromwell became Vicegerent in Spirituals, the king's deputy in charge of religious affairs, effectively giving him authority over the Church of England. The First Fruits and Tenths Act of 1534 redirected the traditional payments of first fruits (the first year's income of a benefice) and tenths (one-tenth of annual income) from the papacy to the English Crown. Cromwell also sent out his agents to enquire into the character and value of all ecclesiastical property in the kingdom, for Valor Ecclesiasticus, the greatest survey of ecclesiastical property since 1291.

In that same year, 1535, Bishop Veysey made Kate's uncle, George Carew, a Canon of Exeter Cathedral. George may have assisted Veysey in responding to the commissioners' inquiries. Like some other bishops Veysey was late submitting the requested information, and on 28 October 1535 he wrote to Cromwell. The bearer of the letter was Sir Philip Champernowne. Veysey wrote: 'The bearer, Sir Philip Chamberis, knight, will explain why the books of valuation of the spiritual possession has not come sooner into Cromwell's hands.'[24]

Unfortunately we don't have a record of the conversation between Sir Philip and Cromwell when he delivered the message, but Veysey's letter confirms that Cromwell knew Sir Philip. In May 1535, Sir Philip was named as one of a list of feoffees appointed to hold lands for the use of Gertrude and Henry Courtenay.[25] At their October meeting, Cromwell may have pumped Sir Philip for information about the state of Courtenay's affairs.

At Christmas Queen Anne was pregnant again. Elizabeth was with the court at Greenwich when, in early January 1536, according to *Hall's Chronicle*, her mother wore yellow when news was received of the death of Catherine of Aragon at Kimbolton Castle. Ambassador Chapuys, writing to his master in Spain, maintained that the king also dressed in yellow, save for a white feather in his cap, and made a great display of his 2-year-old daughter Elizabeth, carrying her around in his arms. But their joy was to be short-lived. On 24 January the king fell from his horse during a jousting tournament. Five days later Anne miscarried. Although optimistic that she would conceive again, Anne knew the king's eye had fallen on Jane Seymour. Tensions were also growing between Anne and the king's chief minister, Thomas Cromwell. The atmosphere at court that spring must have been electric, but no one expected Anne's downfall to be so sudden, or so brutal.

Anne's final brief triumph came when she forced Chapuys to acknowledge her when, on 18 April, she intercepted him at the entrance to the royal chapel at Greenwich, and bowed to him. He had no choice but to recognise her. Deliberately engineered by the king, this was his last desperate attempt to pressure the Holy Roman Emperor Charles V, Chapuys's employer, to recognise Anne as his wife and queen. Only a few weeks later, Anne was conducted to the Tower of London.

Anne may have guessed that something was going on. Matthew Parker, her reform-leaning chaplain, later confirmed that she charged him to care for Elizabeth should anything untoward happen. In his book in the 'Very Interesting People' series, Elizabeth's biographer, Patrick Collinson, mentions William Latymer's chronicle.[26] This flattering account of Anne's life, written around 1560, reports Anne's intention for her daughter to be well-trained in languages, including Hebrew, Greek, Latin, Italian, Spanish and French.

Alexander Ales, a Scottish theologian who attended the court around this time, later suggested that Elizabeth last saw her mother on 30 April.[27] There are differing views as to whether Elizabeth left Greenwich on the day of Anne's arrest, or later, after her execution.[28] It seems Elizabeth and her attendants were at Hunsdon by mid-May, along with Mary, as matters hurtled towards a chilling conclusion.

Cromwell was building his case, gathering evidence which included statements from some people Anne might have considered friends. For example, her first cousin Francis Bryan famously described by the king as the Vicar of Hell, a name echoed by Cromwell in a letter, turned against her and helped Cromwell.[29] Bryan was also a second cousin to Jane Seymour, and he actively promoted her. Long before Anne's downfall, Bryan had spotted that the king's interest in Jane meant the Seymours were growing in power and influence. He wanted to align himself with them.

Another who spoke against Anne was Anne Shelton, whose discomfort when ordered to mistreat Mary may have shaped her testimony when Cromwell questioned her.[30]

Kate's Courtenay kin also added to the growing body of damning reports. Chapuys reported that the Marchioness of Exeter had told him that Boleyn had used witchcraft to 'ensnare' the king and that her failure to bear him a surviving son was proof that God condemned their marriage. Proof of witchcraft could form grounds to dissolve a marriage. Gertrude was probably simply stirring the pot by spreading rumours that could reflect badly on Anne, rather than expecting any charges of witchcraft would actually follow.

Nicholas Carew, a staunchly Catholic courtier, and a distant relative of Kate's Carew uncles, had, on the king's instructions moved Jane from his country estate at Beddington, to Chelsea, near the king's own lodgings. He had been coaching Jane on how best to encourage the king's advances while remaining chaste and virtuous. To allow Edward Seymour and his wife to chaperone Jane before her marriage, Cromwell happily gave up his court lodgings, with their connecting stairs to the king's apartments. The Seymours were positioning themselves as the most powerful family in England.

Anthony Denny was by this time established as a valued royal servant. In December 1535 the king recommended him as Member of Parliament for Ipswich, a sure sign of his growing favour with the king.

The details of the case and trials, the dreadful executions, are well-known. They need not concern us here. On the orders of King Henry VIII, Anne Boleyn, Queen of England, met her death on Tower Green at the hands of a French swordsman on 19 May 1536. Five men, including Anne's brother George Boleyn, Viscount of Rochford, also perished.

King Henry married Jane Seymour just eleven days after Anne's execution. Before another week passed, he promoted Jane's brother Edward to the peerage as Viscount Beauchamp. Thomas Seymour became a Gentleman of the Privy Chamber, serving alongside Anthony Denny and coming into contact with Peter Carew and Kate's brother John.

The fallout following Anne's removal and Henry VIII's marriage to Jane Seymour changed the course of Kate Champernowne's life.

PART II

KATE'S CAREER

Chapter 5

In the Household of the Lady Elizabeth

1536–1537

In the summer or early autumn of 1536, Kate Champernowne travelled through the leafy lanes of Hertfordshire to Hunsdon. She had likely been living in London, possibly with a place at court. Perhaps she was pleased to escape the city, noisome and rife with infections in summer's heat, and looking forward to enjoying a quiet life in the Hertfordshire countryside. Alternatively, her assignment to the household of a child, far from court, the centre of the Tudor world, may have left her disappointed. All we know is that Kate was one of the women appointed to serve Anne Boleyn's daughter, who was to be known as 'the Lady Elizabeth, the king's daughter'.[1]

Kate joined a dysfunctional household where the king's elder daughter, Mary, had been uncomfortably situated for almost three years. Henry, egged on by Anne Boleyn, had forced Mary to give precedence to her younger sister, a state of affairs Mary resented. He had repeatedly tried to force her to acknowledge that his marriage to her mother was invalid, that Elizabeth and any other children he had with Anne Boleyn were the legitimate heirs to the kingdom.

Mary hated giving precedence to the daughter of the woman she held responsible for her mother's fate. At first, she refused to sit with the maids in the dining hall. Instead, she took her meals in her rooms until Anne instructed her aunt, Lady Shelton, to make her eat in the hall. According to Chapuys, Anne also instructed Lady Shelton to treat Mary badly; on one occasion, ordering her to 'box Mary's ears'.[2] Placed in an invidious position, Anne Shelton had little choice but to comply.

Elizabeth and her household moved regularly between Hatfield, her chief residence, Eltham and Hunsdon, all places deemed sufficiently far from London to be 'wholesome'. There were also occasional visits to the royal court at Richmond or Greenwich. In the summer of 1534, en route to Hunsdon,

Chapuys reported that Mary drove her horse forward so she could arrive at Greenwich an hour before her sister's litter.[3]

The atmosphere at Hunsdon must have been fraught while Mary stubbornly refused to acknowledge Anne Boleyn as queen, or Elizabeth as the rightful heir. This caused a great rift between Mary and her father. She frequently fell ill, probably because of the enormous stress she was under. Henry VIII had treated Mary poorly, even denying her the chance to see her dying mother.

In the summer of 1536 the two girls were suddenly on an equal footing – both declared illegitimate, standing beside, or even behind, the king's illegitimate son, Henry Fitzroy, Duke of Richmond.

In the immediate aftermath of Anne Boleyn's sudden downfall, it was Mary, not Elizabeth, who drew the king's attention and ire. Mary and her supporters, people like Gertrude Courtenay, may have hoped that Anne Boleyn's demise would improve her position and might even reinstate her mother's marriage as lawful. Mary blamed Anne for all her woes and on 26 May she wrote to Thomas Cromwell, seeking permission to send a letter to the king, saying she would have written sooner,

> to have obtained his Grace's blessing and favour; but I perceived that nobody durst speak for me as long as that woman lived, which is now gone; whom I pray our Lord of His great mercy to forgive.[4]

Mary then wrote to her father congratulating him on his marriage to Jane, in the hope of a reconciliation. But Mary's hopes soon faded. The king introduced a new act which made it treasonous to argue that either of his marriages to Catherine of Aragon or Anne Boleyn were valid, or that Mary and Elizabeth were legitimate; Jane's children had first claim to the throne. To accept her father as Supreme Head of the Church in England was contrary to Mary's own deeply held religious beliefs. She also felt that accepting that her parent's marriage was invalid was disloyal to her mother. So Mary continued to resist. Cromwell orchestrated a campaign of intense pressure on her to submit, including visits from the Duke of Norfolk and other officials. The threat of being accused of treason eventually persuaded her to capitulate. This brought about a slight thawing of Mary's relationship with her father and she seems also to have developed some kindly feelings towards Elizabeth. On 21 July she wrote to the king saying: 'My sister Elizabeth is well, and such a child toward, as I doubt not but your Highness shall have cause to rejoice of in time coming; as knoweth Almighty God, who send your Grace, with the Queen my good mother, health, with the accomplishment of your desires.'

Mary may have offered kind words about her sister, but while attention focused on her, Elizabeth's needs went unnoticed. No one gave any instructions to those charged with caring for Anne Boleyn's daughter, who was not quite 3 years old. The king had other matters on his mind – his new marriage and his determination to force Mary to his will. Another sad event soon preoccupied him, one that caused him great grief. Only two days after Mary's letter, on 23 July, 17-year-old-old Henry Fitzroy died, probably of consumption.

Lady Margaret Bryan, Elizabeth's Lady Mistress, still had no instructions as to her charge's new status. The child was growing out of her clothes fast, but no replacements were forthcoming. In early August her patience ran out and she wrote to Cromwell complaining:

> Now, as my lady Elizabeth is put from that degree she was in, and what degree she is at now I know not but by hearsay, I know not how to order her or myself, or her women or grooms. I beg you to be good lord to her and hers, and that she may have raiment, for she has neither gown nor kirtle nor petticoat, nor linen for smocks, nor kerchiefs, sleeves, rails, bodystychets, handkerchiefs, mufflers, nor begens.[5]

Anne Boleyn had doted on her daughter, but her job was to produce a son. As was usual, from the age of 3 months, she had to place Elizabeth in the care of others. The little girl was used to receiving regular consignments of fine clothes and presents from her mother. Although Anne rarely saw her daughter, she spent vast sums on her. For example, in a reckoning of the late queen's expenses in the five months before her death, drawn up by her mercer William Locke, the total came to £68 4s 1½d, (worth around £30,000 today).[6] The list includes many items 'for my lady Princess': costly velvet's and silks in rich colours to make partlets, mufflers, kirtles, sleeves and caps. By often ordering purple fabric, recognised as a 'royal' colour, Anne was underlining Elizabeth's royal status.[7] One of the last purchases was for a 'white cap of taffeta laid with a rich caul of gold'.[8] It cost £4 (roughly equivalent to £1,700 today).

To Elizabeth, her mother must have seemed a distant, unfamiliar figure; someone who visited occasionally and spoiled her. Suddenly the presents and the supply of costly clothing dried up. The switch from being showered with pretty things by her mother to barely having enough to wear must have been upsetting and confusing for Elizabeth.

Elizabeth arrived at Hunsdon Manor around the time of her mother's execution, or shortly after.[9] King Henry had purchased the Hertfordshire manor, with associated land, from the Duke of Norfolk in 1525. He had spent a considerable sum on improvements, including the addition of a long gallery, and it was said to be one of his favourites of all the homes he owned. It's said he even created two additional deer parks so that he could enjoy hunting there. Hunsdon may have been among the properties gifted to Anne Boleyn when Henry created her Marquess of Pembroke in 1532. By 1536, the king primarily used it as a residence for his children.

Following Anne's downfall, King Henry was determined to eliminate all symbols and emblems relating to his disgraced queen from the royal palaces. Elizabeth, a bright child, likely spotted unusual activity as they removed her mother's images. She also noticed that people addressed her differently. Sir John Shelton reported that Elizabeth addressed these words to him: 'How haps it, Governor, yesterday my Lady Princess, and today but my Lady Elizabeth?'[10]

If she did indeed make this remark, she showed remarkable insight for a child of her age. Although too young to understand much about the underlying cause, she was clearly well aware of the upheaval unfolding around her. Children are quickly aware of any tension among the adults who care for them. In the confusion, a power struggle broke out between Lady Bryan and Sir John Shelton, comptroller of Elizabeth and Mary's joint household. Even a small child could see that her Lady Mistress and Sir John were at odds. Lady Bryan's frustration shouts from the page in her letter to Cromwell.

> Mr. Shelton says he is master of this house … What fashion that shal be I cannot tel, for I have not sen it afore. … I trust to your lordship, who, as every man reports, loveth honor, to see this house honorably ordered … howsom ever it hath been aforetime … If the head of [the same] know what honor meaneth it will be the better ordered; if not, it will be hard to bring it to pass. Mr. Shelton would have my lady Elizabeth to dine and sup every day at the board of estate. It is not meet for a child of her age to keep such rule. If she do, I dare not take it upon me to keep her Grace in health; for she will see divers meats, fruits, and wine, that it will be hard for me to refrain her from. Ye know, my lord, there is no place of correction there; and she is too young to correct greatly. I beg she may have a good mess of meat to her own lodging, with a good dish or two meet for her to eat of; and the reversion of the mess shall satisfy her women, a gentleman usher, and a groom; which been eleven persons on her side. This will also be more economical.

Lady Bryan's letter seems to have had the desired effect. The king ordered that Elizabeth should take meals suitable to her age in her chamber, rather than seated at 'the board of estate'.

On Wednesday, 16 August, Shelton wrote to Cromwell, assuring him he would follow the king's orders and complaining about the lack of funds.

> I perceive by your letter the King's pleasure that my lady Elizabeth shall keep her chamber and not come abroad, and that I shall provide for her as I did for my lady Mary when she kept her chamber. Have me in remembrance for the King's warrant you commanded me to deliver to Master Wrisley for money for the household, otherwise I cannot continue it.[11]

The quarrel is interesting, as it shows not only the tensions and uncertainty in the household Kate joined, but also that Shelton did not question Elizabeth's status as the king's daughter.[12] Indeed, he thought she should eat in a place of honour. It's sometimes argued that Henry's neglect of Elizabeth's needs in the summer of 1536 was deliberate, because he could not tolerate reminders of his former wife. But as he later showed in his dealings with others like Henry Courtenay and Nicholas Carew, close friends from childhood he sent to the executioner's block, the king could move on rapidly. It is more likely that he simply forgot about Elizabeth's needs.

Despite the allegations of her mother's infidelity, it seems Henry never doubted that Elizabeth was his child. She continued to be accorded the status of a king's daughter, albeit illegitimate. He later gave every appearance of being fond and proud of her, and Elizabeth seemed to bear him no ill will for her mother's execution. Instead, she idolised him, later calling herself the 'Lion's cub'.

In that fateful summer of 1536 Elizabeth was fractious because she was teething. Most children have all their baby teeth by the time they are 2-3 years old. The emergence of the second molars can be painful. Elizabeth was suffering, and Lady Bryan was evidently spoiling her. She writes: 'My lady has great pain with her teeth, which come very slowly. This makes me give her own way more than I would. … For she is as toward a child and as gentle of conditions as ever I knew any in my life.'[13]

The 'motherly' tone of Lady Bryan's letter, her heartfelt concern for her charge, hints at a warm and caring relationship with Elizabeth.

If anyone stood 'in place of a mother' to the orphaned child at this time, it was Margaret Bryan.

Sir John and Lady Shelton continued in post until 1538.[14] The joint household was reordered, split into two, and new staff, including Kate, arrived. Although the records of the new appointments are filed under June 1536, the exact date these women joined Elizabeth's household remains uncertain. Kate was definitely in post at Hunsdon on 10 October when she wrote to Thomas Cromwell, thanking him for her new position.[15] In her letter, given in full below as transcribed from the original by Miss Champernowne, Kate helpfully clarifies her identity, by making it clear her father is still living. Since their fathers died before 1526, that rules out her mother and her future sister-in-law, Catherine Blount:

> To the Rght Honorable Lord Privy Seale deliver this
>
> Right honorable and my singular good lord, after my duty remembrid this may be most humbly to thank your lordship for the great goodness y fynde yn you dyvers wayes which is not only yn that you were the very means to prefer me to the rome that y am now yn and by your letters yn the same the better accepted and regarded myche more than y am worthy to be but also as I ryghte well perceve by my fryndes your lordship perceveth yn your goodenesse yn reporting the best of me to the King's grace whereyn y have gode cause to thynke myself as myche bounde to your lordship as y am to my father of any frynde that I have levinge…

Kate thanks Cromwell for recommending her to the king, and then continues with a request for funds:

> … and for as myche as hyt hathe pleased the Kyng's majestie, by your mean to call me to that rome, whych y am not able to mayntayne to his honour onlesse his grace appoynt me sume yerely stypent towards my levyng y thought therefore meytt most humbly to desyre your lordship to have me in remembres for the same to the Kyngs highness at suche convenyent tyme as your lordship thynke best for y wold have been lothe to have trobled your lordship wt thes rude wryting except very necessitie had inspired me so to doo and loeth y wilbe to charge my father who hath as myche to do wt that lytell levyng he hathe as any man that I knowe as knowith God who ever preserve your good lordship and send you longe lyff wt myche increase of honour
>
> from Hunsden the xth of October
> your dayly bedeswoman
> Kateryn Champnon

Kate confirms it was Cromwell himself who recommended her for the position. However, we don't know for certain who suggested her to the king's chief minister, or what prompted his decision to place her in Elizabeth's household.

Perhaps Kate's father mentioned Kate's name in passing, and commended her exceptional humanist learning, her facility in languages and Latin, when delivering Bishop Veysey's excuses in October 1535. Kate's brother John was a favourite of the king,[16] and may well have nominated her for the post.[17] However, John was young, held a junior position, and lacked the 'gravitas' to influence decisions.[18] He was by now a close friend of another wit at court, his cousin Peter Carew, who, although popular, was similarly unlikely to have been the one to recommend Kate. Kate's uncle, Gawen Carew, another possible sponsor, was linked by marriage to the king's friend, Charles Brandon, and may have had access to the royal circle. However, Gawen's career did not progress quickly, although the king did grant him a licence to import wine and timber in that year.[19] He was hardly a prominent courtier who could advocate strongly for Kate.

Of all those of Kate's inner circle, it is most likely it was Anthony Denny (Plate 4) who first put her name forward to Cromwell. Denny probably also put in a good word with the king. He had been steadily working his way up the hierarchy and gaining the king's trust. Denny may have learned a lot from his time working for Sir Francis Bryan, whose ability to change his views to suit those of the king had, in the main, kept him out of trouble. There can be no doubt of his commitment to reform, but Anthony Denny put his career before religious conviction. He never antagonised King Henry by taking an extreme stance. A yeoman of the royal wardrobe, Denny was also keeper of the royal Palace of Westminster, a post he held informally for a couple of years before being officially given the job in 1538. In his post in the wardrobe he had charge of jewels and costly clothing. The king trusted him with his personal spending money. He was likely also already courting Kate's sister Joan, although they did not marry until 1538. Denny was close to Edward Seymour, their paths crossing many times in the course of their respective careers. He also knew the younger Seymour brother. Like Denny, as we have seen, Thomas Seymour, had begun his career with Sir Francis, acting as a messenger in 1530. With all these connections, Anthony Denny was well placed to speak for Kate.

On 9 September 1536, Anthony Denny received a substantial grant of lands as Groom of the Privy Chamber.[20] He was developing a role as an intermediary between the king and courtiers. As Denny's biographer, N.P. Sil, points out, there are many entries in the king's letters and papers recording correspondence addressed through Denny or his junior colleague and brother-in-law, John Gates.[21, 22] Like the Civil Service mandarin 'Sir Humphrey' portrayed in the BBC series *Yes Minister*,[23] Denny quietly exercised power 'behind the scenes'. However, whereas Sir Humphrey was manipulative and, although outwardly deferential, had an adversarial relationship with those he served, Denny gained King Henry's trust. Everyone who knew Anthony Denny liked him.

Denny was also a member of the set of Cambridge-educated men who were prominent in the coming years. He was a friend of Matthew Parker, whom Anne Boleyn had asked to watch over Elizabeth, should anything happen to her. Aware of Anne Boleyn's wish that her daughter be fluent in many languages to enable her to stand her ground at the courts of any foreign prince she might marry, Parker was perhaps keen to ensure linguists were among Elizabeth's teachers, even at such a tender age. Kate – respectable, well connected intelligent, fluent in several languages and – like her sister, Joan – already leaning towards reform, was the ideal candidate. Who better than Denny, who had the king's goodwill, and knew her well, to act as her advocate?

However, we might wonder why Anthony Denny and others, including Cromwell himself, suddenly took such an interest in Elizabeth's upbringing. Henry Fitzroy's death may have focused their minds. While everyone hoped the king's marriage to Jane Seymour might produce an heir, Henry's track record was not encouraging. No one dared to express such thoughts openly, but the king's brother, Arthur, and his illegitimate son, Fitzroy, had both died as teenagers, probably from consumption or a similar disease. Henry's two marriages had lasted for over twenty-seven years, but resulted in a string of miscarriages, stillbirths, short-lived infants and two girls. If Jane did not give birth to a son, Mary might inherit, and she would not be a friend of religious reform. Although she had reluctantly accepted her father as head of the church, Mary's rigid allegiance to the Catholic faith and her mother's memory did not bode well. Elizabeth, however, was a blank sheet, a child with no fixed views.

Cromwell was quietly gathering reform-minded people around him, and also wanted to build a circle of educated humanist gentry.[24] No one at this stage thought there was any realistic prospect of Elizabeth ruling. However, Cromwell may have argued that with the right education, the king's younger daughter could prove a useful bargaining chip in a future diplomatic alliance. Henry's split from Rome might one day mean the two major Catholic powers, France and Spain, would join forces against England. Cromwell may already have been exploring the idea of an alliance with one of the Protestant European states, like the one he later pursued with disastrous consequences with the House of Cleves.

Kate's humanist education made her an ideal candidate. Her family also had close ties to the Courtenays who Cromwell already had in his sights. It is tempting to wonder if he also wanted Kate as an informant. He had eyes and ears everywhere.[25]

Whatever the reasoning, Cromwell recommended her, and Kate wrote to thank him. To write in such terms to the most powerful man in the land beneath the king, showed extraordinary self-confidence.[26] Kate boldly asked if Cromwell could ask the king to pay her for her services. Kate's may have been intended as an unpaid appointment; that was often the case. However, Shelton had already complained of a lack of funding for the household needs. It's possible that other staff were in similar plight.

Kate's mention of her father's 'little living' subtly alludes to Sir Philip's financial difficulties, something Cromwell knew all about. At the time Kate took up her pen, Sir Philip had been called to muster his men at Ampthill to help put down the Pilgrimage of Grace, a northern rebellion led by a lawyer named Robert Aske.[27] The rebels didn't want to overthrow the king, but they wanted him to change his mind about getting rid of Catholicism and the monasteries. Rising prices and failed harvests, rumours of tax rises all added fuel to the fire. The rebel forces were gaining strength, and the king was worried. So he called men like Sir Philip to 'step up' to support him.

Kitting his men out placed an added burden on Sir Philip's already stretched resources. He had shouldered a portion of the Carew family debts for many years, and had to provide dowries for his daughters, at least three of whom were already married. The elder Joan's marriage to Robert Gamage, a member of a wealthy Welsh family, required a considerable dowry. Elizabeth had married a local landowner, William Cole, while Katherine was the wife of Otho Gilbert. John Gilbert's will of 1539 indicates that Philip had not yet paid the money agreed as dowry due when his daughter married his heir, Otho (Otes) Gilbert.[28] The marriage must have been before January 1536, when their eldest son, John Gilbert, was born. In time, Philip also had to make provision for Joan, the younger, and Frances. He was perhaps relieved that at this time there was no prospect of a wedding for Kate. Instead, she took up her duties at Hunsdon.

With the new appointments, Mary's attendants swelled to forty-two, including gentlewomen, chamberers, gentlemen, a physician, a chaplain, yeomen, footmen, a laundress, grooms of the chamber and of the stable. Being younger, Elizabeth's needs differed from those of her sister, and did not require quite so many servants. The list included gentlewomen, chamberers, gentlemen, a chaplain, grooms of the chamber and of the stable, yeomen, a laundress and a wood-bearer. Kate soon got to know everyone.

The gentlewomen were not there to deal with Elizabeth's domestic needs; those tasks fell to the chamberers, named as Alice Huntercombe and Jane Broadbelt.[29] Gentlemen ushers had oversight of the lower servants (cooks and maids), grooms of the chamber kept the rooms clean, yeomen and woodmen kept the fires in kindling, while laundry maids dealt with the linen. A chaplain named Sir Ralph Taylor was there to oversee Elizabeth's spiritual guidance. The gentlewomen kept Elizabeth company, played games with her, oversaw her first attempts at sewing, entertained her with music, and at all times modelled the high standards of courtesy and manners demanded in Tudor society.

Lady Bryan continued as Elizabeth's Lady Mistress, with Lady Troy serving under her as 'governess'. (These two terms are confusingly interchangeable.) Brought into the royal nursery by her aunt, Lady Troy, Blanche Parry also remained in post. She was in her late twenties or early thirties, close in age to Kate, who was one of the four serving gentlewomen added to Elizabeth's staff.[30]

Elizabeth, Countess of Kildare – named as Lady Garrett – was the daughter of Thomas Grey (Elizabeth Woodville's son). Kate's Poyntz relatives had a connection to the Greys through Thomas Grey's brother, Anthony, whose illegitimate daughter, Margaret, married Robert Poyntz. Elizabeth Grey, had served as maid of honour to King Henry's sister, Mary, when she was Queen of France.[31] Like Anne Boleyn she remained in France for a time, serving Queen Claude, before returning to England to join Catherine of Aragon's ladies. After her marriage she lived in Ireland, but returned to the English court in 1533 with her husband, Gerald Fitzgerald. He was accused of corruption, and already in poor health, imprisoned in the Tower of London. Fitzgerald had lost the use of his limbs from wounds sustained in earlier battles and died in the Tower a year later. The king took pity on his widow and sent her to serve his daughters. There is every possibility that Kate knew the Countess of Kildare well.

The Countess of Kildare's younger daughter, another Elizabeth, accompanied her mother.[32] Elizabeth Kildare, later known as 'the fair Geraldine', had a lot in common with Elizabeth Tudor. She was six years older, and the difference in their ages probably meant they rarely shared lessons. However, both had a turbulent childhood, including losing a parent in catastrophic circumstances. The two girls became close friends, and it is thought Elizabeth Kildare may have acted as an intermediary between Mary and her sister Elizabeth when relations were fraught.[33]

We don't know the identity of the woman named as Elizabeth Candysche for certain. She may be Elizabeth Cavendish, a relative of George Cavendish, former usher to Cardinal Wolsey.[34]

Also joining the nursery was Mary Norreys (Norice, or Norris – once again, many variations in spelling occur). Around 10 years old, Mary was the daughter of Henry Norreys, one of those accused and executed alongside Anne Boleyn. Mary may not have remained in Elizabeth's household for long. In 1537 she attended the funeral of Jane Seymour, and received gifts of jewels after the queen's death, suggesting she was one of Jane's maids of honour. In 1541 Mary became the second wife of Kate's nephew, Sir George Carew, and after his death on the *Mary Rose* in 1545, she married Kate's brother, Sir Arthur Champernowne.

Although Kate's duties did not yet involve formal teaching – in 1536 she was merely one of Elizabeth's gentlewomen – informal training to prepare

Elizabeth for her future role in life had already begun. Childhood as we know it was not really a concept in Tudor England. The birth of a child was an event to be celebrated in high-status and royal families. Parents often considered marriage prospects before a girl could walk or talk, as had been the case for Elizabeth. By that eventful summer, Lady Bryan and Lady Troy had begun to instil the complex set of social 'rules', the fundamentals of good manners and etiquette, that governed the behaviour of the Tudor elite. Lady Troy had almost certainly already taught Elizabeth her letters using a hornbook by the time Kate arrived.[35] Hornbooks were single sheets of paper mounted on boards and covered with cattle horn to make them durable. They often had handles, making them easy for children to hold or hang from their belts or necks. Bea Howell describes this as 'a delicate little horn book of silver filigree'.[36]

Dressed as a miniature adult in clothing not at all comfortable for play, Elizabeth was already being groomed to fulfil her allotted role in life, much like any other well-born girl. She may have had some toys, an amber baby rattle, perhaps a doll or a cup-and-ball or as she grew, a hobby horse. However, playtime must be earned through good behaviour and attention to her lessons.

It is hard to say what it was about Kate that enabled her to forge a special bond with her charge so quickly. She was a spinster in her thirties with no discernible experience of childcare or teaching.[37] It couldn't have been her academic prowess that so impressed a 3-year-old – respect for that might come later. It may simply be that Kate paid attention to a lonely little girl, gave her time, sympathy and love. In the tense atmosphere at Hunsdon, Kate may have appeared as a new, friendly face when those she had known since birth had become distracted and impatient. Elizabeth never mentioned her mother in later life, and it's impossible to discover whether or when anyone explained to the child what had happened. She may have heard whispers as the servants gossiped about the shocking events. It's unlikely Kate or anyone else gave the child the full details until much later. Perhaps Kate earned Elizabeth's trust and respect by answering her questions with honesty and sensitivity in a way appropriate to the child's age. The hint of a smile in Kate's portrait (Plate 1) suggests she had a sense of humour. Perhaps she was one of those rare teachers who can capture a child's imagination, and make learning fun. Unfortunately the historical record is silent. Characterisations of Kate as jolly, fun-loving, and a gifted teacher have been inferred from slim evidence.

Vives, commissioned by Catherine of Aragon to advise on her daughter Mary's education, had recommended that royal children should have companions in the schoolroom. Elizabeth did not share her learning with children her own age as Henry Fitzroy did, whose fellow students proved a distraction. However she had the company of girls only a few years older – Mary Norreys must have been only around 10 years old, and Elizabeth Fitzgerald, 9. Yet it is thought that Kate was the one who instantly became a favourite.[38]

The Pilgrimage of Grace and the Inner Circle

While Kate was getting to know Elizabeth, her cousin – the recently knighted Sir George Carew – like Sir Philip, joined the king's forces in readiness to put down a northern rising. Sir George had taken over responsibility at Mohun's Ottery, following his father's death that momentous summer.

An uprising against the split from the Church of Rome, the dissolution of smaller monasteries and the policies of the king's chief minister, the so-called Pilgrimage of Grace, began in Yorkshire in October 1536 and had rapidly spread throughout the North. The background to the rebellion, the first to seriously threaten Henry's VIII's rule, was complex. Disquiet about a number of issues came on the back of several poor harvests and rising grain prices. The initial spark that ignited ordinary people was the suppression of a short-lived Lincolnshire rising, led by a local cobbler, Nicholas Melton. A well-connected lawyer, Robert Aske, soon emerged as the leader of the growing rebellion.[39]

The king sent the Marquess of Exeter with the Earls of Norfolk and Suffolk to quell the rebellion. He suspected both Exeter and Norfolk of sympathy with the rebels, so this was a test of their loyalty.[40] After a short time he dismissed most of the other assembled nobles, including Sir Philip.

Kate probably accompanied Elizabeth as she and her sister Mary went to join the king at the court in Windsor which was considered safer until the rebellion ended. With promises that he would address their grievances, Henry entertained the rebel leader, Aske, at Greenwich during an exceptionally cold Christmas with the Thames frozen over. But the show of bonhomie did not last. As Robert Aske began his journey north, fighting broke out again. Accusations of treason were followed by arrest and a death sentence, horrifically carried out by hanging Aske in chains from Clifford's Tower in York.[41] The Dukes of Norfolk and Suffolk played their part in quelling the uprising, Norfolk albeit reluctantly. Some sources suggest that Henry Courtenay, Marquess of Exeter, failed in this task and retreated with his men to Devon.

The kingdom stabilised, and the royal sisters resumed their round of moves between different palaces. During this time Mary showed some affection for her younger sibling, often buying her gifts.[42] Mary often joined the king and queen at court, while Elizabeth saw less of her new stepmother. Then, to King Henry's joy, Queen Jane became pregnant. She delivered a healthy baby boy on 12 October 1537, an event which had a significant impact on the lives of both Elizabeth and Kate.

Chapter 6

Governess

1537–1539

On 15 October 1537, 4-year-old Elizabeth played an important part at her brother's christening in the magnificent chapel at Hampton Court Palace. She carried the chrism, a 'richly garnished' baptismal cloth symbolising the cleansing of sins, used to anoint the baby with chrism oil. Thomas Cranmer, Archbishop of Canterbury, performed the ceremony, welcoming Henry's heir into the Church in England, on a platform high enough for everyone to see.

Sir Francis Bryan, wearing an apron, and no doubt delighted to have backed the Seymours, waited at the font as the procession wound its way across the courtyard. Elizabeth was too young to walk alone, so the prince's uncle, Edward Seymour, carried her. Seymour's brother, Thomas, held a corner of the splendid canopy held high over the baby's head. Gertrude, Marchioness of Exeter, chosen to be the prince's godmother, carried the precious child. Her husband walked beside her with the Duke of Suffolk. Gertrude was now the godmother of two royal children, and it seemed the Courtenays had regained royal favour. The Champernownes and the Devon Carews likely breathed a sigh of relief.

Henry's other daughter, Mary, also played a prominent part in the christening ceremony, as the second godmother, while Cranmer stood godfather, as he had for Elizabeth. As was usual, Edward's parents did not attend. We know that Lady Bryan, the Lady Mistress, and Lady Troy joined Mary and Elizabeth to bear the prince's train as the procession left the chapel.[1] It is possible, but not certain, that Kate was also among those caring for Elizabeth.

Fearing a plague outbreak – with London's death toll rising and a death recorded at Kingston, near Hampton Court – the king was anxious to restrict numbers at the christening ceremony. He allowed only those with official letters to attend, and set limits on the numbers accompanying the 'great and the good'. He ordered that,

> no duke is to bring more than six persons in his company, no marquis more than five, no earl above four, no baron above three,

> no knight or squire above two, no bishop or abbot above four, and none of the King's or Queen's chaplains above two.[2]

With that in mind, the party accompanying the Lady Elizabeth, who likely travelled to Hampton Court in late September, had to be small. We do not know how many attendants accompanied her. Nor does the record tell us how long Elizabeth remained after the ceremony, or if she was there when, on 15 October, the king raised Edward Seymour from Lord Beauchamp to become the Earl of Hertford. On that same day, the king knighted Thomas Seymour (Plate 8).

The celebrations came to an abrupt end when Henry's joy turned to sorrow. Queen Jane died, just twelve days after giving birth to her son. She survived a long labour and initially seemed to recover. Historians have suggested many theories to explain Jane's death shortly after childbirth, a fate shared by many women of that era.

No sooner had she passed away than lists were compiled of her jewels and dower lands. We find Kate's father listed at Curry Mallet. (See Chapter 2, p.15.)

It is unlikely Elizabeth understood the significance of her brother's arrival or her stepmother's death. Jane had been kind to both of Henry's daughters, but unlike Mary, who had spent a good deal of time with Jane before the birth, Elizabeth saw her only rarely. Perhaps in later life she reflected on the dangers of childbirth, reinforcing her reluctance to marry. But at 4 years old, she probably only remembered a party where Lord Delaware offered her spices, wafers and wine, and everyone wore glittering clothes.[3]

However, Edward's arrival heralded changes which may have seemed devastating to the little girl. Lady Bryan was to become Lady Mistress in charge of Prince Edward's nursery. She had been a constant presence, a grandmotherly figure who had comforted, loved and cared for Elizabeth since birth. We might wonder how happy Elizabeth was to share Lady Bryan with her brother, although there is no evidence of sibling jealousy. Indeed, Elizabeth came to love Edward.

At first, baby Edward joined his sisters' household as they moved between the Hertfordshire palaces and Eltham, an arrangement that mirrored his father's childhood with his sisters. Sources disagree on exactly when Lady Troy officially replaced Lady Bryan as Elizabeth's Lady Mistress. It seems both women also had a hand in the early upbringing of young Edward. Lady Troy is rarely mentioned in the surviving records, so it is difficult to establish exactly how important a figure she was in young Elizabeth's life.

It was usual for servants and attendants to sleep near those they served to be nearby when needed at any hour of the day or night. Elizabeth was used to having Lady Bryan sleeping in her chamber. Now, so that she could keep a constant watch over the precious prince, Lady Bryan moved to Edward's bedside, leaving Lady Troy to occupy the bed beside Elizabeth's. Lady Troy was no stranger and Lady Troy's niece, Blanche Parry, was another familiar face. Lady Troy may have hoped Blanche would succeed her on retirement.[4] However, it was Kate who became the fixed point in Elizabeth's world.

In another change, the Sheltons left in March 1538, and after Lady Kingston, who was in charge for a short time, Sir Edward and Lady Baynton took their place with oversight of Elizabeth and Mary's households.[5] By the end of 1538 Kate was playing a larger part in Elizabeth's education.

Historians and writers have credited Kate with teaching Elizabeth a long list of subjects including mathematics, geography, astronomy, history and several languages – Latin, French, Italian, Flemish and Spanish – as well as music, dancing, sewing and good manners. However, she did not teach in isolation, along the lines of a Victorian governess. Kate may herself have introduced young Elizabeth to some of these subjects, and taught the rudiments of English and Latin grammar. However, others – we know the names of some of them – also provided specific tuition. Rather than Elizabeth eventually exhausting Kate's academic abilities and needing a male tutor, as Elizabeth's learning progressed, Kate's role evolved.

The Lady Mistress had oversight of not only her charge's education but also the running of her household, rather like a headteacher does in a twenty-first century school. Working under her guidance, like a modern-day deputy headteacher, a royal governess devised and delivered a broad curriculum for her pupil. That meant she must coordinate input from specialist teachers of the right calibre to meet the child's needs. As Kate's new role expanded, she took on more responsibility, and the other aspects of the Tudor governess's role, as a protector, mentor and adviser, became more important.

At 4 years old, Elizabeth likely moved on from the hornbook to a primer, a small book of basic prayers and simple religious readings. Lady Bryan and Lady Troy would have followed the king's lead in religion and accepted the break from Rome. However, we might speculate that Kate encouraged Elizabeth gently towards a more reformist viewpoint. Cromwell may have had that in mind when he recommended her. Anne Boleyn's chaplain, Matthew Parker, preached in Elizabeth's presence at Hunsdon in 1535 when she was only 2 years old, and preached to her again at Hatfield in 1540, suggesting his interest in Anne Boleyn's daughter continued.[6] Elizabeth's own chaplain, named as Sir Ralph Taylor in the 1536 list of appointments, assisted with her early spiritual care.

There were practical life skills to learn too. Of these, riding was not only essential but seen as an excellent form of exercise. Elizabeth became a skilled horsewoman and in later life enjoyed hunting too. There is no evidence that

Kate was particularly fond of riding, unlike her husband who later wrote a book on horsemanship. It may have been Blanche Parry who joined Elizabeth on her early riding excursions.[7]

As soon as Elizabeth could hold a needle, Kate, and the other gentlewomen introduced her to sewing. Women of their social standing often dedicated hours to needlework, crafting exquisite embroidery and sometimes even undergarments like the shirts Catherine of Aragon made for King Henry. Needlework was an especially suitable occupation for girls, as it fostered concentration, precision and patience. Young minds could not wander to unsuitable topics while focused on a complicated blackwork embroidery pattern.

It is likely that Kate inherited her father's love of music, which was an integral part of the royal children's world. Mary's Privy Purse accounts show that she paid the prince's minstrels several times in 1537.[8] Elizabeth became an excellent musician, playing the virginals and the lute, and she enjoyed singing and dancing. While Kate covered the basics, Elizabeth would soon have needed music teachers as she progressed. One of them may have been the accomplished lutenist and composer, Philip van Wilder, who is known to have taught her siblings.[9]

A love of reading passed down through Kate's family to her nephew, Sir Walter Raleigh, who was renowned for taking a chest full of books with him everywhere he went. Another nephew, Sir Humphrey Gilbert, was reportedly reading More's *Utopia* on his ship, the *Squirrel*, when it sank off the Azores in 1583.[10] So it is likely Kate herself loved to read, and introduced Elizabeth to the joy to be found in books.

Kate had a good grasp of Latin and other languages, and Elizabeth was soon making progress. But it was not all hard work. Jane the fool was there to entertain them, Elizabeth Fitzgerald, a few years her senior, was there as a playmate, her sister Mary treated her kindly, and her little brother fascinated her.

The Inner Circle

Marriage was in the air among the inner circle in 1538. A muniments book at Lambeth Palace Library records a marriage licence granted by the Archbishop of Canterbury.[11] Translated from the Latin, the entry dated 4 February 1538 reads: 'Anthony Denny, gentleman of the King's household and Joan Champernowne, daughter of Sir Philip Champernowne. Dispensation for marriage in any church without banns 10s.'

The date of Joan's wedding to Anthony Denny is further confirmed in an entry in the Letter and Papers of Henry VIII which shows that in February 1538, the king granted several prestigious properties, including Cheshunt, to

'Anthony Denny and Joan Champernowne, one of the daughters of Sir Philip Champernowne, whom the said Anthony is going to marry'.[12]

Because of Anthony's position at court, the wedding may have taken place on one of the royal chapels in the presence of the king himself. Hampton Court is a possibility, for Henry VIII spent a lot of time there that year. Work was also starting on new building projects, including a new palace at Nonsuch, near Eltham. This burgeoning fascination with the newest architectural styles, and the construction of even more magnificent palaces, might have distracted the king from the pain of losing his wife. With no queen at court, Joan Denny could retire to the country to start her family. The Dennys had five sons and four daughters in what seemed to be a happy marriage.[13] Of the six Champernowne girls, Kate was the only one who remained unwed. Frances married Roger Budockside, a Devon gentleman, before 1540.[14]

By late 1537 Kate's brother John was married to Catherine Blount, Gertrude Courtenay's younger half-sister. John and Catherine's only son, Henry, was born on 19 June 1538, as confirmed in his grandfather's Inquisition Post Mortem.[15] With Kate and her mother, John's wife became the third woman named Katherine/Catherine Champernowne alive at the same time.

It seems the Champernownes pressed the Blount family for a generous marriage settlement. Either deliberately or inadvertently, they may have passed on details of these negotiations to Cromwell including potentially damaging references to Henry Courtenay. Courtenay wrote to Cromwell in March 1538, complaining that he had been misrepresented to the king as being responsible for paying £1,000 (over £400,000 today) for Catherine Blount's dowry. The king had also been told that Catherine's mother had secretly delivered jewels and plate to the value of £1,000 to the marquess for the same purpose. This was a perilous time for Courtenay, coming only three weeks after Cromwell had personally interrogated two of his servants: William Parr, his bear ward, and John Payne. Unfortunately, details are scant, but the two men were attainted of high treason and executed.[16] Courtenay's letter seems to have convinced Cromwell to back off, at least for a short time. But Henry Courtenay's days were numbered.

John Champernowne continued to serve a court as did his cousin Peter Carew. Henry Champernowne was not Kate's first nephew; her sister, Katherine the younger, already had two boys with her first husband, Otho (Otes) Gilbert.[17]

Things were not going well for Kate's uncle, Gawen Carew (Plate 9). In April 1538, he was in trouble after he and a servant killed a man in a sword fight. Perhaps his connections at court allowed Gawen to escape serious charges, though he spent a short time in the compter, a jail primarily used for debtors and petty offenders. This brawl was one of many breaking out in the city that year, where lawlessness was becoming a serious problem.

Gawen's release soon followed, but this sort of behaviour did not help his career prospects. However, his nephew was forging ahead. Knighted in 1536, Sir George Carew had taken his maternal uncle, William Courtenay's place in parliament as knight of the shire for Devon, and served as sheriff of the county in 1537. Later that year he had his first taste of command at sea when, with John Dudley, he was deterring pirates in the English Channel. Sir George married Thomasine Pollard, daughter of Sir Lewis Pollard, an eminent lawyer who had served under both Henry VII and his son. Several members of Sir Lewis' large family connected with the Champernownes.[18]

Later in 1537, Sir George undertook a mission for Cromwell. Disguised as merchants, he and a man named John Butler, were to investigate the strength of Charles V's defences in the Netherlands. Sir George was also involved in a dispute with Arthur Plantagenet, Lord Lisle, regarding the acquisition of Frithelstock Priory in Devon. Like St Nicholas' in Exeter, Frithelstock was one of the smaller religious houses in the first wave of Cromwell's reforms.[19] Eventually they reached an agreement and Lord Lisle received Sir George in Calais, where Lisle served as constable. Sir George's star was rising, and he became a Justice of the Peace and served on commissions alongside Kate's father during 1538. In 1539, as Cromwell's appointee and likely as his spy, Sir George took up the post of Captain of Rysbank Castle, serving under Lisle. George's wife, Thomasine accompanied him.

In January 1538, Sir Philip Champernowne wrote to Cromwell with some concerns about the Abbot of Tavistock, who was ill. But as the year progressed, Sir Philip kept his head down. It was becoming clear that the Marquess of Exeter was heading for trouble.

The Courtenays had, to some extent, worked alongside Cromwell to bring Anne Boleyn down, hoping for Mary's reinstatement. However, they found it hard to swallow Cromwell's interventions in religion. It was never a good idea to get on the wrong side of the Lord Privy Seal, and Courtenay's links through birth to the Pole family made him an easy target. In addition, Reginald Pole was emerging as the king's arch enemy. Pole, now Cardinal Pole, had published a treatise condemning Henry's policies and denying the royal supremacy. Henry suspected him of encouraging Europe's Catholic powers to act against him. In 1537, Henry sent Sir Francis Bryan to France, ostensibly to persuade King Francis I to refuse to see Pole, but in reality to abduct or kill Pole. Pole escaped because he had received a warning.

In July 1538, Francis I and Emperor Charles V, signed a peace treaty and were rumoured to be plotting a joint invasion of 'heretical' England. In early November Courtenay was arrested, along with Reginald Pole's brother, Lord Montagu. They were accused of plotting to aid the attack and depose the king and return papal authority in England. The accusations stemmed from vague gossip about overheard conversations. Little actual evidence existed, but the court swiftly convicted the men, primarily because of Geoffrey Pole's testimony after he broke under questioning. Geoffrey pleaded guilty to treason, attempted suicide twice, and suffered a complete mental breakdown before his release the following year. But Henry Courtenay, Marquess of Exeter, King Henry's close friend since childhood, met his end on the executioner's block on 3 December 1538. Montagu followed him on 9 December. Courtenay's estates were attainted, Gertrude and her son, Edward Courtenay were held in the Tower of London.

Kate's father desperately feared that, despite having nothing to do with any plots, his longstanding loyalty to the Courtenays and his continued service as the marquess's deputy in the Stannary Court might implicate him. It is interesting that he approached the Duke of Norfolk, not Cromwell himself. Norfolk wrote to Cromwell: 'This night after I supped, Sir Philip Shamborne desired to speak with me. He said he was in danger for my Lord Marquis in divers bonds and only used familiarly with him till they were discharged, when he intended to give up the office of the Stannary under him.'[20]

His plea evidently succeeded, and Sir Philip faced no charges. However, Sir Nicholas Carew was not so lucky. Accused of treasonous activity based on letters found at Exeter's home which implicated him in the supposed plot, he faced trial on 14 February 1539. After a guilty verdict, on 3 March 1539 he followed his friend Henry Courtenay to the block at Tower Hill. Gertrude's release in 1540 came with the loss of her court position and most of her lands, while her 12-year-old son Edward remained in the Tower of London until 1553. The king granted Gertrude an annuity of £163 15s 11d in March 1540 (worth around £70,000 today) and she returned to court under Queen Mary.[21]

This brutal episode, known as the Exeter Conspiracy, must have sent shockwaves through the court and country. A fickle king could turn on his friends on the flimsiest of evidence. In the event, Kate's family eventually benefited from the marquess's fall, securing lands from the breakup of the Courtenay's West Country estates. They may have held some remaining loyalty to their former patrons, holding lands with the intention of safeguarding part of the birthright of the marquess's 12-year-old son.[22] In 1541, Kate's brother, John, received some Courtenay lands around Glastonbury,[23] and the manor of Okehampton, while by 1542 Sir George Carew was steward of extensive Courtenay lands and purchased several more. After John Champernowne's death, Peter Carew added Okehampton to his tally of properties.

Sir Philip enriched his estate following the dissolution of religious houses in Devon. He acquired the lease of Plympton Priory after the priory was dissolved and surrendered on 1 March 1539.[24] He immediately set about selling a number of the buildings for demolition to William Strode of Newnham.[25]

Kate's world

Life continued as before for the royal children, although Prince Edward had his own separate nursery at Hampton Court Palace.[26] (Sources differ on the timing and staffing.) The three royal siblings continued to spend time together as they moved from palace to palace, and Elizabeth particularly enjoyed her brother's company. She loved giving him gifts, and at New Year 1539 she presented him with a cambric shirt she had made herself. For a 6-year-old to make a shirt was a prodigious achievement.

In December 1539, Thomas Wriothesley, a courtier who had served as Cromwell's chief clerk and personal secretary and was moving up in the king's service, visited the royal children at Hertford Castle. After he delivered the king's token to the Lady Mary, he greeted Elizabeth. Her abilities astonished him; he wrote to Cromwell, saying she 'replied to the King's message with as great gravity as if she had been 40 years old. If she be no worse educated than she appears she will be an honour to womanhood.'[27]

Elizabeth's impressive confidence and skills were a testament to the excellent care and education she had received. Alison Plowdon credits Kate with teaching Elizabeth to read and write.[28] However, in the two years since her arrival at Hunsdon, Kate had built on sound foundations already laid by Lady Bryan and Lady Troy. Kate may have extended Elizabeth's learning, even introducing the basics of Latin, but all three women deserve credit for Wriothesley's favourable report.

Chapter 7

Royal Brides Come and Go

1540–1543

At the time of Wriothesley's visit, preparations were underway for the arrival of the king's fourth bride. Cromwell had urged Henry to remarry and this time to make a diplomatic match to cement a useful alliance with one of the Protestant states. Cromwell saw this as providing a necessary buffer against the growing threat from the two major Catholic powers, particularly should France and Spain ever join forces. However, Henry was reluctant to marry without first seeing his future wife. He agreed to marry Anne of Cleves only after a sort of royal beauty contest based on paintings of prospective brides by royal painter, Hans Holbein. In December 1539 Anne was slowly making her way to England. Members of Kate's family joined the welcome party.

Kate's nephew, Sir George Carew, had been Captain of Ruysbank Castle in Calais since the preceding spring. He was among the party that greeted Anne when she arrived with her entourage en route to her wedding. Gawen and his nephew, Peter, were among those who accompanied the Lord Admiral to Calais. The group of courtiers and soldiers also included Sir Thomas Seymour and Sir Francis Bryan, both of whom are described in *Hall's Chronicle* as being magnificently attired with chains of great value and strange fashion.[1] It is interesting to note that the Carews were in company with Thomas Seymour; these men knew each other well.

'Asheley the younger', also mentioned in the Calais party is probably John Astley the younger, son of Sir Thomas Astley of Hilmorten and Melton Constable; the same John Astley (Plate 3), who would later marry Kate.[2] Sir Thomas had three wives, all named Anne, and sources differ as to the order in which he married them, or which offspring came from each union. Adding to the confusion, he had two sons, both named John. If 'John the younger' – Kate's future husband – was Anne Wood's son, then her sister Elizabeth (John's aunt), was Sir James Boleyn's wife, and therefore Queen Anne's aunt by marriage.[3] This rather convoluted relationship came under the umbrella of 'cousin', a term used very flexibly in the sixteenth century. Elizabeth herself accepts John's connection to the Boleyn family when she refers to him as her 'kinsman' in her letter to Edward Seymour, Lord Protector, of 7 March 1549.[4] Sir James Boleyn was in the Duke of Norfolk's party at the welcome for Anne of Cleves, and that may explain 'young Asheley's' presence.

The December weather was not favourable for a crossing to England, so Anne's retinue was entertained with jousting and feasting while they waited for better conditions. On 5 December, Sir George Carew took part in a joust, which Gregory Cromwell records as follows: 'To-day after dinner Sir Geo. Carowe and Knolles ran together at the tilt, Knolles breaking three staves and Carowe one. Tomorrow certain Spears of the town are determined to assay themselves against the coming of lady Anne.'[5] This must have been difficult for Sir George as his wife was ill. Thomasine, died in Calais during the festivities.

Another list of those greeting Anne of Cleves shows John Champernowne (named as Chamburn) as among the squires.[6, 7]

On English soil at last, Anne's first surprise meeting with the king at Rochester did not go well. When he appeared, in disguise, she failed to recognise him and was not impressed with the ageing, corpulent man who greeted her. From that moment on the union was doomed to failure. On his return to London, the king announced to Cromwell: 'I liked her before not well, but now I like her much worse.'

Anthony Denny, was one of the few people to whom Henry confided his concerns, even sharing his doubts about Anne of Cleves' virginity. Anthony and his wife were also among the noble people preparing a warm reception for Henry's new queen. Members of the newly revived troop of fifty splendidly dressed 'Gentlemen Pensioners', armed with ceremonial pole-axes, lined Anne's route as she approached Greenwich on 3 January 1540.[8] Gawen and Peter Carew were among them. Lady Mary and Lady Elizabeth are also on one of several lists of people at Greenwich for a feast in the great hall. Other lists omit them, however, so it is not entirely clear whether they met Anne on her arrival, or whether Kate was there. If she was, she might have come across John Astley, among the welcoming party.

The king's marriage to Anne of Cleves went ahead on 6 January, but, distracted by the Duke of Norfolk's niece Katheryn Howard, Henry was soon seeking an annulment. Anne joined him when he visited the royal children at Richmond in March 1540. However, perhaps she already saw which way the wind was blowing, for she did not strike up a strong relationship with the royal children. The March visit to Richmond may have given Kate an opportunity to catch up with her sister, who was likely carrying her second child. Joan Denny served Anne of Cleves until the young Katheryn Howard became queen.

Kate continued to oversee Elizabeth's learning. She had considerable freedom in setting a humanist curriculum for her bright pupil, who was now nearly 7 years old. Fewer constraints were placed on Elizabeth's early learning than for her sister Mary, who had been educated as the Princess of Wales, although Mary was not educated in statecraft as her brother would have been.[9] There is every indication that Elizabeth flourished under Kate's guidance.

At first, Cromwell seemed to have survived the disaster of the Cleves marriage, despite the king blaming him for it. Henry made Cromwell Earl of Essex on 18 April, and Kate clearly thought he still had influence. She wrote to him on 30 April requesting a position as 'Yeoman of the Bottles' in the prince's household for a friend of hers.[10] She gave no names, and we do not know whether the request was successful:

> Thanks him for his goodness to her. Hears the Prince will have many more officers. Asks for the place of yeoman of the bottles for a friend of hers, or some other place, if the grant of that is passed. There is no honester man, which is well known in this house.

Yeoman of the Bottles was a prestigious position in the royal Privy Chamber, with responsibility for the care and service of the king's drinks, particularly wine. By 1540, through Anthony Denny, Kate knew many Cambridge-educated forward-thinking scholars. Among them, she had almost certainly made the acquaintance of John Astley. John was assessed for the subsidy at £11 (around £5,000 today) in wages in 1543 as a gentleman waiter in Prince Edward's household.[11] It is possible that he gained his position following Kate's appeal to Cromwell.

Despite Cromwell's recent elevation, the conservative faction at court led by the Duke of Norfolk, who considered Cromwell an upstart, soon saw their chance to bring him down. They staged a dramatic ambush at a meeting of the Privy Council in June accused him of treason and heresy, stripped him of his honours in front of his peers, and escorted him to the Tower. Henry kept him alive long enough to complete the paperwork to annul the Cleves marriage. Cromwell's execution on 28 July sent shock waves through the land. The king married Katheryn Howard on the same day.

In the main, the humanist circle Cromwell had gathered around him survived his downfall. Kate's position remained secure, even though Cromwell had recommended her.

Anne of Cleves came out of the affair surprisingly well. She kept her personal jewels, and Henry granted her several prestigious properties and gave her the title of the king's sister, second only in rank to his queen.

Anne's replacement, Katheryn Howard, only a teenager herself, seems to have been fond of the young Elizabeth. When Elizabeth was at court, Katheryn gave her the place of honour closest to her own person, and a gave her gifts of jewellery. In May 1541 the young queen sent her barge to collect the 8-year-old, and they enjoyed a few days together at the royal palace of Chelsea. We do not know whether Kate accompanied Elizabeth, nor if she approved of the bright, beautiful young queen.

Besotted as he was with Katheryn Howard, claims about her questionable conduct before her marriage devastated Henry. Gawen Carew played a minor part as one of the courtiers who gave evidence that they had heard of her unchaste behaviour before her marriage.[12] Allegations of liaisons after her marriage sealed her fate. On 13 February 1542, Henry had his fifth wife executed.

While the gruesome details of her mother's death may have been withheld from Elizabeth until she was older, by the time Katheryn Howard met the same fate, Elizabeth was 9 years old. It would have been much more difficult to keep her in the dark. Historians speculate that Katheryn Howard's death affected Elizabeth profoundly. Some suggest that, taken alongside her own mother's execution and Jane Seymour's death after giving birth, the fate of Henry's fifth wife influenced Elizabeth's aversion to marriage. However, her father's cruel actions do not seem to have changed Elizabeth's view of him, rather she adored her larger-than-life father, despite his having been a largely absent parent.[13]

Elizabeth's bond with Kate may have strengthened during this difficult period. Elizabeth's household staff were the fixed point in her life, more important to her than her blood relatives, whom she rarely saw. No doubt Kate and the other attendants did all they could to distract her. Elizabeth likely relied heavily on Kate for comfort, a familiar, unchanging presence, in a confusing and frightening time. She likely found solace in her studies. Humanist teaching often used double translation to enhance students' language skills and understanding of texts. This involved translating a text from one language (often Greek or Hebrew) into Latin, and then translating it again, either back into the original language or into another vernacular language. Such translations demanded intense focus. Needlework or mastering an elegant script also required concentration. These are exactly the sort of activities experts recommend in the modern world for lowering heart rate and reducing anxiety and stress.

Kate wrote in the old-fashioned cursive style (Plate 5), so she sought other tutors to help Elizabeth perfect a distinctive italic script. Henry Fitzroy's first letter to his father, written from Pontefract Castle when he was barely 8 years old, shows that lessons in handwriting began at an early age for the royal children.[14] Letters Elizabeth wrote during her incarceration at Woodstock in 1554 mention a tutor named John Picton. John Guy suggests that Anthony Denny, who later recommended John Cheke as tutor to Prince Edward, may have introduced Picton to teach Elizabeth handwriting and possibly Italian.[15]

So, under Kate's direction, with specialist input from others, Elizabeth continued her education. Agnes Strickland suggests that in the months following Katheryn Howard's death she joined her sister Mary, at the Royal Palace of Havering, on the outskirts of London.[16]

The Inner Circle

Soon after the reception of Anne of Cleves, Peter Carew sought the king's permission to travel overseas with Kate's brother, John. The victories of the Ottoman Sultan Suleiman the Magnificent in Eastern Europe were the talk of the court. Stories of Suleiman's impressive court captivated the king so much that he sometimes wore Turkish clothing. Many young men professed themselves keen to see the sultan's court for themselves, and Peter Carew was never one to miss out on an adventure. His enthusiasm was infectious, and soon John was joining him in pleading with King Henry to be allowed to go.

John Champernowne was popular with the king. According to Richard Carew of Antony, whose *Survey of Cornwall* was published in 1602, 'through his pleasant conceits … won some good grace with the king'. Carew relates in humorous terms how John knelt alongside other supplicants for lands and although he had made no formal request, persuaded the king to grant him a share, depriving the others of some of theirs.[17]

Eventually, Peter and John overcame the king's initial reluctance and, suitably funded, they set off in the spring of 1541. Writing after the events, Exeter recorder and antiquary John Hooker has left us a colourful account of their journey.[18]

After many adventures, Peter and John made for Vienna, intending to return home. There they met up with a man named Wingfield, and all three men went down with the 'bloody flux' (dysentery). John Champernowne and Wingfield died, but Peter somehow fought off the illness. After recuperating in Venice, he came back to England in the spring of 1542 to dine out on tales of his adventures. We do not know when Kate learned of John's death, which reportedly saddened the king.[19] Losing the son and heir was a severe blow to the Champernowne family. John left a widow and a 7-year-old child, Henry, initially cared for by his mother and grandfather at Modbury.

Meanwhile, in Calais, at about the time of Cromwell's arrest and Peter and John's departure for foreign parts, Sir George Carew's increasingly Protestant views put him at odds with Lord Lisle, and also with the king's more conservative religious convictions. Commissioners reported that Sir George favoured heretics, and he confessed to eating meat in Lent. Sir George took part in the May Day tournament at Westminster Palace, along with Thomas

Seymour and other knights. But in mid-May Lord Lisle was recalled and arrested on suspicion of involvement in a plot to betray Calais to the French or Cardinal Pole. Sir George also came under suspicion briefly and may have spent a short time in the Tower. However, the king could not afford to lose an effective and loyal soldier, so George went free while Lisle remained in the Tower and died on 3 March 1542, possibly of a heart attack after hearing the news he had been found not guilty.

In the late autumn of 1540 Sir George Carew remarried. His bride was young Mary Norreys, who had for a short time been one of Elizabeth's waiting women. Like Joan, Lady Denny, Mary served Anne of Cleves and probably also Katheryn Howard. The newly married couple settled at Polsloe Priory near Exeter, where George's aunts had once been nuns.[20] Sir George became prominent in Devon affairs, besides his duties in Calais, and sat for a royal painter, Hans Holbein, in the winter of 1542/1543.

Gawen Carew's first wife, Anne Brandon, died before 1540. In July of that year Gawen married Mary Wotton, widow of Sir Henry Guildford. She had served at court for many years, and had connections to Catherine Parr's family. Holbein painted Mary with a Book of Hours and a rosary, formal references to a wife's piety.[21] She likely set aside the rosary, since Gawen now openly favoured religious reform. Like most of Kate's family, he was no longer bound by allegiance to his former patron, the Marquess of Exeter. The king's views, however, veered back towards more conservative ways of worship while remaining Head of the Church in England. Gawen, like his nephew George, came close to grief for alleging he had a royal licence to eat meat during Lent.

On a date after 12 January 1542, the other George Carew, Kate's uncle, was pursuing a career in the church in Devon. He briefly re-enters Kate's story via a perplexing document. In an appeal to Lord Audley against charges of trespass, he names his niece, Katherine Champernowne, as having the use of a property in London's Greyfriars.[22]

The abbot surrendered the Franciscan Friary of the Greyfriars on 12 November 1538. After a brief closure and looting, the City of London acquired the church. Reopened as Christ Church Hospital, it became a school for disadvantaged children and a parish church. Leases were also granted for private dwellings within the precincts. When he visited the city, it seems Uncle George regularly stayed at one of these dwellings, which his brother Gawen had secured from the tenant, John Lympanye for the use of his niece, Katherine Champernowne, on payment of 5 marks, (roughly equivalent to £1,400 today).[23]

Further research is needed to discover the background and outcome. The printer Robert Grafton, who had worked with Coverdale on translations of the Bible in Paris, set up his printing press in the precincts at Greyfriars and began printing the Bible in English there. Kate's Uncle George was an advocate of the Bible in English. However, a definite link cannot be confirmed.

Carew explicitly refers to Katherine Champernowne as his niece, which eliminates Kate's mother. Nor would he use that term for John Champernowne's wife. Gawen had demised the tenement and garden for Kate's use for a year from the Feast of the Annunciation of Our Lady (25 March 1541). Kate normally lodged with Elizabeth. It is not clear why she also needed this property.

Kate's father was now mostly in Devon managing the family estates, which had grown after acquiring lands from dissolved monasteries. He also served on various commissions in the early 1540s.

By 1542, Anthony Denny was keeper of the royal Mansion of Hatfield, giving him opportunities to visit Kate and her charge when they were in residence there.

Chapter 8

Tutors

1543–1547

Both Elizabeth and her sister Mary were present when, on 12 July 1543,[1] their father married for the sixth and last time. Anthony Denny was among the select group who gathered in the queen's closet at Hampton Court Palace. It was a quiet affair with no lavish celebrations. Catherine was proclaimed Queen of England on the same day, but there was to be no great entry into London, nor any talk of a coronation.

King Henry's new wife could hardly have been more different from her predecessor, being older, (she was 31 years old) wiser, bookish and pious. Twice widowed and highly respectable, Catherine Parr had no children of her own. However, she had a stepdaughter, Margaret Neville, from her marriage to Lord Latimer, whom she had nursed through the final stages of a debilitating illness. Before the king selected her to be his next queen Catherine had met and fallen in love with the dashing Thomas Seymour, who remained unwed at 35. Whatever her feelings, Catherine Parr knew her duty. She married the 52-year-old king, whose infected leg had forced him to give up jousting and hunting, contributing to his becoming grossly overweight – his waistline reportedly measured 52 inches. He often needed a stick when walking, and the suppurating ulcer on his leg was frequently painful, making him bad tempered. Yet Catherine went to her marriage cheerfully, understanding she needed to moderate her own increasingly Protestant views.[2] Henry had followed the Act of Six Articles, which reinstated many aspects of Catholic worship, with new laws restricting who could read the Bible in English. Women were barred from reading the Bible, though noblewomen could do so privately – but they couldn't discuss it.

Catherine already knew Henry's elder daughter, Mary, well; some sources suggest she had a place in Mary's household from February 1543.[3] Elizabeth and Edwards's first meeting with their new stepmother at the time of her marriage went well, and they seemed to like her very much. However, Catherine had little time to get to know them.

After the wedding, Mary remained at court while Elizabeth was sent to join Edward's household, taking Kate, Lady Troy and Blanche Parry with her.[4] She still had her own household, but followed her brother's movements, sometimes coinciding at the same place. Life for Kate and her attendants settled back into its usual pattern, moving between the royal palaces in Hertfordshire and Buckinghamshire, where Kate continued to oversee Elizabeth's lessons. However, Queen Catherine did not forget the children. Her stepdaughter, Margaret Neville, delivered messages just before Christmas 1543. Elizabeth may have been out of favour with her father and banished from court for a time, but Queen Catherine corresponded with her.[5]

Queen Catherine took up her royal duties. In the spring of 1544, Gawen Carew's wife was one of the ladies who assisted her on her first Maundy Thursday; washing the feet of poor women, and distributing alms.[6] In April, Catherine published her first book, an anonymous translation of John Fisher's *Psalms and Prayers*.[7] She soon took on an even more demanding role.

A short-lived reconciliation between the Emperor Charles V and Francis I in 1539 had raised the possibility of an alliance between Spain and France, the two Catholic powers. Of course, it did not last. However, when another conflict erupted, Henry felt he should decide which side to back. With money in the coffers from the dissolved monasteries, he pledged to join the action alongside the emperor, against the French. After the Scottish parliament rejected a marriage between Mary, Queen of Scots, and his son Edward in December 1543, Henry was furious. King François proposed that 6-year-old Mary should marry the Dauphin, his eldest son, instead. Henry sent Edward Seymour with an invading English army into Scotland in May 1544, and Seymour burned Edinburgh to the ground. With the Scottish threat quelled, at least for the moment, the king prepared to go to war.

With his ego battered after Katheryn Howard's betrayal, Henry saw a new war as his last chance to shine as a military leader. To the astonishment of his council, the ailing king announced his intention to lead his forces into battle himself. He was, however, realistic enough to recognise the dangers that entailed, and set in place new arrangements for the succession. In February 1544 he introduced the 3rd Act of Succession. Though still labelled illegitimate, he reinstated Mary and Elizabeth in the succession. Edward was the next heir, but should he have no children, any children Henry had with Catherine Parr would be next, then Mary and her heirs, then Elizabeth and hers.

King Henry appointed Catherine Parr as regent and entrusted the care of his children to her, a decision that brought changes for Kate and Elizabeth.

The queen may have been the one to suggest, early in 1544, that it was time for 6-year-old Edward to have a new tutor. However, Anthony Denny's role in shaping the royal children's education should not be underestimated. Just as he had persuaded King Henry to appoint Kate as Elizabeth's governess, so Denny almost certainly had a hand in John Cheke's arrival as the prince's tutor.[8]

Anthony Denny was at the heart of a group of scholars and friends – well-educated thinkers who were all moderate reformers; men Kate and her sister Joan knew well. Most, like Denny, had studied at Cambridge, which had become something of a hotbed for innovative thinking and reform. Among others, the group included the king's physician William Butts, and his doctor, Thomas Wendy; Thomas Smith, the son of an Essex sheep farmer; and John Cheke, a younger son of an Isle of Wight gentry family. Butts had nominated both Cheke and Smith as king's scholars, and they both believed in the importance of classical learning and language. They sought to revive the pronunciation they believed was closer to the original sounds used by the Ancient Greeks. Smith's brilliant academic career led him to become vice chancellor of Cambridge University in 1543 at the young age of 30. William Cecil was one of Cheke's students, and in 1541 he married Cheke's sister Mary.[9] Roger Ascham, whose reputation as a brilliant scholar was spreading, also studied with Cheke and became a close friend of John Astley.

Denny was in an excellent position to influence the king's choice of a tutor for his son. He had become one of Henry's most trusted advisers and had unparalleled access through his position in the Privy Chamber. David Starkey describes him as 'one of the smoothest operators of the era'.[10]

In the early days of her marriage, Catherine Parr likely preferred not to be the advocate of reform-leaning scholars lest she alarm the king. Much better to leave that task to the silver-tongued Denny, who Cheke described as 'a man able to mould Henry's mind, now mixing the useful with the sweet, now weaving serious things with light ones, great with small'.[11]

On 26 June, just before he left for France, the king dined with Edward, Elizabeth and Mary, with 'divers other lords and ladies' at St James's Palace.[12] A few days later, Henry ordered Prince Edward's household to be moved to Hampton Court and reordered to become predominantly male, Lady Bryan retired, although she retained the title of 'Lady Mistress'. She lived quietly in Essex and died in 1552, having lived long enough to see Edward on the throne of England.

Richard Cox, provost of Eton, who had begun teaching Prince Edward the basics of Greek and Latin, became almoner, and on 10 July 1544, on Denny's recommendation, John Cheke took up his appointment as Edward's tutor.

Jean Belmain, a French Huguenot scholar and a zealous Calvinist, joined him to polish Edward's French. Belmain, a refugee from France, likely had a powerful impact on the young prince's developing ideas on religion.

The prince records this significant change in his chronicle that during his early years he was:

> brought up among the women, [but] In the sixth year of his age he was brought up in learning by Dr Cox, who was afterwards his Almoner, and John Cheke … two learned men, who sought to bring him up in learning of tongues, of scriptures, of philosophy, and all liberal sciences.[13]

The king sailed for Calais with Charles Brandon, Duke of Suffolk, leading an English invasion of France for the second time in his long career. Soon after the king's departure, Elizabeth wrote her first surviving letter from St James's Palace on 31 July 1544.[14] Addressed to her stepmother in Italian, a language in which Catherine Parr may not have been fluent, the letter is a scholarly exercise. It shows off an early version of the italic script she perfected under the tutelage of Giovanni Battista Castiglione and later, Roger Ascham. Castiglione, an Italian soldier who fought with the English in France, accompanied the king's soldiers when they returned from France. So the letter of 31 July must be the product of John Picton's tuition, overseen by Kate.

Since Edward was based at Hampton Court, the queen moved there and brought Mary and Elizabeth to join their brother. Kate would have been among those who accompanied Elizabeth, and she may have renewed her acquaintance with John Astley, who continued to serve as waiter to the prince. John clearly shared Kate's family's interest in music, for he is credited with teaching Edward to play the virginals when the boy was older.[15]

During this time Elizabeth shared Edward's lessons, and also forged a closer relationship with her stepmother. All the indications are that they got on well, and there is no evidence that Kate was in any way jealous of this relationship. Elizabeth observed how Catherine exercised royal power as regent, a role model that proved instructive. As regent, Catherine handled the provisioning of Henry's French campaign, signed five royal proclamations, and monitored the complex and unstable situation with Scotland, showing skill and diplomacy.

Following the principles laid down by Vives for his sister's education, other boys around Edward's age joined him in the schoolroom.[16] While at Hampton Court, among the prince's fellow students, Elizabeth may have met young Robert Dudley, who later claimed he had known her since she was 8 years old. When Elizabeth joined the classroom in the all-male household, Kate would also have been there to act as 'chaperone'.

The royal children remained at Hampton Court with the queen through August, and in September accompanied her on a short progress in Surrey and Kent. Kate was likely with them at Enfield when they heard the news of the king's victorious entry into Boulogne.

The Inner Circle – War with France

Edward Seymour joined the king on 13 August to play his part in the siege of Boulogne. His brother Thomas had performed well as second in command to Sir John Wallop in the Netherlands in 1543, and the king rewarded him by making him Master of the Ordnance for life in the spring of 1544. If he was aware of his wife's interest in Seymour, Henry did not show it, for he awarded Thomas Seymour a salary four times higher than that of his predecessor. Thomas took part in the capture of Boulogne, and afterwards the king ordered him to harry the French fleet in the channel.

Although Henry came home in triumph, he already knew that Charles V had signed a peace treaty with France, Charles knew that the English forces were all but spent in the action in Boulogne and would not help him in the planned expansion of the war. King Henry expected King Francis to retaliate.

Kate's father had responded to the king's call to muster his men in Devon on 21 May, 1543.[17] However, Sir Philip was likely considered too old or in poor health to fight. He remained in Devon, occupied with various commissions and looking after his grandson and heir. It is possible, but not certain, that brother Arthur went to France, perhaps with his uncle, Gawen Carew. Gawen accompanied the Duke of Norfolk to the Netherlands in 1543, bringing with him four horsemen and four footmen. In the following year he joined Henry's forces for the Boulogne campaign.

Kate's cousins were also in the thick of the fighting. Sir John Wallop gave colourful reports of the Carew brothers' exploits. Sir George Carew was Lieutenant General of the Horse and, not wishing to miss out, Peter funded and captained a troop of a hundred footmen, dressed in black, known as the Black Band. Ironically, one the places where Peter and George saw action was Thérouanne, where their grandfather had died in 1513.

Eventually French forces took Sir George prisoner, along with several other English gentlemen, their fate for some time unknown.[18] Hooker says Sir George was 'more forward than circumspect'.[19] Peter sought to secure his brother's release by capturing a French officer he could trade but he was too trusting and the Frenchman did not provide the ransom money he promised. Sir George remained in French custody for several months until the king intervened and negotiated his release. After Henry's triumphant entry into Boulogne on

14 September 1544, he knighted Anthony Denny.[20] This was probably not for any specific act of bravery during the siege, but because the king, elated by victory, wished to honour his loyal servant. When the king returned to England, Peter Carew joined Sir John Dudley's fleet as captain of the *Primrose* and was involved in action which for the time being kept the French navy out of English waters.[21]

Elizabeth's education

In the schoolroom at Hampton Court, John Cheke was struck by Elizabeth's early brilliance and suggested she have a tutor of her own. Kate and Lady Troy, who was presumably still involved in such decisions,[22] had already recognised the need for additional tutors to stretch Elizabeth's remarkable talents, bringing in people like John Picton.[23] That Elizabeth needed an academically gifted tutor does not imply any failure on Kate's part, rather the reverse. She had done well to bring her charge up to such an impressive standard.

Kate was likely included in discussions with Cheke and Denny about a suitable tutor for Elizabeth. One of Cheke's former pupils, the scholar Roger Ascham, was a man with a growing reputation. Ascham later sought the position for himself, but in October 1544, along with Cheke, he recommended William Grindal. Kate seems to have approved of the appointment. She may even have recommended him.[24]

After the king's return, Elizabeth returned to Ashridge and began her studies with Grindal, under Kate's supervision. It was not appropriate to leave a young girl completely alone with her tutor, however well-respected and trusted he was. A room that overlooks the great hall at Hatfield Old Palace survives from when Elizabeth lived there. We might imagine that this was where Elizabeth studied with Grindal, while Kate sat quietly in the corner with her sewing, perhaps chipping in with a word or two here and there. Elizabeth liked Grindal, who was probably in his twenties. Elizabeth's tutor also had a good deal of respect for Kate, who he believed had given Elizabeth a sound grounding, particularly in her Latin studies.[25]

At this time, as far as we can tell, Kate and Lady Troy continued to share responsibilities for Elizabeth's overall development, overseeing her household and balancing academic tuition with other suitable activities like needlework, music and dancing. Kate had by now developed a strong bond with Elizabeth, acting as a mentor and protector in the fullest sense of the definition of the Tudor royal governess. Perhaps Kate helped Elizabeth to plan her New Year's gift for her stepmother, a translation of *The Mirror of the Sinful Soul*, which showed Elizabeth's linguistic and literary abilities, as well as her needlework, since she embroidered a cover with the initials 'KP' and a design of pansies.[26] Elizabeth must have dedicated many hours to producing this very personal gift for her stepmother.

Life settled into the old pattern, moving from palace to palace while Elizabeth flourished under Grindal's guidance. The next year, 1545, would bring the threat of invasion, and changes both sorrowful and joyful for Kate.

Chapter 9

Gentle Mrs Astley

1545–1547

Reports from France, where English soldiers remained to defend Boulogne, confirmed that the King of France had 200 ships ready to sail for England; a fleet far larger than the Spanish Armada of 1588. Diplomatic efforts to bring Charles V back into the conflict to support Henry had failed, and Henry knew he must prepare to fight off an invasion unaided. He gathered his navy at Portsmouth.

Joan, Lady Denny, was often at court and may have been among the ladies in attendance when the queen accompanied Henry to Portsmouth to review the fleet in June 1545. Joan and Anthony had five boys, and four girls, over the eleven years of their marriage.[1] Joan must have been almost constantly pregnant. However, the queen's ladies were expected to take only a short period of leave of absence around the time their children were born. They were back in post soon after.

Joan was one of the group of intellectual ladies around the queen, all strong supporters of reform. They included the queen's sister Anne Parr, Lady Herbert; her cousin Maud Parr, Lady Lane; Elizabeth Oxenbridge, Lady Tyrwhitt; and an old friend of her mother, Mary Wotton, Lady Carew (Gawen's wife); Mary Arundell, Countess of Arundel; Anne Calthorpe, Countess of Sussex; Mary Howard, Dowager Countess of Richmond; and Mary Scrope, Lady Kingston. These women shared a scholarly interest in the new religion, and Joan Denny was becoming one of the strongest advocates of reform. Queen Catherine had embraced the reform agenda before her marriage to the king, and often left the English Bible open in her chamber, allowing her ladies to read it.[2]

Joan made no secret of her views, and appointed a reformist as her chaplain. William Hugh, a Yorkshireman, gained his MA at Oxford in 1543. He held controversial opinions about transubstantiation (whether bread and wine transform into the body and blood of Jesus Christ); Joan's patronage helped him pursue his studies without interference.

By mid-July, the ships of the English fleet awaited the French in Portsmouth Harbour. On the evening of Saturday, 18 July, three of Kate's Carew relatives dined with the king on board the *Henry Grace à Dieu,* a ship under the command of Admiral Sir John Dudley, who Henry had created Lord Lisle on the death of Arthur Plantagenet. Each man had command of one of the king's ships; Gawen the *Matthew Gonson*, Peter the *Great Venetian*, while Sir George had the honour of commanding the newly refitted *Mary Rose.* During the dinner, the French fleet was sighted; according to Hooker, it was Peter Carew who climbed the mast and spotted them first.[3] As Henry went ashore, he presented Sir George with a gold whistle, signalling his appointment as vice admiral in the coming battle.

The next morning was calm, ideal conditions for the French galleys to attack. The English sailing ships waited for the wind to pick up, as the galleys tried to draw them out into open waters. Henry watched from the battlements atop Southsea Castle, one of his new defences commanding views over Portsmouth Harbour and the Solent. Charles Brandon, Duke of Suffolk, recalled from France, had stationed his army around the castle; it is thought there were around 12,000 English soldiers at Portsmouth, heavily outnumbered by a French force of 80,000. Several ladies joined the king to watch the battle unfold at sea. Among them was Mary Carew. Towards evening, the wind got up and at last, two of the largest ships, the *Henry Grace à Dieu* and the *Mary Rose*, led the attack. Suddenly, the *Mary Rose* keeled over, and disappeared from view, taking all those on board to the bottom of the sea. Estimates of the number of men on board vary – *Hall's Chronicle* says 400.[4] The king reportedly exclaimed, 'Oh, my gentlemen! Oh, my gallant, gallant men!' As he watched the pride of his navy disappear from view. Only forty men survived.

Many theories are advanced to explain the sinking of the *Mary Rose*, including water rushing in through open gun ports as she turned. One theory questions Sir George Carew's competence, suggesting this was the first time he had been in charge of so large a vessel. However, Sir George was an experienced sea captain, having sailed with Sir John Dudley as early as 1537. Dudley, who was directing operations that day, had made many improvements and modernised the English navy. George's desperate last words, called out to his Uncle Gawen aboard the *Matthew Gonson* that 'he had a sort of knaves he could not rule', suggest problems with discipline on board.

For Mary Carew, this must have been an agonising moment, knowing that in full armour, there was no chance George could survive. No wonder she fainted. After her husband's death, Mary remained at court, probably serving Henry's daughter, Mary. Sir George's loss was a significant blow to the whole of Kate's family, and we can only imagine his brother and uncle's feelings as they watched helplessly from their own vessels. Fortunately, the rest of the

English fleet drove the French back, forcing them to land instead on the Isle of Wight. There, they encountered such strong resistance that they were soon heading back to France. The invasion had failed and England was safe.

Peter Carew may have been involved in the first frantic attempts to salvage valuable guns and armaments from the sunken ship. However, by September, he and Gawen were at sea again, conducting retaliatory raids on the French coast. Unlike his uncles, George and Gawen, Peter never came directly under the conservative influence and patronage of the Courtenays. Towards the end of the year, he was in trouble for having seditious books in his possession, showing that he was by now taking a more radical reformist stance.[5] However, the king liked Peter, and soon forgave him. Following his brother's death Peter inherited the family estates in Devon, and was sheriff of the county in 1545.

Hard on the heels of the news of her cousin's death at sea, Kate received more sad news from Devon. Her father, Sir Philip Champernowne, died at Modbury on 2 August, having made his will two days earlier.[6] He named Kate and her uncle, George Carew (the priest), as joint executors should his wife, also named executrix, be unable to complete all his bequests. This rather strange arrangement suggests Katherine, his wife, may have been ill.[7] John Champernowne's widow married Sir Maurice Berkeley, between July and November 1545, when an Inquisition Post Mortem identified Kate as Sir Philip's eldest daughter.[8]

Kate's Marriage

After November 1545 when her father's IPM was conducted, but probably before the end of the year, Kate married John Astley. John was distantly related to Elizabeth through the Boleyns, and Kate had known him for some years. They were intellectually well matched, and had mutual friends and acquaintances among the Cambridge Set.

Marriage certainly came at a convenient time for Kate. Lady Troy was probably in her late sixties (her first marriage was in 1494), and was due to retire. The position of Lady Mistress traditionally went to a married woman. Kate's marriage may have made her more 'suitable', giving her an advantage over Lady Troy's niece, Blanche Parry, who was unmarried.[9] The timing of Kate's formal appointment and Lady Troy's retirement is uncertain (Roger Ascham mentioned Lady Troy in a letter tentatively dated shortly after Kate's marriage).[10] Kate had in effect assumed the role of Lady Mistress as well as governess by 1547. It has been suggested that Kate's overbearing ways eventually prompted Lady Troy, who had hoped her niece might succeed her, to retire.[11] However, evidence of acrimony is slim, and Blanche Parry, continued to work alongside Kate for many years with no outward signs of discord. Lady Troy was receiving a pension from Elizabeth in 1552 and living at Troy House in 1552, when she is mentioned in her son's will.[12] She likely continued to receive her pension there until her death around 1557. More details of Lady Troy's departure are given in the Appendix, pp. 174-177.

As a married couple in royal service, John and Kate did not settle into a quiet married life together, but continued in their respective posts, always on duty. John may have continued to serve in Prince Edward's household, only switching to Elizabeth's after King Henry died. At that time John was named as one of those 'that do remain unplaced and served the King's majesty'.[13]

John's friend Roger Ascham wrote in Latin to Elizabeth in 1545. Using Kate's maiden name, he praised her teaching and care and that of William Grindal.[14] Ascham wrote again to Kate, probably shortly after her marriage.[15] He begins by expressing his friendship for both Kate and John, and then offers Kate some advice about teaching Elizabeth.[16] His letter opens with the salutation, 'Heartie Commendations and health to Him that is the Author of all Health, my Gentle Mrs Astley.'

This letter from a man of Ascham's undoubted scholarly standing provides interesting insights.

Fulsome in his praise of her achievements, Ascham writes:

> So pleasing a thing as to him in will is most ready, and in wishing most desirous to have her grace come to that end in perfectness with likelihood of her wit, painfulness in her study, true trade of her teaching, and your diligent overseeing doth most constantly promise.

Diligent overseeing doesn't quite fit with the image of Kate as a gossipy nanny.

Ascham then says how much he values John's friendship, welcomes their marriage, and offers thanks for Kate's gentle kindness to Grindal and himself. He then gives advice, which reinforces the impression that Kate might push her pupil too hard:

> If you pour too much drink at once into the goblet, the most part will dash out and run over if you pour it softly you may pour it even to the top, and so her Grace, I doubt not, by little and little may be increased in learning, that at length greater cannot be required.

None of this calls to mind a foolish woman.

At Christmas 1545 Elizabeth showed off her progress with a magnificent gift for her father; her own translation of her stepmother's *Prayers or Meditations* in not one, but three languages: French, Italian and Latin. The book, in its beautifully embroidered cover with Henry and Katherine's initials entwined, stitched by Elizabeth herself, can still be seen at the British Library.[17] Kate had equipped her pupil with a range of skills, including needlework.

The end of an era

On 20 September 1545, in a clear sign of Henry's acceptance of his increasing ill health and infirmity, Sir Anthony Denny became one of three men authorised to use the 'dry stamp', a facsimile of the king's signature on documents. The other two men given this powerful role were Sir John Gates, Anthony's brother-in-law, and William Clerk. Between them, Denny and Gates held an unrivalled position of power and influence.

Edward Seymour, the Earl of Hertford, recognised how strong Anthony's position was. Their interests converged, and they planned to collaborate. They wanted to ensure that if Henry's son, as was becoming probable, succeeded to the throne while still young, he would rule as a Protestant king. Edward's reformist-leaning tutors had prepared the ground.

However, the more conservative faction did not cede control without a fight. Having failed to oust Archbishop Cranmer in 1543 – the king sent Anthony Denny with a warning – the traditionalists turned their sights on Catherine Parr. Bishop Stephen Gardiner, who Alison Plowdon describes as 'a brilliant, but tricky lawyer and diplomat',[18] thought a woman called Anne Askew might provide ammunition for him to use against the queen.

Anne was a Lincolnshire gentlewoman with strong Protestant beliefs. Her husband, Thomas Kyme, was a devout Catholic; he threw her out of the house and she went to London and began to preach. In March 1545 Kyme had his wife arrested and brought back to Lincolnshire. She escaped and, back in London, continued preaching. In early 1546, she was arrested again, but released. In May 1546, she was arrested for the third time.

Bishop Edmund Bonner and later Chancellor Wriothesley and Gardiner himself, interrogated Anne Askew about a group of Catherine's ladies, including Joan Denny. According to Miss Champernowne, Archdeacon George Carew, Joan's uncle may also have been questioned.[19]

Anne steadfastly refused to incriminate anyone, only admitting that Lady Denny and Lady Hertford (Edward Seymour's wife) had sent her money. Even after being tortured in the Tower of London, Anne refused to betray her beliefs or denounce others.[20]

Gardiner overheard the querulous king complain in a fit of pain-fuelled temper that he did not relish being taught by his wife. Catherine had not noticed the king's irritation when she overstepped the bounds of prudent wifely duty in her enthusiasm to debate matters of religion. Gardiner seized the opportunity and persuaded Henry to order the queen's arrest. However, perhaps Henry had second thoughts and confided in Dr Wendy, his physician, one of the moderate reformers in the Cambridge Set. Perhaps it was pure chance that Wendy intercepted the mislaid order for the queen's arrest; or perhaps, as Elizabeth Norton suggests, Henry had set her a test.[21] If that is so, then Catherine Parr passed. After quickly removing any forbidden books among her belongings she cleverly won Henry round, saying she was a weak woman, whose only wish was to learn from the king's superior knowledge and intellect. Joan Denny must have been relieved.

In July 1546 Henry signed a peace treaty with France, having triumphed in keeping Boulogne. Kate's cousin Peter Carew and her brother Arthur were among those who went to France to receive the King of France's oath.[22] Prince Edward played his part in the lavish celebrations when the French admiral paid a return visit to England in August, and the king's elder daughter was also involved. Elizabeth may have been there too.

In September 1546 Denny applied the king's stamp to a letter to Mary Carew, Sir George's widow, in favour of her marriage to Kate's younger brother, Arthur.[23] After the wedding, the couple settled at Polsloe Priory, near Exeter, where Mary had previously lived with George. Shortly after that, in October 1546, Henry appointed Anthony Denny as his Groom of the Stool, replacing Sir Thomas Heneage. Henry clearly liked and trusted Kate's brother-in-law, and probably preferred a man he considered his friend in this most intimate of roles.

As the year drew to a close, everyone recognised Henry was very ill. Protestants and traditionalist factions continued to jockey for position, each wanting control of Henry's son. The pendulum swung dramatically in the reformist's favour in December 1546 when the king had the Duke of Norfolk and his son, Henry Howard, Earl of Surrey, arrested and charged with treason, on suspicion of planning to usurp the throne. Gawen Carew was one of those whose depositions sealed Surrey's fate.[24]

Surrey's sister Mary Fitzroy, Duchess of Richmond and Somerset (widow of Henry's illegitimate son Henry Fitzroy), fell out with her brother when he suggested she should seduce the ageing king and become his mistress. Gawen Carew reported conversations when the duchess made her position entirely clear, saying 'she would rather cut her own throat than do as her brother suggested'.[25] Even more damaging to both Norfolk and his son, Gawen reported overhearing Surrey claim his father was best placed to 'have the governance of the prince and the realm'.

On Christmas Eve, Henry sent his wife and most of the court away. Catherine Parr spent a dreary and anxious Christmas at Greenwich with Henry's daughter

Mary. The two younger children were at Hertford and Enfield, respectively, unaware of the dramatic changes the New Year would bring.

At Whitehall Palace on 26 December 1546, King Henry VIII asked to see his last will. He had not updated it since his departure for France in 1544, and it likely named his wife, Catherine Parr, as regent. Recognising the reality of his situation, but still in control of events, Henry ordered the drafting of a new will. After removing Stephen Gardiner from the list of executors, Henry approved the new will, which was witnessed by three physicians. It was Henry himself who removed the strongest Catholic supporters, Norfolk and Gardiner. Denny argued for Gardiner to keep his place. Ever a more moderate reformer, he may have thought Gardiner was a useful counterweight, should Seymour become too radical in pushing the reform agenda forward. The king overruled him and removed Gardiner's name. The dry stamp affixed, the will was sealed, to be kept in a box to which only Edward Seymour had the key.

After becoming very ill over New Year, Henry rallied and in mid-January was sufficiently recovered to send the Earl of Surrey to the block. Furious that Surrey had quartered the attributed arms of King Edward the Confessor into his family coat-of-arms, Henry showed no mercy. Thirty-year-old Henry Howard, Earl of Surrey, erstwhile favourite of King Henry VIII, childhood companion to Henry's illegitimate son, the Duke of Richmond, met the executioner on 19 January, 1547.

After 16 January, the only people allowed into the king's chamber were members of the Privy Council. The king's new will named sixteen executors to form a Regency Council until his son came of age. Sir Anthony Denny was one of them. Sir Thomas Seymour was not. However, Thomas's brother had him admitted to the Privy Council on 23 January 1547, despite King Henry reportedly crying out 'no, no, no' at the suggestion. At this stage, there was little sign of animosity between the brothers, and Thomas remained ignorant of the will's contents.

On 26 January, during Henry's last hours, Edward Seymour and the king's secretary, Sir William Paget, spent a long time in the cramped bedchamber with the dying king. According to Foxe Sir Anthony Denny, told Henry that his end was near and called for Archbishop Cranmer:

> when the rest were in dread to do, Master Denny, who was specially attendant upon him, boldly coming to the king, told him what case he was in, to man's judgment not like to live; and therefore exhorted him to prepare himself to death, calling himself to remembrance of his former life, and to call upon God in Christ betimes for grace and mercy, as becometh every good Christian man to do.[26]

Beyond speaking, the king could only squeeze the Archbishop's hand to show his faith before he slipped quietly away. He had reigned for thirty-seven years and nine months. Many in England had no memory of a time when the larger-than-life King Henry was not on the throne. He died just hours before the Duke of Norfolk's scheduled execution, thus saving the old man from the scaffold.

Seymour, Paget and Denny took control. Denny's privileged access to the private apartments made it easy for him to keep the king's death secret for several days.[27] That gave the three plotters time to fine tune their plan. The old king's will did not specify that anyone should head the council. They were to govern as equals. However, Edward Seymour, King Edward's closest living relative, and a man with a dazzling list of military achievements to his name, was intent on becoming Protector. He had the support of Kate's brother-in-law, Anthony Denny.

Seymour, set off for Hertford with Sir Anthony Browne, to inform Henry's son of his father's death; he had been working on Browne for some time, hoping to secure his support for a bid to become Protector.

Having collected Edward, in a rare act of compassion Seymour took the 9-year-old boy – now, although he did not yet know it, King of England – to Enfield, where his sister Elizabeth had spent Christmas. Young Edward had his sister's support when he learned of his father's passing. A less charitable explanation is that Seymour needed a little more time to persuade Browne to support him.

Kate had spent a quiet Christmas at Elsyng, also known as Enfield House, with Elizabeth.[28] The magnificent complex of buildings had been constructed for Sir Thomas Lovell in the late fifteenth century on the site of an earlier manor house. After he acquired the palace, Henry occasionally went to hunt in the vast deer parks of Enfield Chase. Nothing remains above ground, but archaeological investigations suggest that there were two courtyards, with the brick-built palace resembling St James's Palace in London. Surrounded by extensive gardens, with a moat and fishponds, the house boasted extensive royal apartments.[29] Elizabeth's father had made repairs at Elsyng in 1542, when all three royal children enjoyed Christmas there together. That Christmas of 1546 may have rekindled memories of happier times with her siblings.

John Astley, an accomplished horseman, had likely joined the party at Elsyng to enjoy some hunting in the deer park when the weather permitted.[30] There is no evidence of Kate sharing John's love of equestrian sports, although, like all women of her time, she had to be a proficient rider. Hunting was not solely a male activity. In later life, Elizabeth enjoyed hunting, and the 13-year-old princess may have joined the chase at Elsyng on fine days. However, toward the end of January, cold weather set in, and she was likely waiting indoors when Seymour and Paget clattered into the frosty cobbled courtyard unexpectedly, bringing her brother with them.

We can imagine how Elizabeth's heart lifted when she recognised Edward, for they were close; her brother had written to her in December, saying how much he missed her. Her delight in the reunion soon turned to sorrow. In the great hall at Elsyng, Seymour startled both children by suddenly kneeling before Edward to declare his loyalty. Realising this meant their father was dead the children wept in each other's arms.[31] Edward noted the occasion without emotion in his own journal.[32]

Kate was there to offer what comfort she could, while Seymour and Paget concluded their discussions. With Paget's support secure, Seymour could take the king to London. But he left Elizabeth behind. She must have realised that from that moment on she would see much less of her brother as he took up his royal duties. Kate's future, intertwined with Elizabeth's, was uncertain.

Chapter 10

Handsome Admiral Seymour

1547–1549

Thomas Seymour was no stranger to Kate Astley. She had come across him frequently when at court with Elizabeth. More significantly, as we have seen, the men in her circle also knew him well. During his long career in the king's Privy Chamber, Anthony Denny often came across him. Kate's cousin, Sir Peter Carew, and her Uncle Gawen served with Thomas in the Gentlemen Pensioners. John Champernowne was there when Thomas showed off his magnificent attire in Calais in 1539. Peter likely swapped stories with Thomas about the Habsburg court and the Turks.[1] Kate's other cousin, the now deceased Sir George, rode against Thomas in jousts, including the one on 1 May 1541 recorded in *Hall's Chronicle*.[2]

Edward VI's biographer, Sir John Hayward, whose work was published posthumously in 1630, described Seymour as 'fierce in courage, courtly in fashion, in personage stately and in voice magnificent', but 'somewhat empty in matter'.[3]

David Starkey says Thomas Seymour was 'tall, well-built with a dashing beard and auburn hair; he was irresistible to women.'[4] Yet he was nearly 40 and still unmarried. The only match seriously contemplated with Mary Firtzroy, Duchess of Richmond, did not go ahead.

Thomas Seymour had a reputation for being 'more of an opportunist than a gentleman where women were concerned'.[5] Some thought him a fool, but for many his overpowering 'charisma' overcame doubts about his reckless ambition. He was also King Edward's uncle. Kate's reform-minded advisers might conceivably have considered Thomas Seymour a suitable English husband for Elizabeth.

However, Thomas's unrealistic vision for the post-Henrican world was that his brother Edward would govern the country while he had charge of his nephew.

Henry had appointed Thomas Master of the Hunt and keeper of the palace and steward of Enfield Manor on 21 April 1545. This was a lucrative appointment bestowed when Thomas was doing well in the king's service. He kept rooms at Elsyng and visited occasionally. However, there is no evidence that he was there during January 1547. Early in the month he was busy with ordnance at the Tower of London, following instructions from the Privy Council to oversee the despatch of arms to the North.[6]

Soon after the king's death, Thomas paid his respects to the grieving widow. His visit rekindled the attraction between them set aside when Catherine Parr married the king.

On 6 February Paget announced that the old king had believed fresh blood should replace a decaying nobility. The old, more conservative, regime had fallen: Norfolk was in the Tower, and Gardiner was excluded. A new era was dawning. Edward Seymour rose to become Duke of Somerset, a dukedom previously reserved for royalty; John Dudley became Earl of Warwick; Thomas became the 1st Baron Seymour of Sudeley and stepped up to take Warwick's place as Admiral of the Fleet. Although Thomas relished the role of admiral, it was not nearly enough to satisfy his ambitions.[7] His anger and jealousy smouldered as he watched his elder brother being accorded all the airs and graces as the Lord Protector. In Thomas Seymour's eyes, only an accident of birth prevented him having all the power in his hands.

Sidelined and smarting at his exclusion from the regency council, Thomas launched his own bid to have care of his nephew. John Dudley probably egged him on; the former admiral was adept at playing the brothers off one against the other and likely saw an opportunity to sow the seeds of division. If so, he succeeded in setting the Seymour brothers further at odds. Thwarted and having angered his brother, Thomas sought to woo others to support him. He sent his servant John Harrington to the Marquess of Dorset with a message concerning the wardship of the marquess's 9-year-old daughter, Jane Grey. Jane was first cousin once removed to the young king, being the granddaughter of Henry VIII's sister, Mary. The message Harrington delivered interested Dorset. Since Thomas Seymour was the king's uncle, Dorset may have thought it could do no harm for his red-haired daughter to become Seymour's ward. He may even have hoped it could pave the way for Jane to marry King Edward.

However, any marriage between little Jane Grey and Edward was a long way off. Thomas was also considering a royal marriage for himself. His thoughts first turned to the king's elder daughter, the staunchly Catholic Mary.[8] She was 33 years old and heir to the throne. However, Somerset was having none of that and reproached his brother. Mary is said to have laughed when told about it.

Anthony Denny remained one of Somerset's strongest allies. The Imperial Ambassador reported on 10 February that Anthony Denny was 'the most confidential of any of the gentlemen of the chamber'.[9] Only a few days later, on 16 February Denny's intimacy with the late king was emphasised when he rode with the queen's brother-in-law, Sir William Herbert, 'at the head and foot' of the late king's body, which was borne on a chariot as the funeral procession made its way to St George's Chapel at Windsor.[10] Henry VIII was buried with suitable pomp and tradition alongside Jane Seymour, his third wife, although the elaborate tomb he had planned was never completed. Elizabeth did not attend the funeral. Catherine Parr observed from the queen's closet.

While Kate packed up Elizabeth's goods and the household headed for Hatfield, only four days after his father's funeral in Windsor, on 20 February 1547, Edward was crowned in Westminster Abbey. Archbishop Cranmer shortened the ceremony, using the youth of the new king as an excuse, but also changing the service to reflect the new way in religion. It must have been a daunting occasion for young Edward. Elizabeth, Mary and their stepmother did not attend.

The Seymour brothers played a prominent part in the ceremonies and celebrations. Thomas acquitted himself admirably when five men took on all comers in the jousts. One of the five was Sir Peter Carew, who, on the day of the coronation, had married Lady Margaret Talboys, wealthy widow of Lord George Talboys. Peter had been seeking King Henry's permission to marry her since 1546, but the king had been reluctant. That may have been because Peter was asking him to approve the marriage of a former mistress. There is some evidence that Margaret's first marriage to the 16-year-old George Talboys in 1538 was arranged in some haste, with the king urging secrecy. It is thought Margaret was the 'Mrs Skipworth' named in a letter from John Husee.[11] At last, on 14 February, Peter had consent to marry Margaret, and wasted no time doing so. Her wealth was a godsend to the cash-strapped Carews, but it may also have been a love match. Hooker's account refers to Peter being 'trapped in Venus Bands'.[12] Margaret would support Peter through difficult times to come.

Meanwhile, the dowager queen, who had expected to be appointed regent, assembled a distinguished legal team, led by Sir Roger Cholmeley, who played his part in Kate's later life, to argue her case.[13] Catherine Parr soon understood it was useless. However, Henry's will left her well provided for, and she seemed the obvious person to have care of Elizabeth, with whom she had already established a bond. So, towards the end of February, Elizabeth's household were on the move again, this time to join Catherine, initially at Greenwich, where Thomas Seymour was already a regular clandestine visitor.[14] Catherine had patiently endured three arranged marriages. Now, with thc handsome admiral, she convinced herself everything would be different. Accounts suggest Thomas had genuine feelings for his old flame. However, a man of his nature could easily persuade himself to make a match elsewhere if he found another bride who could bring him the power and position he craved. Although he was soon visiting Catherine, professing his love, at first he avoided talk of marriage.

Elizabeth had lived a sheltered life, protected by Kate and her loyal household. The only men in her orbit were Kate's husband John, her tutors William Grindal – an earnest and respectable young man; another tutor, Castiglione; her chaplain, the recently arrived dour Welshman, Thomas Parry who looked after her accounts; and various lower-ranking servants. When joining lessons with her brother's tutors, Kate or other ladies always chaperoned her. Visits to court, where she may have encountered other noblemen, were carefully choreographed to ensure due decorum. Catching glimpses of the handsome admiral defying all convention to visit her stepmother in secret must have seemed incredibly exciting and romantic to the teenager.

Kate's charge had grown into a slender girl on the brink of womanhood, with her father's fair colouring and her mother's arresting dark eyes. In the twenty-first century, a girl of 13 or 14 is a child; thoughts of marriage may seem shocking. However, in the sixteenth century, it was not at all unusual for girls, especially those from noble and well-to-do families, to be married by 14.

It does not reflect well on Thomas that, while already romantically involved with Catherine, he also actively sought the council's approval to seek first Mary's and then Elizabeth's hand in marriage.[15] Despite his requests being denied, letters cited by the seventeenth-century Italian biographer Leti indicate that Thomas proposed in writing to Elizabeth. Many historians dispute whether the letters Leti quotes are genuine, since none of the originals have come to light. If Thomas Seymour did write as Leti suggests, he was prepared to marry Elizabeth in defiance of the council, in flagrant conflict with the terms of King Henry's will. Considering his many other reckless decisions, that seems quite plausible, and the letters are therefore considered here.[16]

On 25 February, soon after she arrived in Greenwich, Elizabeth is supposed to have received Seymour's letter, claiming to be in love with her and offering marriage. The proposal, if made, would have posed a dilemma for Kate. She must consider not only Elizabeth's personal best interests but also the wider political aspects. A king's daughter was normally a valuable commodity in the marriage market. However, Elizabeth's marriage prospects were not all that rosy in 1547. Although Henry's will restored her succession rights, she remained illegitimate. In addition, as Anne Boleyn's daughter, she carried a certain unwelcome reputation in some quarters. A match with a foreign prince might prove difficult, and was not necessarily desirable. The council might favour an English nobleman, but Somerset was unlikely to accept his brother. However, leaving aside the unfortunate jealousy festering between the brothers, some might see Thomas Seymour, the king's uncle, as a strong candidate for Elizabeth's hand. Kate might have been inclined to advise a holding response.

Robert Dudley claimed Elizabeth told him when she was 8 years old she would never marry. However, in 1547 she knew that this was not a realistic prospect. Leti includes a mature and considered reply, dated 27 February 1547. The letter does not exactly refuse Seymour outright. After thanking him, she is supposed to have replied, expressing her surprise at receiving such a proposal: 'I would never have believed that anyone would have spoken to me of nuptials, at a time when I ought to think of nothing but sorrow for the death of my father.' She supposedly went on to say she intended to mourn her father, to whom she owed so much, for two years. Despite the doubts about Leti, this seems a plausible response.

Catherine Parr remained blissfully unaware, secure in her own happy bubble of happiness, sure that Thomas would soon be her husband. And so it proved. Just days after Leti says he received Elizabeth's response, Thomas secretly married Catherine. The date, 3 March 1547, was only thirty-four days after King Henry's death. When she heard about the wedding, if he really had proposed, Elizabeth may have felt hurt by Seymour's duplicity. Kate may have intended to soften the blow when she assured her he really cared for her by saying, 'He would have had you before the Queen.'[17]

Edward Seymour was strengthening his position as Lord Protector. Anyone who disagreed had to go. In March he abruptly dismissed Thomas Wriothesley from the chancellorship on charges of selling off some of his offices to delegates. He also he lost his seat on the Privy Council.

Amid all this upheaval, Kate heard that her brother-in-law Otho Gilbert, husband of her sister Katherine, had died in Devon. A month's mind – a special requiem mass for the deceased – held in St Thomas's Church, Marldon on 13 March caused a controversy. The month's mind was a traditional Roman Catholic rite and largely suppressed by the end of 1547 due to its association with the theology of purgatory and prayers for the dead. It is not surprising that the staunchly Protestant Sir Peter Carew objected strongly when Richard Crispin, former chaplain to the Marquess of Exeter, preached an inflammatory, anti-Lutheran, sermon. Crispin was one of those involved with the Marchioness of Exeter in 1534 in the Nun of Kent affair.[18] With Seymour established as Protector, further progress on religious reform was certain, and Peter could flex his muscles. He asked a layman, Philip Nichols to write a rebuttal of Crispin's words, and Crispin was later arrested for seditious preaching.[19]

Only a few weeks later, Kate lost another brother-in-law when Elizabeth Champernowne's husband, William Cole, also died. We do not know what caused the deaths of these two relatively young men, but records show several outbreaks of the plague around this time.

There is no indication that Kate travelled to Devon to comfort her sisters. She was fully occupied with her duties as Elizabeth settled in with her stepmother, who planned a move to more suitable lodgings. Privacy was impossible in elite or royal households. Servants were ever present, even sleeping in their masters' rooms, and gossip spread quickly. Catherine Parr's sister, Anne Herbert, soon guessed what was going on between her sister and Seymour.[20] It is likely that Kate and Elizabeth already knew about the secret marriage when they briefly stayed at St James's Palace in April, while Catherine was finalising her plans for a more permanent move to Chelsea.[21] Kate later recalled meeting the admiral in St James's Park when taking her exercise there.[22] She boldly challenged him, asking about his intentions towards Elizabeth. He replied he did not intend to lose his head for a wife, but he would have the queen. He made no reply when a laughing Kate told him she had heard he had already married Queen Catherine.

The dowager queen headed a lively household, where many of her former ladies congregated. Elizabeth had witnessed her stepmother acting as regent in 1544. Now she saw her heading a household as a woman in her own right, and enjoying literary and philosophical discussions with like-minded women, including Joan Denny.

Soon Kate had to supervise yet another move, this time to the relatively small red-brick manor house on the banks of the Thames at Chelsea, which was part of Catherine Parr's jointure. A little distant from the city, Chelsea offered fresh air, pleasant gardens and orchards.[23]

Elizabeth continued her studies with Grindal, and while Thomas was fulfilling his duties as admiral in Cornwall and the Scilly Isles dealing with pirates, she enjoyed her conversations with the queen as they studied and read together. Kate remained as Elizabeth's Lady Mistress, having overall responsibility for her welfare and education, although under Catherine's roof, she had to give up a little of her autonomy. She remained Elizabeth's closest confidante, the one who knew all her secrets, and saw to all of her most intimate needs.

The house was not large, and with over 200 people in the joint households, space was at a premium. Even though Elizabeth had her own room, it may have been too tiny to also hold Kate's bed.

Later testimony from four other gentlewomen suggests Kate ousted Lady Troy from the pallet next to Elizabeth's bed some time before, or at the time of, the move to Chelsea. In his letter of 31 January 1549, Sir Robert Tyrwhitt told Protector Somerset that Kate had removed Lady Troy and insisted that she herself must sleep next to the princess's bed: 'She could abide nobody there but herself.' A full transcript of Sir Robert's letter and further analysis is included in the Appendix (pp. 174-177).[24, 25] Historians differ on the interpretation of Sir Robert's letter, some believing Kate continued to insist that she alone should sleep in Elizabeth's room because she was alarmed by the admiral's visits,[26] while others suggest Elizabeth was left to sleep unattended.[27]

It is hard to believe that after making a fuss about ousting others from Elizabeth's room, Kate was happy with a highly unusual arrangement that left Elizabeth without a chaperone at night.[28] As she later showed in her outrage when gossip circulated about her charge, Kate knew very well how important it was to protect Elizabeth's reputation.

One explanation might be that Elizabeth herself insisted on Kate removing the bed. Teenagers can be difficult and often want to stretch the boundaries. As Elizabeth grew, the relationship between the two women had to evolve as Kate gradually ceded authority to Elizabeth herself. Alternatively, we might speculate that Kate wanted to share the marital bed with her husband, and slept even further from Elizabeth's room than in the crowded maids' room next door. However, given her dedication to Elizabeth, that seems far-fetched. Similarly, it is highly unlikely a direct instruction from the master of the house led to the highly unusual situation of a young princess alone in her room. If Kate did leave Elizabeth to sleep unattended it was a severe error of judgement on Kate's part. However, in her deposition Kate confirms that when the household was at Hanworth she 'lay with her grace', suggesting she was taking what precautions she could to protect Elizabeth.[29] It is difficult to see how Kate could have included so many details about events at Chelsea if she had not been in the room.

In June, the peaceful interlude at Chelsea shattered when, after the marriage became public knowledge, Thomas moved in. Somerset and the council were shocked. Princess Mary was so appalled she wrote to Elizabeth expressing concern that the dowager queen was not a suitable guardian. While politely declining Mary's offer to live with her – she was happy at Chelsea – Elizabeth similarly expressed her shock. Anne Somerset, who was on friendly terms with Mary, despite the difference in their religious views, was horrified to learn of the hasty marriage. A long-running row ensued about Catherine's jewels, which Anne had kept, adding more fuel to the flames of Thomas's resentment of his brother. Many accounts suggest that Anne and her old friend had a complete falling out, and engaged in a bitter feud over social standing. However, most reports come later, in the 1550s, and may represent efforts by pro-Catholic factions to discredit the Duchess of Somerset, a prominent Protestant figure.[30]

With Thomas's arrival, the entire power dynamic at Chelsea changed. In Tudor society, a man held absolute authority in the home, and as his wife Catherine – even though as the king's widow she was of higher rank – had to defer to him. Everything she owned was now his. He asserted his authority by ordering sizeable sums of money to be transferred from Catherine to him, so that he could support an extravagant lifestyle. As well as using much of Catherine's money, he borrowed from Sir William Sharington, who was Under Treasurer of Bristol Mint, with oversight of daily operations there. Thomas poured a fortune into renovating Sudeley Castle, furnishing and decorating it lavishly. Whether he was thinking only about pleasing his wife or was envisioning a royal lifestyle for himself is open to debate. Thomas liked to dress in the latest fashions and he lorded it over everyone.

Thomas brought his own household with him to Chelsea, including his ward, 10-year-old Jane Grey, who had been at his house on the Strand. Elizabeth and Jane were both highly intelligent and loved their studies. However an age gap of four years can seem large at that age, and they did not become close. Jane brought her own servants with her, including John Astley's sister Elizabeth.[31]

Almost everything we know about what happened in the twelve months from June 1547 to June 1548 comes from the later depositions taken from Kate and Thomas Parry. Historians have generally taken them at face value as an accurate description of events.

When Thomas began showing an inappropriate interest in Elizabeth, Kate's situation became very difficult. As she approached her fourteenth birthday, Elizabeth was as much prey to mood swings and hormonal outbursts as any modern teenager. Kate's job was to protect her, but Thomas was master of the house, and one of the most powerful men in England.

Kate might have hoped for support from the dowager queen. However, Catherine Parr, the intelligent, independent woman who had survived the ageing and irascible Henry VIII, was completely in Thomas Seymour's thrall. She dared not risk her slim chance of happiness by crossing him. Thomas picked little quarrels to test her, once even accusing her of impropriety with a groom who had carried coals for the fire into her room. Under questioning in January 1549, Thomas Parry, Elizabeth's cofferer, claimed he had heard that the admiral was an oppressor who cruelly and dishonestly used his wife.[32] We might, in modern parlance, view the way Seymour treated his wife as bordering on 'coercive control'. However, in a Tudor household, the relationship between husband and wife differed from that of our time. Husbands had the upper hand, and wives sometimes suffered. At least Seymour did not treat Catherine as badly as the Duke of Norfolk treated his wife. Elizabeth, Duchess of Norfolk wrote to Cromwell in 1538 complaining of her husband's ill treatment which included physical violence.[33]

Unfortunately, we know little of the arrangement of rooms at Chelsea Manor, which was demolished in the mid-eighteenth century after the death of its final owner, Sir Hans Sloane. Corridors did not become common in buildings until the late seventeenth century, so the rooms may have interconnected. Thomas had secured the keys to all the rooms in the house and could come and go as he pleased. Within days of his arrival, he was making early morning visits to the room in which Elizabeth now slept. If Elizabeth was in her bed he would 'make as though he would come at her'. Elizabeth would shrink back, but he reached out to 'strike her on the back or the buttocks familiarly'. Seymour would 'come up every morning in his nightgown, barelegged in his slippers'.

Elizabeth began to rise earlier so that he wouldn't find her in bed, but up and reading her book. Elizabeth rose even earlier. If she were dressed, he would bid her good morning and then go on his way.[34]

Kate surmised Elizabeth did not really welcome his advances, since she took precautions like rising early to avoid them. But the girl was understandably confused, prey to a tumult of emotions; flattered to have such an attractive man pay attention to her, she was excited and terrified all at the same time. Elizabeth could not hide the fact that she found her stepfather alluring. When later questioned, Kate recalled her husband mentioning how Elizabeth blushed if Thomas touched her hand in the dance. Kate's husband warned Kate she must 'take heed, for he did fear that the Lady Elizabeth did bear too much affection to my Lord Admiral'.[35]

There was clearly gossip in the wider household, since Kate says she heard of a time when the admiral waited for Elizabeth to come out from her hiding place from Elizabeth's gentleman usher, Robert Porter.[36]

If Seymour's wife noticed – and it is hard to believe she did not – she turned a 'blind eye'. Besotted and under her husband's controlling eye, she blotted such thoughts from her mind.

Kate was horrified when she understood the situation, yet she hesitated. Many historians have suggested that Kate too had come under Thomas's spell. Even if she did like him, even if she thought that at some future date, if he were free, he might be suitable as a suitor, it is inconceivable Kate condoned Seymour's actions. Allowing Elizabeth's stepfather to take such liberties not only imperilled Elizabeth's reputation, but could lead to Kate's own dismissal – or a more severe punishment.

Yet Kate was powerless. Without Catherine Parr's support, she dared not confront him. However, the morning came when Thomas climbed into Elizabeth's bed and tried to kiss her. That was too much for Kate, who exploded in fury, crying, 'Go away for shame!'[37]

What had perhaps begun as an exciting adventure had become threatening for Elizabeth. She knew that, for a young woman in her position, particularly one who was Anne Boleyn's daughter, reputation meant everything. She resorted to even more desperate measures to avoid him, running to her serving women when she heard his key in the lock. Thomas simply waited for her to come out.

In July, Kate packed up their belongings once more to move to Hanworth, so that Chelsea could be thoroughly cleaned. Thomas was probably pleased to make the move. A day's ride from London, and a larger property, Hanworth was conveniently situated, closer to Hampton Court. Thomas could visit the young king there, trying to wheedle his way into the boy's affections as the 'fun uncle' who was generous with his gifts of money. (Edward often complained about Somerset not allowing him pocket money.) Over a long period, Thomas cultivated his contacts among King Edward's servants. For example, he bribed John Fowler, a Groom of the Privy Chamber, to sing his praises to the king and pass on messages and gifts. Fowler had already played a crucial role in the political manoeuvring that led to the marriage of Thomas Seymour and Catherine Parr, by persuading the king to support the match. Another on Thomas's 'payroll' was John Cheke, the king's tutor. Initially reluctant, Cheke later admitted that on one occasion, at Christmas 1547, Seymour gave him £40 (a substantial sum, roughly £11,000 today). Cheke claimed he distributed most of the money to the king's servants. Thomas Seymour had a way of winning over even the most upstanding characters. Thomas also wasted no opportunity to tell his nephew that as the king, he wasn't being given enough say in things.

At Hanworth, Thomas showed no sign of giving up his visits to Elizabeth's bedchamber. On two occasions he even brought his wife with him to tickle Elizabeth in her bed. Catherine cannot have been comfortable, but she went along with it, making his actions look less sinister. In her deposition Kate said she had witnessed these visits herself.[38]

Damaging gossip was circulating, and Kate had had enough. She accosted Thomas in the gallery and told him in no uncertain terms he was ruining Elizabeth's reputation, crying, 'My Lady is evil spoke of.' Thomas was furious replying, 'God's precious soul! I will tell my brother how I have been slandered.' Then, ominously, 'I will not leave it, for I mean no evil.'[39]

To our twenty-first century eyes, given the large age difference, and his powerful position in the household, Seymour's behaviour fits the description of sexual grooming and harassment of a child. However, attitudes and perceptions vary over time. For example, Mumby writing in the early twentieth century dismisses the affair, saying 'It is possible that there had been nothing worse than unseemly romping.'[40] Writing in the 1950s, J.E. Neale apportioned some of the blame to Elizabeth: 'Judged by Victorian standards, Seymour may well appear a lewd man, and Elizabeth a shameless hussy.'[41] Neale goes on to suggest it was all innocent fooling, and that Thomas had no idea it could be misconstrued.

Even judging by sixteenth-century values, Thomas had overstepped the mark. As her stepfather, he was effectively Elizabeth's guardian; she was a royal princess and he had abused her trust.

Kate's protest had no effect. Worse was to come.

One late summer or early autumn afternoon, when Elizabeth was walking in the pleasant gardens at Hanworth with her stepmother, Thomas suddenly appeared in their path, brandishing a dagger. Alarmed, Elizabeth turned to her Catherine Parr. Inexplicably, Seymour's wife held the teenager, while Thomas cut Elizabeth's gown to shreds.[42]

Kate does not specify the colour in her deposition, but some sources suggest the dress was black, meaning Elizabeth was still mourning her father. Elizabeth often wore black; it was a colour that flattered her slim build, fair skin and red hair. If we were certain she was wearing mourning attire, and if we accept Leti's account, we might interpret the dress-cutting incident as Thomas reminding Elizabeth of her rejection letter, when she told him she intended to mourn her father for two years. Perhaps he wanted to prove how much power he had over the two women. Whatever the motivations, according to Kate, Catherine Parr helped her husband remove much of Elizabeth's dress, leaving it in pieces on the grass and Elizabeth in her underwear.

Wriggling out of Catherine's grip, Elizabeth ran headlong to find Kate, who found Seymour's wife's involvement deeply worrying. It seems Catherine Parr was not, however, at all comfortable. She was becoming alarmed at her husband's interest in her stepdaughter. Not long after the dress incident, she summoned Kate. Catherine alleged the admiral had told her he had seen Elizabeth in the gallery with her arms around a man's neck. When Kate quizzed her, Elizabeth tearfully denied the allegations. All of Elizabeth's other gentlewomen told Kate there was no man in the gallery. Apart from the intense, scholarly William Grindal, whom Kate discounted immediately, there were no other gentlemen at Hanworth. Kate concluded Catherine Parr had made the story up to warn her to keep a closer eye on Elizabeth.[43]

Soon after, an opportunity arose for Catherine to separate Elizabeth and Thomas. She went with her husband to his London house when he went there to attend parliament, while Elizabeth remained at Hanworth. In November, Thomas tried to get his nephew, King Edward, to sign papers for the House of Lords, giving Thomas the governance of the king. On the advice of his tutor, John Cheke, young Edward refused to sign.

Thomas had been steadily acquiring lands, and with those lands went parliamentary seats. In this way, he could influence the composition of parliament, hoping to get the bills he favoured passed. He flattered the country gentlemen and knights elected to the Commons and won them round with gifts. Some of Kate's relatives were among the MPs who attended Edward VI's first parliament; brother Arthur was elected for Barnstaple in 1547, as was Sir Peter Carew for Dartmouth and Sir Gawen as senior knight of the shire for Devon. No evidence has emerged to suggest Seymour approached any of them, but it remains a possibility. Arthur was unlikely to have supported Thomas. He owed his seat to the backing of his friend John Chichester, but also probably to the influence of Protector Somerset, who purchased Berry Pomeroy, a prestigious estate in Devon in December 1547. Somerset had praised Arthur's service in Boulogne in 1546, for which Arthur received £40 (more than £10,000 today) towards his expenses.

Thomas also tried to gain support from members of the House of Lords, but for all his machinations he had little impact in parliament. When a bill was presented in the Lords confirming Seymour's Protectorate, Thomas and his ally the Marquess of Dorset were the only ones to vote against. Thomas spent Christmas in London complaining. It was about this time that, at the age of 35, Catherine became pregnant.

Despite all the distractions Elizabeth continued to progress well in her studies during the bitterly cold winter of 1547. She spent the Christmas season away from court and away from her stepmother and Thomas. In January, her kindly tutor William Grindal became ill and died. It is easy to imagine how terrified Kate and the rest of the household were to learn he had died of plague. Miraculously, no one else succumbed, but a saddened Elizabeth needed a new tutor.

Roger Ascham wrote a touching letter on 22 January.[44] His suggestion that the 'other' Grindal (probably William's kinsman Edmund), might be a good choice, veiled his own ambitions for the post. Ascham was in his mid-thirties and was on friendly terms with Kate and John Astley. He was keen to get away from Cambridge, where disputes were rife. However, when he paid Elizabeth a visit, she had to admit to him that Catherine and Thomas favoured another man, Francis Goldsmith. Ascham withdrew gracefully, praising his rival. However, he stayed on for a few days, listening to Elizabeth's translations. They got on well, and on this occasion Elizabeth's will prevailed. Ascham became her tutor and went with Elizabeth when she joined Catherine and Thomas in London towards the end of February 1548.

Following the death of Francis I of France, relations with the French began to deteriorate again. There was talk of the French reclaiming Boulogne, or supporting the Scots. Thomas had been abusing his power over the navy, his actions becoming distinctly piratical. In his greed for more riches, he took advantage of his position as admiral as ships in the channel became fair game. He disobeyed direct orders from the council, kept the waters around the Scilly Isles under his own control, and allegedly filled his houses with stolen goods.

The row about the queen's jewels continued. Meanwhile, work began on Somerset Place, and Edward Seymour's extravagant lifestyle and construction projects stirred his brother's intense envy.

If Kate had hoped that Thomas had lost interest in Elizabeth, she was wrong. When he returned, the morning visits began again.

Thoughts of motherhood preoccupied Catherine. The household was back at Hanworth and packing was underway, readying to leave for Sudeley in early June.

As Catherine prepared to move to Sudeley, Edward Seymour's mind was on the religious reform agenda. He saw Stephen Gardiner as a barrier to progress. Gardiner had written at least twenty-five letters to Seymour, arguing against reform. When he resisted the visitation of his Winchester diocese by the ecclesiastical authorities, Seymour had him thrown into the Fleet Prison. Gardiner was released in January 1548, but on 29 June he preached against the reforms and was sent to the Tower, where he remained until 1553.[45]

Meanwhile, Elizabeth continued to be both fascinated and terrified by Thomas. Perhaps Kate did not see the message inscribed by Elizabeth on a package given to her by Catherine, which was to be delivered by messenger to Thomas in London. She scratched out 'Thou touch me not', written in Latin, and replaced it with 'let him not touch me'.[46] It sounds as though she wanted someone to help extricate her from Thomas's attentions.

On 11 June, Catherine caught Thomas with Elizabeth in his arms; that moment confirmed all of her worst fears. She turned her anger first on Kate, accusing her of failing to watch her young charge.

Soon after, Elizabeth moved to the Dennys' house at Cheshunt. When questioned, Thomas Parry could not recall whether Elizabeth was sent away or whether it was she who decided to go. The Dennys were the ideal choice to act as guardians, being both discreet and practical. Joan probably already knew from Kate what had been going on. At the time, no one hinted that Elizabeth had left in disgrace, and Thomas even accompanied her for part of the journey, Elizabeth and Kate keeping him engaged in conversation. They never revealed what they talked about.

Chapter 11

The Noblest Man Unmarried in This Land

1549

That summer at Cheshunt should have provided a pleasant respite in the happy family atmosphere of the Dennys' home. Joan and Anthony's family was growing. Their eldest sons were a little younger than Elizabeth and about to go to university. Anthony had helped make Edward Seymour Protector, and the two men remained political allies. We might wonder if Anthony spoke to Somerset about the circumstances of Elizabeth's move to Cheshunt.

Fuller described Joan Denny as 'a lady of great beauty and parts, a favourer of the Reformed religion when the times were most dangerous'.[1] She was Catherine Parr's friend and a firm proponent of religious reform, having sent money to Anne Askew in the Tower.[2] Roger Ascham likely got on well with Joan; he was pleased with the move to Cheshunt because it brought him nearer to Cambridge, while still preserving his independence. Some years later in a letter to John Astley, Ascham recalled:

> friendly fellowship together at Cheston [Cheshunt], Chelsea and at Hatfield, at her grace's house, our pleasant studies in reading together Aristotle's rhetoric, Cicero and Livy; our free talk, trim conferences of the present world and too true judgements of the troublesome times that followed.[3]

Ascham's words bring to mind cozy fireside chats, or long summer evenings in a garden, time shared with learned friends, as they put the world to rights. However, Elizabeth didn't enjoy the scholarly discussions. She was often unwell during her time at Cheshunt. Symptoms that plagued her all her life: headaches, irregular periods, migraines, problems with digestion and jaundice – symptoms often linked to stress – marred that warm sunny summer. Later suggestions that Elizabeth's illness was because she was pregnant with

1. Kate Astley, by an unknown artist, believed to be sixteenth century. (Photographer: Rich Schaapkens. Reproduced with the kind permission of Lord Hastings)

2. Joan Champernowne, wife of Sir Anthony Denny, oil painting dating from at least the eighteenth century, thought to be a distant copy of a sixteenth century likeness of Joan. (© Victoria and Albert Museum, London)

3. Portrait of John Astley, Master of the Jewel House, dated 1555 when John was in Europe. It is, one of the earliest full-length portraits of a non-royal Briton. (© National Portrait Gallery)

4. Sir Anthony Denny – stipple engraving W.T. Mote, possibly after Hans Holbein the Younger. (© National Portrait Gallery)

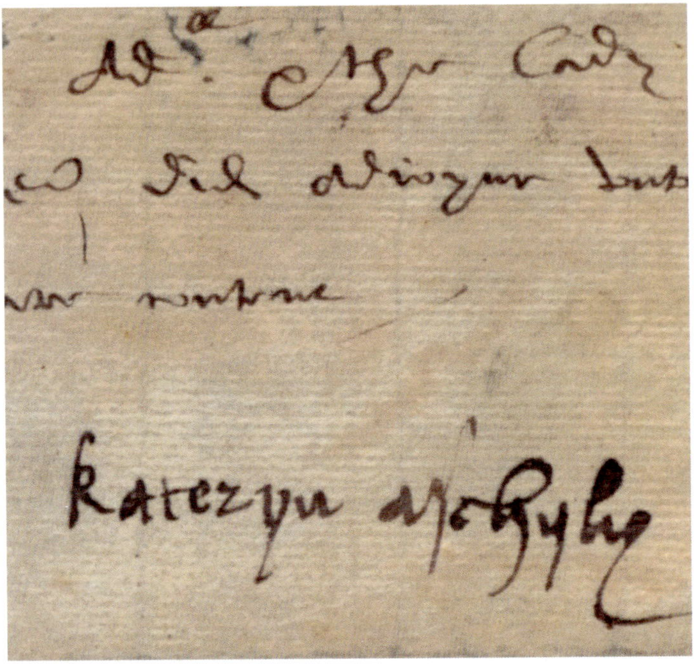

5. Signature of Kateryn Astley at the foot of her 'confession' which is recorded in the handwriting of Sir Thomas Smith. (Reproduced with the kind permission of the Marquess of Salisbury)

6. Hatfield House Old Palace. (Photographer: Pete Seaward, reproduced with the kind permission of the Marquess of Salisbury)

7. Sir Peter Carew, by Gerlache Flicke. (National Galleries of Scotland, via Alamy)

8. Admiral Sir Thomas Seymour, stipple engraving after Hans Holbein. (© National Portrait Gallery)

9. Sir Gawain Carew, British School. (National Trust Collections, Anthony House, via Alamy)

10. Sir Arthur Champernowne. (Private collection, reproduced with the kind permission of the owners)

11. The Elizabethan Maundy, Levina Teerlinc. (Beauchamp Collection, via Alamy)

12. The author at the King's Chapel of the Savoy, near the Strand, London. Kate Astley was buried either within the chapel or in the churchyard. (Author's own)

Seymour's child, far-fetched stories of blindfolded midwives called at dead of night, or newborns destroyed in a fire, do not stand up to scrutiny. The most damning rumours surfaced long after the events, including an account given by Jane Dormer, one of Queen Mary's ladies.[4] Almost certainly, Elizabeth was simply a young girl recovering from an unnerving brush with temptation and danger at the hands of an unscrupulous, but very handsome man.

No doubt Kate enjoyed catching up with her sister and spending time with her nieces and nephews. However, she was worried, aware that harmful gossip could damage Elizabeth's reputation.

Elizabeth plucked up courage to write to Catherine soon after she arrived at Cheshunt, and it appears there was a reconciliation. Catherine and Thomas went to Sudeley to await the birth of their child, but Catherine became increasingly unwell as her pregnancy progressed. On 30 August she gave birth not to the son they had hoped for, but a daughter, who they named Mary. At first all seemed well, but Catherine, like so many other women of this time, became ill a few days after the birth. Feverish and distraught, she turned to her faithful friend, pious Lady Tyrwhitt, and cried out:

> I am not well handled, for those that be about me careth not for me, but standeth laughing at my grief and the more good it will do them, the less good that they will to me.[5]

That outburst sounds like a heartfelt expression of Catherine's feelings about Seymour's 'affair' with Elizabeth. On 5 September, two days before Elizabeth celebrated her fifteenth birthday, Catherine Parr died.

Kate has come in for a good deal of criticism for encouraging Elizabeth to write to Thomas soon after the sad news reached Cheshunt. In an additional statement taken under interrogation in January 1549, Kate gives us the details. 'Madam,' she said, 'now you may have the husband that was appointed you at the death of the king.' Without registering Elizabeth's reaction, she went on: 'If all the council will agree, why not! For he is the noblest man unmarried in this land.'[6]

To us it seems premature and callous that Kate approached the matter so soon. Some writers have interpreted her early intervention as stemming from her own infatuation with Thomas Seymour. Equally, Kate might have been voicing the wishes of others who thought that, now a widower, Seymour was a good match for Elizabeth. She also knew that Elizabeth was attracted to the handsome admiral. It was not unusual for a man whose wife had died following childbirth, as so many women did, to waste little time in taking another wife. Kate may have felt it her duty to advise Elizabeth that she must prepare for Seymour to renew his suit. She may even have searched for some words of comfort for Elizabeth. Catherine's death must have come as a devastating blow, especially since Elizabeth had parted from her stepmother in unfortunate circumstances.

Whatever Kate's motivation, Elizabeth refused to write, saying people might think she 'sought to woo him'. It was Kate who wrote to Thomas Seymour, as she said, 'to remind the admiral that they remembered him'.[7]

At first, Seymour seemed genuinely shocked at his wife's death. The funeral went ahead at Sudeley with Jane Grey as chief mourner. Had she been there, Elizabeth would have taken that role, but she was once more ill at Cheshunt. After first deciding to send Jane back to her parents Thomas changed his mind, saying he intended to keep the household together. At first, Jane's parents, the Dorsets, were not keen. However, using a bribe as a sweetener, Thomas persuaded Jane's father to let her go back to Sudeley, with a vague promise that one day she would marry the king.

The Protector and his wife had other plans for Jane; a marriage with their eldest son. Thomas's relations with his brother were getting worse, although Edward Seymour had sent one brotherly note of congratulations on the birth of Thomas's daughter. Unfortunately, it arrived after Catherine's death. Thomas was as ambitious as ever, soon demanding of his brother that the Protector should allow either Mary or Elizabeth to wed.

Anne Somerset sent Mary Cheke, wife of the king's tutor, to Thomas with messages of comfort in his loss.[8] In reality, Anne was hoping for a thaw between the brothers. But Thomas was not to be mollified. He assembled his late wife's women and servants, effectively rebuilding a royal household. Meanwhile, the dispute about Catherine Parr's jewels resurfaced. Particularly incensed with his sister-in-law, Thomas boasted that when his daughter Mary grew up, she would have precedence over 'my Lady of Somerset' as a queen's daughter.

During the summer, as well as raising a series of complaints with his brother, Thomas had become more and more embroiled with William Sharington, who he was effectively blackmailing. Sharington had been debasing the coinage using church plate from the Somerset villages. He also sheared and clipped coins. To conceal his actions, he made false copies of the mint account books, destroying the originals. Fearing discovery, he sought Thomas Seymour's help. In return for protection, Sharington lent Thomas money and gave him access to the Bristol Mint, and offered to mint sizeable sums in coinage for Thomas to use in recruiting followers to his cause. Funded by all these fraudulent dealings, Sharington added properties in Wiltshire to Lacock Abbey, which he had bought in 1540.

Thomas was also drumming up support among the West Country gentry, who were becoming concerned about Somerset's high-handed approach to government. The Protector was pushing forward the reform agenda at an alarming rate, while his aggressive stance had strengthened the bond between France and Scotland and the costly wars continued. Ordering investigations into the legality of enclosure, particularly in the Midlands and southern England, did not win the Protector many friends among the nobility and gentry either. Thomas was notorious for being able to charm women, but he could also appeal to the pockets and interests of their menfolk, country landowners who felt under threat. He boasted he had as great a number of gentlemen that loved him as well as any nobleman in England.[9] It began to look as though Thomas was trying to raise an army for an insurrection against his brother. Marrying Elizabeth was probably part of his plan.

While Thomas was plotting, Elizabeth's health improved and she felt ready to leave her hosts, the Dennys. In something of a dilemma about where to go, she consulted Anthony. On his advice, she took up residence at Hatfield, which had many fond childhood memories for her. It was a handy location for both Cheshunt and London, and she was eager to revisit the sprawling palace and its grounds.

Thomas sent a man, named as Edward, to help with the move – it seems he was keeping in touch. Thomas's man told Kate his master was 'a heavy man in his grief for the queen'. John Seymour, the Protector's eldest son by his first marriage, also turned up. His uncle had sent him, he said, to enquire of Elizabeth 'whether her great buttocks were grown any less or no'.[10]

Being second in line to the throne and approaching an age for serious marriage negotiations, Elizabeth knew her future: an arranged marriage, perhaps to a foreign prince. That was her expectation, though she and Kate talked about her future husband. It's likely Thomas Seymour's name cropped up rather often.

Elizabeth now had independent means, but it soon became apparent that her finances were a mess. She needed to keep up appearances with a lifestyle fitting for her status, but her spending outstripped her income. Thomas Parry, the thickset Welshman, was her comptroller. Sir Robert Tyrwhitt later recognised he wasn't doing his job properly. Elizabeth soon had to cut costs by reducing wages.[11]

Towards the end of October Elizabeth gave Kate permission to make a mysterious visit to London. At first Kate said she was going to speak with Thomas himself. Her story then shifted. She said she planned to ask the gatekeeper at Durham Place, a property of the princess's she hadn't yet secured, for lodgings. Whatever the true reason for the visit, Elizabeth gave her permission, and Kate set out.

While Kate was in London, the Duchess of Somerset summoned her. The duchess told her in no uncertain terms that she was too close to Thomas Seymour. Kate, she said, had been lax in her supervision, allowing Elizabeth to go out on the river at night.[12] She was not fit to be Elizabeth's Lady Mistress. Someone should take her place.

Kate did not seem overly concerned that she might lose her position. She returned to Hatfield and told Thomas Parry all about it. Kate also met Mary Cheke, who passed on a message from the admiral that he planned to visit Elizabeth soon. Kate brought back all the latest gossip about Thomas Seymour. This does not imply that Kate was by nature a 'gossipy woman', rather that if she was to protect her mistress it was imperative she and Elizabeth knew what people were saying. The word was that Thomas was keeping all Catherine Parr's ladies on, ready for Elizabeth's arrival as his wife.

Elizabeth wrote a seemingly innocuous letter to Thomas, seeking his favour for her chaplain, Edmund Allen. It was quite usual to seek preferment for servants from a family member or other noble contact. However, Elizabeth added a cryptic note that Thomas should trust her cofferer, Thomas Parry in all other things.[13] Keeping that line of communication open may indicate that Elizabeth might have been seriously considering the merits of marrying Thomas Seymour.

By the time parliament convened in November, the Seymour brothers were eying each other like two dogs about to fight over a bone. One of the 'bones' in question was the marriage of Jane Grey.[14]

Edward Seymour was driving forward sweeping religious changes. A new Book of Common Prayer in English was introduced, and clerics could marry. Two members of Kate's family took advantage. Kate's uncle, George Carew, married Anne, daughter of Sir Nicholas Harvey, a Devonshire knight who had accompanied King Henry at the Field of Cloth of Gold. George had by now collected a list of church appointments. He was a Canon of Exeter and, from 1546, of Wells, and he would soon add the post of Precentor of Exeter to his impressive curriculum vitae. He does not seem to have taken up the leave to travel overseas, granted in the early days of King Edward's rule. Kate's sister Elizabeth, widow of William Cole, also benefited from the new ruling when she married Archdeacon John Pollard.[15]

Kate went to London again in early December 1549. The meetings she had there give us some important clues about what was going on.[16] Kate's excuse for making this second trip was flimsy in the extreme. She said she had a sore arm and needed to go to London to have it bled. Surely there were doctors at Hatfield who could bleed her? Kate's further detailed deposition under questioning clarifies that this was just what she pretended to everyone, including Elizabeth, who then permitted the visit.[17] This seems rather like a 'paper trail', distancing Elizabeth from the circumstances of Kate's visit. The real reason, Kate said, was that she and John had had a 'jarr' (argument) and he had left for London to attend parliament without their making up. Kate had written to him but he had not replied, so she set out for London to see him.

She met John at Slanning's house.[18] This is likely the home of John Slanning, who hailed from Devon, but in 1545 was steward of the Inner Temple in London. In 1541 the Crown granted Plympton Priory to Kate's father, Sir Philip Champernowne. He immediately sold parts of the site for demolition, and some of the priory's lands. John Slanning bought some of the land at Marystow, part of a substantial property portfolio he was amassing in Devon, adding some from Buckland Abbey.[19]

Overnight, Kate and John resolved their differences. After breakfast the next morning, John went on to parliament. He travelled with Elizabeth's cofferer, Thomas Parry, who had joined them at Slanning's house.

Kate had, probably deliberately, packed no court clothes; only her nightgown, the same one she also wore later when taken to the Tower for questioning. She could not therefore deliver in person the token Elizabeth had sent for the Duchess of Somerset. Instead, Kate sent William Russell to deliver it and went herself with Slanning's wife to Lady Berkeley's house in Fleet Street.

Lady Berkeley was the widow of Kate's brother, John. Her second husband, Sir Maurice Berkeley, was a committed Protestant who had served Cromwell and also received 200 marks under Henry VIII's will. Kate's sister, Joan Denny, Sir Peter Carew, Sir Gawen Carew, Archdeacon George Carew, and the as yet unidentified Henry Eliot, also joined the meeting at Lady Berkeley's house.[20] This was more than a cosy family reunion. It was a meeting of some of the foremost advocates of Protestant reform. As Elizabeth Norton points out, Fleet Street was conveniently close to Seymour Place.[21] Sir Peter Carew was Thomas Seymour's vice admiral in Devon. Although Kate protested strongly that she had not spoken with the admiral, they might easily have sent and received messages.

The importance of this intriguing meeting has been largely overlooked. Were they plotting to join Thomas Seymour in a coup? Kate's row with John might even have been a subterfuge to get Kate to the meeting. It seems more likely John was trying to dissuade Kate from going. Unfortunately, it is unlikely we will ever know what they discussed that day in the Berkeley mansion on Fleet Street.

Even though Kate said otherwise, it's obvious she really wanted Elizabeth to marry Thomas, and she was not his only supporter. *The History and Topographical Survey of the County of Kent* by Edward Halsted,[22] which was first published in 1797, refers to another vigorous supporter of Thomas Seymour. After her first husband Robert Willoughby died, Dorothy Grey, aunt of Lady Jane Grey, married William Blount, Lady Berkeley's father. According to Miss Champernowne, on one occasion Dorothy's insistence on pleading the admiral's suit before Elizabeth almost got her thrown out of the house.

Halsted's *Kent* also mentions that Lady Berkeley, Lady Denny and the three Carews 'who all favoured the admiral's design, at no small personal risk, were all at the front rank of the Protestant Party'. It is quite possible they considered Thomas Seymour with Elizabeth as his wife a strong bulwark against any return to Catholicism if Mary ever became queen. Edward was young and they may have had concerns about the longevity of Tudor princes in mind.

Whatever the outcome of the meeting, Kate left on horseback, returning to Hatfield, speaking to no one on the way.

Thomas Parry, Elizabeth's cofferer, now enters the story. Parry began his career assisting Thomas Cromwell with various tasks concerning the dissolution of the monasteries. After Cromwell's demise, he drifted in and out of a few posts until he joined Elizabeth's household. Parry was a friend and distant relative of William Cecil, who had accompanied Protector Seymour on his Scottish campaign in 1547, and was now Master of Requests, an administrative role.

Thomas Parry had not been in post long and was an inefficient accountant, yet both Elizabeth and Kate trusted him. About a fortnight before Christmas, Elizabeth despatched him to the admiral's house to enquire if she might use Durham House at Christmas. Seymour had bad news. Despite Elizabeth's prior claim, Durham House was to become a mint. Turning on the charm with Parry, he offered his own house, Seymour Place, for Elizabeth's use instead. In a few days Parry was back for another interview with Seymour, who this time said he intended to visit Elizabeth.[23]

Although Seymour had won Parry over, Elizabeth was cautious. Kate advised her to seek Anthony Denny's advice. Denny warned her not to accept the offer from Thomas. After quizzing Kate about what she had heard in London, Elizabeth had Kate write to Thomas, refusing his offer, saying 'She thought it not best, for fear of suspicion'.

Thomas blustered and grew red in the face when he read the refusal during Parry's next visit. He called on Mary Cheke, one of his loyal admirers, and soon she was on her way to Hatfield, even though she was pregnant. Mary and Kate met privately, and Mary relayed Thomas's message; he wanted to visit Elizabeth but was afraid people would say 'he came a wooing'.

Kate was noncommittal, but Elizabeth bade her write again, making it clear nothing could happen without the council's consent. Elizabeth later claimed to have been furious when Kate's letter went further than she intended, which does not seem to have been wholly true. Elizabeth felt torn; she clearly wanted to see Thomas, but that might lead to accusations of encouraging him without the council's express consent.

Sir Robert Tyrwhitt and his wife arrived, warning Elizabeth to take heed; the marriage would be to everyone's undoing if it happened without the prior consent of the council. Both John Astley and Anthony Denny also warned Kate and Elizabeth.

When Thomas Parry visited Seymour again on 20 December, the admiral questioned him about Elizabeth's household, the number of servants and where she had lands. He probed the quality and value of her estates, and whether she held full title to them with letters patent. Seymour seemed to want her to exchange some for properties in Wales and the West, nearer to his own base. The interview convinced Parry that Thomas was a serious suitor enquiring about the wealth of a prospective bride. Upon his return, he bravely asked Elizabeth directly whether she would wed the admiral if the council approved it. Annoyed, Elizabeth asked him who had put such thought into his head, and he confirmed that it was when the admiral questioned him about her lands. She insisted he tell Kate everything that had passed between him and Thomas Seymour.

As Christmas approached, William Sharington was a worried man. He had been carefully covering his tracks, destroying account books and changing figures where necessary, but he knew he could not continue. Disturbed by Sharington's unease, Thomas knew he must act soon. We can only guess at his state of mind. At loggerheads with his brother he often fell into rages, and according to the servant Fowler, since Catherine's death he had taken to drinking alone.

It was a tense Christmas at Hatfield. Elizabeth did what she often did when things got difficult; she took to her sickbed.

Parry sought Kate out on Twelfth Night to inform her of everything Thomas Seymour had said to him, just as Elizabeth had instructed. As they sat beside the glowing fire in Kate's chamber, Kate revealed rather more than was necessary about what had passed between Elizabeth and Seymour. According to Parry's later testimony, she announced that she herself would 'rather see her wedded to him than any man living'.[24] Kate swore the comptroller to secrecy, and he confirmed 'he would rather be pulled with horses' than betray Elizabeth.

When Parry saw Thomas next after Christmas, he found him changed. Preoccupied and with none of his usual bonhomie, perhaps worried that the net was closing in on Sharington, he dismissed Parry curtly.

Thomas had not yet fully developed his plans. He took to visiting Fowler, the king's servant, late in the evening, helping himself to drinks from the buttery and asking after the king. People noticed his strange behaviour, and erstwhile friends and supporters avoided him.

Somerset, heard about his brother's peculiar evening visits and put a special watch on all doors leading into the king's Privy Chamber in order to prevent Thomas's clandestine entry.

On 6 January, the council's agents searched Sharington's home, Lacock Abbey, for evidence of fraudulent dealings.[25] Hearing from John Fowler that Sharington was arrested, seems to have galvanised Thomas to take drastic action.

On 16 January, during one of his evening visits, Thomas found the door to Edward's bedchamber bolted. The king's pet dog barked, and Sir Michael Stanhope, who slept in the king's chamber, heard the commotion. Upon finding the king's dog dead outside the door, he raised the alarm. The guards had spotted Thomas hanging around the king's apartments that night, and assumed he had run the poor beast through with this dagger.[26]

Thomas attended parliament the following day, but failed to turn up when ordered to explain himself to the Privy Council. His failure to give a convincing account of himself, fuelled suspicions. Rumours circulated that he had been intent on murdering both the king and Mary, marrying Elizabeth and seizing the throne. On the evening of 17 January, after Thomas dined at the Earl of Huntingdon's house, Henry Grey, Marquess of Dorset, and his brother Lord Thomas Grey were among a group who accompanied him back to Seymour Place. It was Thomas Grey (who will feature in later events) who persuaded Seymour to give himself up.

At around 8.00pm that same evening, Thomas Seymour was on his way to the Tower. William Sharington confessed all in return for a pardon. Council officers searched Thomas's properties and found incriminating evidence: he was stockpiling weapons and recruiting men. Thomas's close friends were questioned. Under interrogation, his servants revealed Parry's visits, throwing suspicion on Elizabeth.

Chapter 12

They All Sing to One Tune

1549

On the morning of 21 January 1549, Sir Anthony Denny and Sir William Paulet caused quite a stir when they rode into Hatfield's courtyard. They had likely left Cheshunt, a mere 10 miles away,[1] before dawn, braving icy roads and bitter cold to get there so early. Time was of the essence if they were to complete their uncomfortable mission that day. They went to prepare the ground for Sir Robert Tyrwhitt, whom the Protector had assigned to question Elizabeth, hoping to uncover evidence to implicate her in Seymour's schemes.[2] Protector Seymour had ordered them to remove Kate and Parry for questioning so that Tyrwhitt could interrogate Elizabeth.

As soon as he spotted them through a downstairs window, Thomas Parry panicked.[3] Climbing the stairs two at a time, he burst into his chamber and, tearing off his chain of office, he turned to his terrified wife crying, 'I would I had never been born, for I am undone'.

As Parry paced up and down, wringing his hands, his wife, Lady Fortescue,[4] tried to calm him. After a few moments he composed himself and they went down together to join a tight-lipped Kate, who was greeting the visitors below.[5] (These details are taken from Sir Robert Tyrwhitt's letter to Somerset the following day, when he reports that many people at Hatfield had witnessed Parry's reaction. We might question the veracity of this hearsay evidence and wonder if the witnesses were primed. However, Parry was indeed a man who might easily panic. In 1560, during the Dudley crisis, Ambassador Breuner found him untrustworthy and timid.)[6]

Kate was likely less surprised to see them. The news of Thomas Seymour's arrest had reached Hatfield almost as soon as it happened. At least one of the people Kate met in London in December had almost certainly been in touch; no doubt they all wanted to distance themselves from Thomas Seymour's schemes as quickly as possible. Forewarned, Elizabeth and Kate had already started to prepare their story.

They couldn't have asked for a better team to launch the investigation. If anyone could devise a strategy to ensure they all came out of the unfortunate business unscathed, it was that smoothest of all political operators, Sir Anthony Denny. His companion, William Paulet, was, like Denny, a career bureaucrat. Having trained in the law, he had served in a succession of posts under Henry VIII and his son. Paulet now held two of the highest offices of state as Grand Master of the King's Household and Lord Keeper of the King's Seal.[7] His star had steadily risen, proving he knew how to navigate the dangers of the Tudor Court.[8] Paulet was one of those named as executors in King Henry's will. Edward Seymour's domineering style and mismanagement was probably already worrying Paulet. Only a few months later, he was one of the instigators of Somerset's downfall.[9]

In January 1549, however, Somerset had full control and it was abundantly clear his brother was beyond saving. Sharington's evidence alone proved he was aiming to overthrow the Protector.[10] Denny and Paulet knew each other well, and were both adept at using all the precepts of humanist rhetoric to present a case. They knew how to 'inflect a narrative to present as truthful witnesses', and how to 'garner most support for their arguments'.[11] They had likely agreed on their approach at Cheshunt.

Kate sat her brother-in-law and his companion down and offered them food. No one recorded the details of their conversation at the table, but after dining, Denny and Paulet left to 'interrogate' Elizabeth.

Parry's wife was in despair, but Kate calmly reassured her that her private conversations with Parry could not damage them. Kate and the Parrys then retired to their separate quarters to await events. A little later, Parry's wife came to Kate to assure her again that her husband 'would rather be pulled by horses' than say anything. It is interesting that this statement appears several times in the depositions. This could be a deliberate ploy to set the scene for Parry to crumble after a few days in custody after which Kate could express her disgust before she too gave her 'confession'.

Denny and Paulet discussed strategy with Elizabeth. They agreed immediately that the greatest danger was in any evidence that Elizabeth agreed to marry Thomas without the express consent of the council. That she had always made it clear that she never considered accepting him without the council's consent was the strongest line to take, to be repeated regularly throughout the questioning they all knew must follow. They would throw the blame onto the already condemned Thomas. Nothing must reflect badly on Elizabeth. Insofar as Seymour's inappropriate approaches during his marriage to the late queen, to some extent Kate must shoulder a portion of the blame and admit her negligence, while also pointing out she had tried in vain put a stop to it. Anne Somerset's declaration that she was unfit to have charge of a king's daughter already supported that line. Kate had to 'fall on her sword' to clear Elizabeth of any wrongdoing. This must have been a terrifying prospect for Kate. She showed brave devotion, which Elizabeth never forgot.

The timing of events on that January day has perhaps become a little confused because Kate mentioned in her further statement, taken in late February, that she was wearing her 'russet nightgown' in the Tower.[12] This has led to suggestions that Denny and Paulet left Hatfield in the middle of the night, hastily removing Kate in her night attire, without even giving her time to dress. However, people in the sixteenth century did not use the word 'nightgown' to describe what they wore in bed. Women slept in linen shifts, (also called smocks and later chemises), while men wore a similar linen nightshirt in bed. A 'nightgown' was a loose-fitting over-gown, compared somewhat misleadingly to a modern-day dressing gown.[13] It was more than that. Fashion historian Janet Arnold says: 'The term is nearer in meaning to the eighteenth-century "dress" and "undress" and the modern "formal" and "informal".[14] More comfortable than a formal 'court' dress, nightgowns were designed for warmth – with only fires to heat draughty palaces and houses, both men and women needed layers of clothing. In a detailed account of the dressing ritual of a French noblewoman, written by Peter Erondell and published in 1605, the lady chides her maidservant asking 'Why do you not offer my nightgown? For I take cold.'[15]

Royalty and the nobility wore highly embellished and fur-trimmed nightgowns on less formal occasions. When queen, Elizabeth often received visitors in her nightgown, as did her father. When George Cavendish told Henry VIII of the death of Cardinal Wolsey, the king greeted him 'in his nightgown'.[16] It is interesting that Kate wore a russet gown. Russet was not only a colour, but also a fabric: 'a coarse narrow wool, undyed and unfinished; broad russet, better quality, might be dyed; London russet as wide and costly as broadcloth'.[17]

The narrow undyed version of russet, usually a subdued grey or brown colour, was generally worn by people of lower status. Kate's nightgown was likely cloth of higher quality, and may have been trimmed or lined with black lamb fur known as budge,[18] or other fur. However, it would not have been ostentatious. When she went to London, no one would notice her in her russet 'nightgown'. It was also a sensible choice for incarceration in a freezing cell at the Tower. This simple garment in sombre tones might also create an impression of a humble servant who had erred, the character that Kate wanted to present before her interrogators.

The minor detail of the nightgown changes the narrative of that January day. Denny and Paulet did not summarily remove Kate and Thomas Parry at short notice, but escorted them with due concern for their comfort. There was plenty of time on the journey for Denny and Paulet to coach Kate and Parry in the tactics and answers they had agreed with Elizabeth.

The Tyrwhitts arrived the next morning. They were unlikely to see the Hatfield household in a favourable light. Lady Tyrwhitt had testified about Catherine Parr's deathbed allegations of her husband's cruelty. She was a pious woman, puritanical in her beliefs, and may have held Elizabeth partly to blame for Thomas Seymour's behaviour.

On the next day, Tyrwhitt reported to Somerset that he has used a rather obvious subterfuge to frighten Elizabeth into believing her servants were already undergoing questioning in the Tower.[19] Tyrwhitt forged a letter, purporting to be from one of Blanche Parry's friends, saying Kate and Parry were being questioned in the Tower. They were in fact taken first to Petty Calais (also known as Petty France) an area of Westminster known for its wool dealers. This area was a stone's throw from the Palace of Whitehall, and also housed court officials. Denny or Paulet may have had people there and hoped to hold the prisoners there, in surroundings less daunting than the Tower.[20] Elizabeth knew exactly where Denny had taken them, and did not fall for Tyrwhitt's trick.

John Astley was in London on 21 January. Considering his protest against Kate's London visit and his repeated warnings that she shouldn't interfere, it seems rather harsh that the Protector ordered his arrest and confinement in the Fleet Prison, where he was held for months. Kate's Carew relatives and Lady Berkeley likely felt relieved when no one questioned them. Thomas Seymour admitted his involvement with Sharington, but did not implicate anyone else.

It was not long before Kate and Parry were taken to the Tower, presumably on the Protector's orders. The potentially friendly Sir Thomas Smith would eventually record their answers there. Smith was clerk to the Privy Council, a member of the Cambridge Set, associate of Denny and friend of John Cheke. Even though Kate was in a cramped, cold and dimly lit cell, she might hope his presence would spare her from the worst brutality. In her additional statement in late February she appealed directly to Smith, saying: 'good Master Secretary Smith, speak that I may change my prison. For by my troth, it is so cold that I cannot sleep in it and so dark that I cannot in the day see, for I stop the window with straw; there is no glass.'[21] Even in her thick nightgown, she was freezing.

What we understand today of the events considered here and in the preceding chapter comes largely from the evidence Kate and Parry gave under duress. Together they told a story that ultimately prevented Elizabeth from being pulled down with Seymour.

The involvement of Denny and Paulet, points to a deliberate plan, which they enacted perfectly. After holding out for a few days to give Elizabeth time to compose herself, Parry, already established as flaky, appeared to wilt under questioning. Kate, after expressing her righteous anger at his having done so, could then give all the salacious details of Thomas Seymour's approaches to his stepdaughter. Although perhaps not viewed quite as harshly as in our time,

Kate established clearly that he had abused the trust of a royal princess in his care. Thomas was the guilty party. Kate's focus on all the titillating details of Thomas' inappropriate behaviour may have been agreed as a distraction tactic. If so it worked.

The depositions rarely attribute events to specific dates. Kate is even vague about her visit to London only a few weeks earlier. They do, however, mention the names of other witnesses who, if questioned, could corroborate statements. Together with many inconsequential details, this established their credibility as witnesses. Like a broken record, they repeatedly insisted Elizabeth never contemplated marrying Seymour without the council's approval. They repeated the same refrain with which Elizabeth, who is similarly vague about dates and places, answered Tyrwhitt: marriage without the council's consent was never considered.

Aware that she may be punished for the negligent care of Elizabeth which she admits, in her final statement taken in late February she explains that she tried to get Thomas to desist, adding:

> And as touching on my lord's [Thomas Seymour's] boldness in her chamber, the Lord I take to my record, I spoke so ugly to him – yea and said that it was complained of to my lords of the Council, but he would swear 'What do I? I would they all saw it!' That I could not make him leave it. At last I told the queen who made small matter of it and said she wold come with him herself.[22]

At Hatfield Elizabeth handled matters with remarkable skill, showing a gift for clever diplomacy that would become the hallmark of her reign. She admitted only minor, non-incriminating details, a much stronger defence than blanket denial. Only 15 years old, yet Tyrwhitt soon recognised that with her composure and ability, she could run rings round him. Robert Tyrwhitt was nobody's fool. He saw exactly what was happening. He wrote in frustration to Somerset on 7 February saying: 'They all sing with one song, and so I think they would not do so had they not set the note before.'[23]

Chapter 13

Rebellions and Losses

1549–1553

Sir Robert Tyrwhitt failed in all his attempts to trap Elizabeth into a confession. She maintained the line and wrote a clever letter to the Protector on 7 February, accepting her servants' confessions but clarifying that while Kate had often spoken to her of marriage, it was in the clear understanding that it depended always on the council's agreement.[1]

By the end of February, the council felt they had enough to charge Thomas Seymour on thirty-three counts, including practicing to marry Elizabeth without consent. They could not however, prove Elizabeth's complicity.

Elizabeth appeared to decry Kate's 'evil doing', while arguing vociferously for her release, which she eventually secured. The Protector would not allow Kate to return as Elizabeth's Lady Mistress. Instead, they appointed Lady Tyrwhitt, which provoked an indignant and angry response.[2]

The 11-year-old king signed the order attainting his uncle for treason without a second thought. This spelled a rude awakening for Thomas, who thought his nephew loved him. Perhaps King Edward had seen through Thomas's attempts to manipulate him. A bill passed rapidly through the House of Lords, but proved more tricky in the Commons, where members asked why there had been no trial. They debated for several days before, on 5 March, they gave their assent.

On 7 March Elizabeth wrote again to Protector Somerset, this time taking a considerable risk. She spoke up in Kate's favour, saying she had not pleaded for Kate before in case the council thought she 'favoured her evildoing'. She praised Kate for bringing her up, and added that keeping her Lady Mistress in the Tower could fuel suspicions about her own involvement, damaging her reputation.[3]

William Cecil, at this time private secretary to Protector Somerset, may have seen her letter. Cecil was not in favour of Kate's reinstatement, thinking her 'the unmeetest woman to be about such a person as your grace is'.[4] We don't know for sure why Cecil held this view. He was related to Blanche Parry so may have felt Kate had pushed Blanche aside.

Somerset had other matters to consider. He now faced the agonising decision about his brother's fate. On 20 March Thomas Seymour met his brutal end on the scaffold on Tower Hill. King Edward showed no regret for his uncle's passing, recording his death in his chronicle with the stark words: 'Also the Lord Sudeley, Admiral of England, was condemned to death and died the March Ensuing.'[5]

They laid Thomas Seymour to rest in the Chapel of St Peter ad Vincula, near to Elizabeth's mother, Anne Boleyn. Somerset was not in London at the time of his brother's execution, and he later had regrets.[6]

Reporting of the 'Thomas Seymour affair' has not only led to assumptions about Kate's character, it also defines what we believe about Seymour himself. He may have had faults, but Kate Astley was not the only one to like him. He had many friends, and Catherine Parr, a highly intelligent woman, loved him. The record suggests he was manipulative, reckless and consumed by jealousy. But some who knew him hinted at other explanations.

An anonymous poem, thought to be written by Nicholas Throckmorton, cousin of Catherine Parr and published by a relative in 1570/1571, includes the following words about Seymour's end:

> Off went his head, they made a quick despatch,
> But ever since I thought him sure a beast
> Who causeless laboured to defile his nest
> Though guiltless, he, through malice, went to pot
> Not answering for himself nor knowing cause.[7]

This suggests Throckmorton believed other men's ambitions were just as much to blame as Seymour's own. John Harrington, Seymour's loyal servant, described him as a,

> Friend to God's truth, and foe to Rome's deceit…
> Yet against nature, reason and just laws
> His blood was spilt, guiltless, without just cause.

Harrington presented 'The Hospitable Oake', written after Seymour's death, after Elizabeth became queen, together with a portrait of Seymour.[8]

The unreliable Leti quotes Elizabeth's words on hearing the news of Seymour's death as: 'This day died a man of much wit and very little judgement.'[9] Whether she actually used those words, and whatever the extent to which the vulnerable teenager was drawn into Seymour's web, there can be no doubt Elizabeth's close brush with disaster due to his attentions had a lasting impact on the future choices she made.

By late spring Kate and Parry were released, although Elizabeth had to put up with the puritanical Lady Tyrwhitt for a little longer. Elizabeth made no secret that she resented her imposition as Lady Mistress in Kate's place.[10] By September, Kate and Parry were back at Hatfield, and the Tyrwhitts had gone. Elizabeth set about restoring her reputation by dressing soberly and living quietly at Hatfield, out of the public eye.

During the summer of 1549, chaos descended upon several parts of the country. Somerset, damaged by the revelations about his brother's treason, had to deal with disruptions, rebellions and riots. An act introduced in April ordered those who had enclosed lands to remove the fences, but not surprisingly, many landowners failed to comply. They did not want to lose their profits from running large flocks of sheep or keeping deer in the newly created enclosures. However, the enclosures curtailed the rights enjoyed by villagers to graze animals on common land, threatening their livelihood. In many parts of England, ordinary people took the law into their own hands, burning down hedges and tearing up fences, killing sheep and deer.

At the same time, on religious policy, Somerset had the full backing of King Edward, who had become evangelical in his zeal to transform England into a fully Protestant land. They introduced sweeping religious reforms that upset the age-old traditions that were the very fabric of people's lives. Introducing a new prayer book in English was the last straw in a long line of grievances for the people of Cornwall, and a catalyst for trouble that soon spread through Devon. While the tension built, Somerset and the council were focused on the long and costly war in Scotland. To deal with the western emergency, the council turned to two of Kate's relatives. They summoned Sir Peter Carew from his wife's Lincolnshire estates, and sent him, with Sir Gawen, who was in attendance at court, to put down the riots.[11]

Unfortunately, Sir Peter, a reckless, swashbuckling character, handled matters badly. When he and Sir Gawen approached Crediton, where the well-armed rebels had dug in, what Somerset had intended as a 'peace mission' turned ugly. Edward Seymour misjudged Sir Peter Carew in selecting him for the commission. John Dudley, Earl of Warwick, probably had a more realistic idea of the likely outcome, having seen Sir Peter's aggressive and flamboyant military escapades in France. Met with a barricade, Sir Peter forgot the peaceful nature of his mission and led the charge. Amid the chaos, roadside barns were set ablaze. After falling back to Exeter, Sir Peter tried to negotiate with the rebel leaders, who presented a long list of demands – including the release of Richard Crispin, the Catholic preacher imprisoned after he was called to account for disrupting the month's mind of Kate's brother-in-law, Otho Gilbert, in 1547. In a tense show-down near Clyst St Mary, someone fired a shot, and the negotiations failed. The rebel forces laid siege to Exeter. In the mayhem that ensued on 22 June, rebel troops captured Kate's brother-in-law Raleigh and imprisoned him for several weeks in St Sidwell's Church.[12]

Sir Peter slipped out of the besieged city and rode to the Paulet family seat at Hinton St George, where Lord John Russel waited with reinforcements. Sent to take charge, Russel had gathered over 1,000 additional soldiers. He put an end to matters in a series of bloody battles culminating in the defeat of the rebels at Clyst Heath on 6 August. During the rebellion over 5,500 men of Cornwall and Devon died.

Their conduct did nothing to enhance Sir Peter's and Sir Gawen's standing among the ordinary people of the Catholic-leaning West. They were already viewed in a negative light for profiting from the dissolution, and they had also identified themselves with radical reform preachers.[13]

Kate's 25-year-old brother, Arthur Champernowne (Plate 10) also played his part in what came to be known as 'The Commotion Time' of 1549. He was rewarded, along with John Chichester, with the lead bell-clappers from Devon churches, ordered removed to prevent the bells calling people to rebellion again. Some sources suggest the two men soon sold the bell-clappers back to the churches and made a tidy sum.[14] Others suggest the clappers were never removed.[15] King Edward knighted Arthur at Westminster on 10 November 1549.[16]

While these events were unfolding in Devon, the Duke of Somerset sent Sir Anthony Denny with the Marquess of Northampton to put down another serious uprising in Norfolk, where Robert Kett, a yeoman farmer, lead a revolt against the enclosures. Kett's Rebellion ended on 27 August when an army under the leadership of John Dudley, Earl of Warwick, defeated the rebels.

Sir Anthony returned to Cheshunt, where he died on 10 September 1549, most likely of illness or infection picked up during the campaign; he was 48 years old. Five sons and four daughters, and an illegitimate son, of whom little is known, survived him. In his will, he left Joan a wealthy widow with instructions to educate their children so that 'the commonwealth may find them profitable members and not burdens as idle drones be to the hive'.[17]

As she returned to Hatfield that September, Kate had lost the adviser who had steered her and, more importantly, Elizabeth through the crisis. Somerset had lost a politically astute ally.

The rest of his council did not share Somerset's sympathetic approach towards the anti-enclosure movement. Alienated by his autocratic style and self-aggrandisement – he was spending vast sums building a palace for himself at Somerset Place – they had had enough of his incompetence as a leader, his costly wars and his mismanagement of the Crown's finances.[18] His failure to deal effectively with the summer uprisings was the final straw. In early October, John Dudley and other Privy Councillors removed Somerset from his position as Lord Protector and imprisoned him in the Tower of London. Somerset himself brought matters to a head by effectively kidnapping his nephew and holding him at Hampton Court. One of those sent to persuade him to give himself up was Sir Thomas Smith, the scribe who noted down Kate's statements.

Had Anthony Denny survived, he might have used his diplomatic powers in Seymour's favour. This time he was released, but Edward Seymour, was living on borrowed time. When he was arrested again in October 1551 and charged with treason, there was no reprieve. Edward Seymour was executed on 22 January 1552. King Edward recorded the event in his chronicle with characteristic coldness: 'The Duke of Somerset had his head cut off upon Tower Hill between eight and nine o'clock in the morning.'[19]

In 1551 Seymour's wife, Anne, was arrested the day after her husband, accused of complicity in his treasons. John Dudley certainly did not want Anne at large to work against him.[20] Anne remained under lock and key until Mary released her in the summer of 1553.

From October 1551, John Dudley, Duke of Northumberland, was in control. He reversed Somerset's liberal agrarian policies and, by continuing the consolidation of Protestant reform, he gained favour with King Edward. To his credit, he tried to stabilise the economy by fighting inflation, stabilising coinage and expanding trade. However, his high-handed methods made him increasingly unpopular.

Seymour's removal was of less importance to Elizabeth and her household; they had weathered the storm, and she was restored in her brother's favour. She spent Christmas of 1549 at court, in great style. Elizabeth then lived quietly, mainly at Hatfield, doing all she could to repair the undoubted damage to her reputation. Kate was at her side, perhaps advising her to dress demurely as she did herself. (In her portrait Kate appears in a dark gown, with few adornments.) In December 1551, John Aylmer, Jane Grey's tutor, said of Elizabeth: 'She goes clad in every respect as becomes a young maiden.'[21]

Dressing plainly in black and white – a colour combination which also showed her slender figure and fair skin off to perfection – Elizabeth was happy to embrace her brother's religious reforms. That also suited Kate, whose family now counted some of the foremost adherents to the Protestant cause in their ranks.[22] Elizabeth's sister Mary, however, held out against the changes; she continued to have her chaplains practice the mass, putting herself in danger.

William Cecil's former association with Edward Seymour earned him a few weeks in the Tower in 1549. He soon regained favour, however, and he served as secretary to the young King Edward VI. Despite his opinion of Kate, Elizabeth trusted him. Gradually, Cecil took Anthony Denny's place as Elizabeth's closest adviser. In spring 1550 Elizabeth took control of the estates left her by her father and appointed Cecil her surveyor. She took a great interest in managing her properties herself, as seen in the only surviving set of household accounts for 1551–1552, which bear her signature on every page.[23] These show Kate's salary was £7 15s (roughly £2,128) per half year. Blanche Parry received, £5 (roughly £1,373) and Lady Troy's much smaller pension was sent by the Knight's Marshall's servant. Elizabeth Ballard, responsible for Elizabeth's laundry, received regular payments. The accounts include a surprisingly large payment of £100 (around £27,000 today) to Joan, Lady Denny, Kate's now widowed sister. This was at about the same time as Joan was involved in litigation concerning her late husband's estates.

Kate held a trusted position, empowered to disburse payments to others, including one to Mistress Slanning on 1 April 'by the handes of Mistress Asheley, for damask and satin'.

These accounts offer a fascinating snapshot of life at Hatfield. Among the records of provisions for buttery, bakehouse, pantry, cellar, squillery and stable, are many entries relating to the purchase of costly fabrics like velvet for gowns and hoods, clothes ordered from Elizabeth's tailor, Warren, and new lute strings and payments to musicians. Scholars also received gifts, and Elizabeth sent a christening present when Mary Cheke's son was born.

The accounts reveal the presence of another tutor in Elizabeth's household, since a payment on 14 April goes to 'Johñes Spithonius'. Johannes Spithovius (John Spithoff), also known as Monasteriensis, is thought to have come from near Münster in north-west Germany. He may have taught Elizabeth German and helped her understand the Lutheran world. Joining the household in 1549, he sat in on the learned discussions with Ascham, who remained with Elizabeth until 1550, and others from the Cambridge Set. Such was the atmosphere of learning at Hatfield, it was dubbed an 'outpost of Cambridge university'. Kate and her husband mixed with the group of intellectuals who congregated at Hatfield, joining their philosophical discussions.

Kate likely accompanied Elizabeth when she spent Christmas 1550 at court with King Edward, and was received with much more favour than her sister. It was the last Christmas Henry VIII's three children spent together. Elizabeth did not join the court celebrations a year later, but spent Christmas 1551 quietly at Hatfield or one of her other residences. At this time Elizabeth kept a low profile, concentrating on her continuing studies and managing her estates.

In early 1552, King Edward fell ill. With Catholic Mary next in line of succession, Northumberland knew his position was precarious should Edward die.

Rumours that he would arrange a divorce for his eldest son, John, so that he could marry Elizabeth came to nothing. Northumberland's younger son Robert had married Amy Robsart on 4 June 1550, with King Edward and Elizabeth both in attendance; the marriage appeared to be a happy one, so he was out of the running.[24] Another son, Ambrose, was on his second marriage. However, Dudley's youngest son, Guildford, was unmarried.

After Somerset's fall in 1552, Dudley offered Somerset House to Elizabeth in return for her townhouse, Durham Place. In December 1552 his son Robert was appointed keeper of Somerset House, but Edward Seymour's grand mansion was still a building site and Elizabeth did not visit.

One sunny morning in May 1553, Kate mounted her horse to ride through the lanes to Cheshunt. On this occasion she did not enjoy the birdsong as her mount ambled along beneath trees dressed in fresh spring green. On that bright May morning, hers was a sad mission. The king was not the only one suffering ill health. Kate had been called, along with her niece, Elizabeth Budockside (Butseyd) to witness Joan Denny's will.[25] Kate's beautiful and learned sister died on 23 May and Kate proved her will four days later. Joan died a wealthy woman and made many bequests of jewellery. Her death came as a blow to Kate as the two women had spent a good deal of time together, especially during the summer of 1549, and shared similar views on religion.[26]

Northumberland decided on drastic action and drew Henry Grey, now Duke of Suffolk, into his plans. Although questioned during the Thomas Seymour investigations, Grey had escaped unscathed and was now game for another brush with danger. On 25 May 1553, while Kate was at Cheshunt, Suffolk's daughter, the 16-year-old Jane Grey, married Guildford Dudley at Durham Place, which he had exchanged with Elizabeth for Seymour's palatial Somerset House.[27]

Northumberland then convinced the severely ill king that the best way for him to avoid the crown passing to Catholic Mary was for him to sign a device cutting both Mary and Elizabeth, deemed illegitimate, out of the succession and settling the crown on Jane. This was contrary to King Henry VIII's will, but Edward went along with it. A late alteration to the 'device for the succession' settled the throne on Jane herself, when the king realised he could not live long enough to see Jane have a child. No one knew exactly what Northumberland had contrived, but the rumour mill was grinding fast.[28] On 6 July 1553, King Edward's brief life ended.

Chapter 14

Intrigues and Plots

1553–1557

Kate found herself caught up in several plots and schemes during the period between King Edward's death and that of his sister Mary. Elizabeth naturally became the focus for disenchanted Protestants and those against Mary's marriage to Philip of Spain. Kate's close relationship with Elizabeth meant she was bound to be suspected, especially when her family and friends were involved in actions that eventually led to open rebellion. Of those in Kate's inner circle, it was Sir Peter Carew who would draw Kate and her mistress into perilous times.

It is uncertain when Elizabeth heard about her brother's death. Edward and Elizabeth had been close, had shared lessons, and he reportedly called her his 'sweet sister temperance'. Elizabeth had hoped to visit her brother in the spring, but his illness prevented it.[1] She must have felt his loss keenly, even though they had seen little of each other recently. His death also left Elizabeth's position in the succession in jeopardy.

No doubt Elizabeth was aware of, and concerned by, Northumberland's machinations to set his daughter-in-law, Jane Grey, on the throne. As the dramatic events unfolded, she kept well out of the way at Hatfield. Kate was with her, perhaps acting as a conduit for information supplied by her contacts.

Jane Grey was the great-granddaughter of Henry VII. With her extreme Protestant views, Northumberland thought Jane could rely on those who feared Mary would return the country to the Church of Rome. However, he miscalculated the loyalty Mary could stir up as Henry's daughter, and therefore lawful heir to the throne. Although members of the council initially proclaimed Jane queen on 10 July 1553, they soon had second thoughts.

Mary confounded everyone by rallying her supporters and sweeping into London to be proclaimed queen on 19 July.[2] She imprisoned Jane, rounded up Northumberland and his sons and sent them to the Tower.

As soon as she was sure her sister had prevailed, Elizabeth wrote to congratulate Mary, then set off for London. At about the same time,

Sir Peter Carew, with Sir Arthur Champernowne at his side, surprised everyone by declaring his allegiance to Queen Mary at Dartmouth and Newton Bushell (Newton Abbot).[3] Peter, a staunch Protestant, had been busy in Devon, assisting in the compiling of inventories of confiscated church goods. With Mary's accession, he faced a total reversal of fortunes. Yet he supported her, at least initially. It's possible that he had heard from Kate that Elizabeth intended to support her sister.

On 29 July 1553, Kate joined the 2,000-strong retinue, with all the gentlemen dressed in the Tudor colours of green and white, as Elizabeth made her entry into London.[4] Kate couldn't help but notice the loud cheers that greeted them. Elizabeth rested at Somerset House with Kate and all her ladies before continuing with a somewhat reduced escort towards a meeting with Mary.

Cheering people thronged the streets a few days later to see Mary enter the city at Aldgate, where colourful streamers fluttered in the light breeze. The Lord Mayor of London greeted Mary, presenting her with the sceptre of office, before the queen set off towards the Tower of London.[5] Elizabeth followed with the Duchess of Norfolk, the Marchioness of Exeter and other ladies. Mary had not forgotten Gertrude Courtenay's loyalty, and had immediately recalled her to court. Gertrude became one of the queen's closest companions, sleeping in her chambers.

On entering the Tower, Mary immediately released Catholic prisoners who had languished there for many years. Among those she freed were Stephen Gardiner, who she would make Lord Chancellor; the 79-year-old Duke of Norfolk; and Gertrude's son, Edward Courtenay.[6] Considering their religious differences, it's perhaps surprising that Mary also released Anne, Duchess of Somerset. Mary and Anne, however, had never let their different ideas on religion come between them; their friendship had endured for over thirty years. Mary allowed Anne to live at Syon House in suitable style. Anne petitioned to recover some of her widow's jointure and secure the inheritance of her children, and later remarried.

In the first heady days of her reign, Mary intended to be generous and pardoned Jane Grey's father, Henry, Duke of Suffolk. Her clemency could not, however, extend to Northumberland, and, after a last-minute conversion to the Catholic faith, he met his end on 23 August. Jane Grey and her husband and many others remained in the Tower, awaiting the queen's pleasure.

Kate was likely in attendance when Elizabeth joined Mary's court that summer. With her connections to some of the strongest proponents of the reformed religion, Kate must have been concerned. Mary had not always been a friend to Elizabeth.

At first, the signs were positive; Mary made a show of unity with her Protestant sister, and issued a proclamation that, although she hoped to bring her people back to the Catholic faith, mentioned no compulsion as yet. However, while in public the two sisters presented a unified front, Mary soon put pressure on Elizabeth to adopt the old ways of worship. Elizabeth pretended to consider it, but said she needed instruction. Mary remained unconvinced.

The sisters presented a striking contrast. Mary was nearing 40, and her features showed clear marks of years spent battling anxiety. Elizabeth, on the other hand, was young, and full of life. As Mary contemplated her future marriage and wished for a child, that disparity might well have caused her to resent Elizabeth.

It is likely that Kate was among the gentlewomen riding on horses trapped with red velvet, dressed in gowns and kirtles of similar bright red velvet, who followed Elizabeth on 1 October in Mary's magnificent coronation procession. Elizabeth rode in a chariot alongside Anne of Cleves during a glittering spectacle designed to impress the people of London. In her own open chariot, draped in gold cloth, wearing a luxurious purple gown trimmed with ermine, Mary wanted to stand out. Later, as she held her head in her hands to support the weight of the heavy bejewelled crown, Mary may have begrudged the loud cheers for her sister, in her gown of silver cloth-of-gold.

Only a few days later, it became apparent that Mary's warm feeling towards her sister had changed. Something had reminded her that Elizabeth was Anne Boleyn's daughter, and her old animosity surfaced. She gave precedence at court to Margaret Douglas, daughter of Henry VIII's sister, Margaret, over Elizabeth. Thus demoted, an outraged Elizabeth asked to return to her own properties. In early December, Mary gave Elizabeth permission to withdraw from court.

The 'Wyatt' Rebellion

To Tudor eyes, it was unthinkable that Mary could rule alone, and, being in her late thirties, she too was keen to marry quickly. For a time it seemed she might favour a match with Edward Courtenay, whom she had restored to the Earldom of Devon after his release. No doubt his mother encouraged it, and Kate's Devon family would have rejoiced to see the son of their former patron on the throne, despite his ambiguous personal religious beliefs; he leaned towards the conservative beliefs his parents had embraced with such vigour. Courtenay, an Englishman with Plantagenet blood, had been locked up for a long time, so he had few enemies. For once, Gardiner's interests aligned closely with those of Kate's Carew relations, for he had befriended Courtenay in the Tower and was keen to promote him. Courtenay took his place in Mary's court and bore the sword of state at her coronation.[7]

However, Mary had relied on advice from Emperor Charles V for years, and she felt a strong connection to her mother's Spanish background. Having his son Philip marry Mary appealed to the emperor, as he could then control England and bring the Protestant nation back to Catholicism. A Catholic England could also be a powerful ally in Charles's struggles with the Protestants in Germany. The Imperial Ambassador, Simon Renard, worked on Mary, extolling Philip's virtues.

Rumours and fears about a Spanish marriage spread, fuelled by pamphlets circulated by the French ambassador, who was keen to thwart a Spanish alliance. The idea of Mary marrying the Prince of Spain met with strong disapproval among the public.

Sir Peter Carew was a member of a group of MPs who hoped to promote the queen's marriage to Courtenay. As holder of the royal purse strings, parliamentarians believed they could influence Mary's choice of husband. They prepared a petition urging the queen to take an English husband.[8] However, before they could present it, Mary chose Philip of Spain. In doing so, she followed her personal inclination, ignoring the pleas of MPs and public opinion, which was by now firmly against the marriage. Her hectoring tone when she told parliament of her decision did not go down well. She said: 'to force her to take a husband who would not be to her liking would be to cause of her death. For if she were married against her will, she would not live three months.'[9]

Thwarted, a group of gentlemen of standing began meeting secretly in London to consider their options. Peter Carew was one of them. While they might have stomached Mary returning the country to some sort of Catholic regime and had all accepted her accession on that basis, they could not accept a Spanish marriage. What started as a plan to persuade Mary to marry Courtenay became a plot to overthrow the queen, marry Elizabeth to Courtenay and put her on the throne. The French ambassador Noailles was likely involved; some plotters were known to frequent his residence.[10] While many of these men tended towards the reformed faith, it was not religion that drove them towards rebellion. Rather, they were concerned about what a foreign prince at Mary's side meant for their influence and position. In Tudor society a husband ruled his wife, even if she was a queen by birth. They believed that the Spanish, once in England, would seize power and act at will, disregarding any treaty terms.[11]

Sir Peter Carew was a well-travelled man. He retained a fondness for France from his youthful exploits, but had developed an intense hatred of the Spanish. He had probably neither forgiven nor forgotten a Spaniard who tricked him during his continental adventures with John Champernowne.[12] Peter had also made his strong belief in reform clear for many years. It was not in his nature to sit idly by and he became one of the prime movers in the plot. At first, Devon appeared to be the key to success. Plymouth was the most likely place for Philip to land, and Peter glibly assumed that the people of the West would join him to keep the Spanish prince out. He was also Kate's cousin and it was through her that he hoped to secure Elizabeth's support.

Courtenay's lands were in Devon, where he ought to have commanded popular support, and the plotters were relying on him to join them. However, since his release, the newly restored Earl of Devon had been making up for lost time in the stews of Southwark and getting drunk. This did not impress Mary. The plotters also realised that he might be a weak link in the plans. In some ways Courtenay's weakness was attractive to the French king. With the easily influenced Courtenay beside Mary, Henry II of France saw an opportunity to bring England within his power. Noailles promised French support if enough English people supported the plan. With her decision to marry Philip, Mary had forced a change of plan. Courtenay knew about the plot, and they couldn't easily exclude him. Although the French still seemed willing to give some support to having Elizabeth and Courtenay on the throne, the plotters were wary of the French, doubtful that the people would welcome French involvement.

With Kate's cousin as a ringleader, and with Elizabeth now critical to the plan, it's hard to believe she did not know about it. Whether Elizabeth ever agreed to marry Courtenay is quite another question.

The conspirators met at the London home of Henry Grey, Duke of Suffolk, on 26 November.[13] Grey and his two brothers, John and Thomas, were the only noblemen to join the group. Henry Grey had been fortunate to be set at liberty after Northumberland's attempted coup. His daughter Jane and her husband Guildford Dudley, convicted of treason, remained in the Tower, awaiting their fate. Yet he was prepared to risk all in joining another plot. Elizabeth was cautious, already suspicious of the French, who might encourage the claims of Mary of Scotland. She also feared Suffolk might press his daughter Jane's claim again.

William Paget, restored to favour after initially supporting Jane Grey, was now one of Mary's advisers. Aware of the growing public disquiet about Mary's marriage, he looked for a way to diffuse matters. Before Elizabeth left court on 6 December, he may have approached her to discuss the merits of a counterproposal whereby the Spanish marriage went ahead, but Elizabeth married Courtenay and was heir to the throne.[14] If he did, the idea went nowhere, knocked on the head by Charles V, who advised Mary to avoid a marriage between Elizabeth and Courtenay. It is extremely doubtful Elizabeth would have consented anyway.

As Elizabeth headed for Ashridge that December, no doubt she and Kate were both reflecting on their experience during the Thomas Seymour affair. Caution was their watchword. If they were in touch with the plotters, they were careful to cover their tracks.

It seems inconceivable that Kate knew nothing. However, John Guy has suggested it was not Kate, but John Astley who was the 'go-between', since Kate's husband felt it necessary to leave England with John Cheke shortly after the plot unravelled.[15] If John was directly involved he may have got to know Thomas Grey, Suffolk's younger brother, who was reportedly the keenest of the three Grey brothers to proceed.[16]

According to the later indictment, besides the Greys the group included Sir Peter Carew, Sir James Croftes (Croft), Sir Nicholas Arnold, Sir William Pickering, William Winter, Sir Edward Rogers, Sir Thomas Wyatt, Sir George Harper and William Thomas.[17] Thomas Wyatt of Allingham, the son of Anne Boleyn's admirer, had developed an aversion to the Spanish government after hearing about the Inquisition when travelling with his father. He claimed to have joined the group at a late stage, although the rebellion now bears his name. Wyatt's cousin, William Brooke, also supported the rebels, although the extent of his involvement is unclear. Nicholas Throckmorton, who Elizabeth would have known from his time in Catherine Parr and Thomas Seymour's household, was also implicated.[18]

The plan was to ignite four simultaneous popular uprisings on Palm Sunday, 18 March 1554: Carew in Devon, Croftes on the Welsh border, the Duke of Suffolk in the Midlands, and Thomas Wyatt in the South. Drawing on his seafaring connections, Peter planned their supply lines and for naval backup if needed. He left for Devon in mid-December and began rather clumsy efforts to prime resistance among the local gentry.[19]

While Peter was stirring up the locals in Devon, Elizabeth was waiting at Ashridge. It must have been a tense Christmas at the former college near Berkhamsted, which her father had turned into a hunting lodge and nursery for his children. The rooms, familiar from her childhood, must have felt like a welcome refuge. Elizabeth was determined not to be drawn into the plot against her sister – at least not until she was sure of the outcome. When Sir James Croftes, who had served in her brother's Privy Chamber and been imprisoned briefly for supporting Jane Grey, arrived with a letter from Wyatt, she had the good sense to take to her bed. She did not receive the missive, which told her to seek shelter in Castle Donnington, in Berkshire.[20]

Elizabeth's illness was genuine; stress almost certainly triggered it. Her face and arms swelled up; she suffered headaches and a cold, and felt weak and nauseous. She lay fearful at Ashridge, with Kate at her bedside, administering herbal draughts and wiping her fevered brow. Kate must have been very anxious herself, especially if John was indeed liaising with the conspirators.

Peter had made himself unpopular during the 1549 crisis and had misjudged the level of support he could muster. Alerted to the danger, Queen Mary's council summoned Peter to report to them in London in early January. When he gave a weak excuse for not complying, suspicions grew. On 17 January, Exeter residents noticed Peter's servant leading horses through the city gates, carrying harness and handguns drawn from his armoury at Dartmouth Castle. A rumour started that he planned to take Exeter Castle.[21]

Renaud, the Imperial Ambassador, also learned of the plot and potential French involvement through his agents. On 18 January, Renaud discovered that the French fleet was gathering on the Normandy coast and told the queen of his suspicions. While Peter's plans were unravelling in Devon, Gardiner spoke to Edward Courtenay and easily extracted details of the plot.

The plotters decided the rising could not wait until March. Wyatt roused his followers in Kent. Queen Mary wrote to Elizabeth on 26 January 1554, suggesting she come to court 'for her own safety'. In her letter, Mary mentioned Donnington, giving away her suspicion that her sister had been in contact with the conspirators. Elizabeth replied that she was too ill to travel and asked the queen to send her own doctors to confirm she was truly ill. Mary's suspicions increased when a copy of a letter from Elizabeth was reportedly found in the French ambassador's postbag.

In Devon, Sir Thomas Dennys went to arrest the Devon conspirators. Sir Gawen Carew, who had joined Sir Peter in the attempt, scaled the walls of Exeter Castle to escape. They later caught him at his nephew's house in Bickleigh.[22] Sir Arthur Champernowne maintained he had quarrelled with Sir Peter and had refused to join his enterprise. He declared his loyalty to Mary saying: 'forasmuch as now he knew the queen's pleasure was to have the prince of Spain into England, that he would embrace the same, and show himself obedient to his power unto the queen's pleasure.'[23] It was to no avail; Arthur was arrested.

Despite having given away the plans to Gardiner, the Earl of Devon remained at liberty and sent a message warning Peter, using a cipher they had agreed. Realising the game was up, Peter travelled by back roads to Weymouth, disguised as a servant. He escaped to France with a few others on board Kate's brother-in-law, Walter Raleigh Senior's ship.[24] The Imperial Ambassador mistakenly reported that Sir Peter Carew 'and his brother' had escaped to France (both Sir Peter's brothers had been dead for a long time).[25] Sir Gawen Carew and Sir Arthur Champernowne were soon on their way to the Tower of London.

Meanwhile, Wyatt had been more successful in finding supporters after calling his relatives, friends and neighbours to a meeting at Allington Castle on 22 January. On 25 January the queen sent a message to the Duke of Suffolk, unaware of his involvement. Perhaps as a test of his loyalty, she intended to ask him to deal with the rebels. However, Suffolk, assuming Mary had discovered his part in the plot, left his house at Sheen and headed for Bradgate in Leicestershire.[26] His brothers had planned to join him at St Albans, but they missed him. The Greys had little success in recruiting supporters in Leicestershire, so Suffolk and his brother John headed for Astley Castle in Warwickshire, intending to travel to Wales and make their escape.[27]

In the grounds of Astley Castle a stone marks the spot where Henry Grey hid for three days inside the hollow trunk of an oak tree. However, his park keeper betrayed him, and he was soon on the road to London with his brother John. Henry Grey, Duke of Suffolk, was executed on 23 February 1554. Thomas Grey, got as far as Oswestry before he was arrested on 7 February by Richard Mytton of Shrewsbury.[28] James Croftes, also arrested, and Thomas Grey were escorted to London. Lord Thomas was beheaded on 24 April 1554,[29] but his brother John, although tried and condemned to die, was released, though still under attainer, after an appeal by his wife's staunchly Catholic brother Lord Montagu. Croftes was imprisoned, tried, and convicted, but later released. Those who escaped death owed their lives to Stephen Gardiner, who urged the queen to clemency, perhaps due to his friendship with Courtenay.[30]

Wyatt reached Rochester, with a force of around 2,000 men, and took the bridge. Queen Mary ordered the 80-year-old Duke of Norfolk to lead a counterforce out of London. Many of his soldiers were sympathetic to the rebel cause and deserted. The duke fled back to London, where nothing had been done to fortify the city. Again, Mary confounded her critics by rising to the occasion. On 1 February she rode to the Guildhall and there delivered a passionate speech, moving the citizens of London to unite to defend the capital. Wyatt continued to advance, repulsed at London Bridge, he marched to Kingston, crossed to the north bank, and again moved eastwards. However, the citizens of London failed to flock to his banner, his own men were exhausted and many were deserting. On reaching Ludgate Wyatt found the gates barred. He turned back but only got as far as Temple. It was Sir Maurice Berkeley, the second husband of Kate's former sister-in-law, and possibly sympathetic to the rebels' cause, who arrested him.[31]

Mary hardened her heart and on 12 February sent Jane Grey and her husband to meet the executioner. Wyatt, held in the Tower, watched as the innocent girl bravely laid her head on the block. Kate's brother and uncle may also have watched the executions from the windows of the grim fortress.

Mary and her advisers now set their sights on Elizabeth. Doctors arrived and pronounced that, though weak, she could travel. With the doctors came several of Mary's councillors, and according to Foxe's rather colourful account, demanded she leave in the middle of the night.

According to some accounts, they separated Elizabeth from most of her servants immediately; others say it was later. On the day of Jane Grey's execution, Elizabeth left Ashridge in a litter to bring her in slow stages to Whitehall Palace. After a painfully slow journey, she arrived at Whitehall, on the same day the Duke of Suffolk was beheaded.

Even under torture Wyatt gave no evidence to implicate Elizabeth. In fact, although Croftes had assumed her compliance, no direct evidence ever emerged connecting Elizabeth with the plot. However, Imperial Ambassador Renaud saw Elizabeth as a grave threat and convinced Mary that she must find reasons to remove her permanently. Elizabeth's life was on the line. Her pleas for a personal audience with her sister went unanswered. Even the carefully worded letter she wrote on the day before Palm Sunday (the letter took so long to complete that the tide was too high for her to be taken by barge to the Tower) could not move Queen Mary.[32] She only achieved a brief delay. On the very day the conspirators had originally earmarked to begin their uprising, Palm Sunday 1554, Elizabeth entered the Tower, passing Jane Grey's scaffold on her way.

Separation

Kate's links to the Devon rebels alone were reason enough for her to be questioned. Mary's adviser's probably thought Kate would yield up information to allow them to convict Elizabeth. She had apparently given way under questioning during the Thomas Seymour business. No doubt they thought she would do so again.

It is not known where or when Kate was removed from her place at Elizabeth's side. No records have survived to suggest Kate was held in the Tower or sent to the Fleet Prison, although both are possibilities. The next time her name appears in the record is a full fifteen months later in the Acts of the Privy Council 1555: 'At Hampton Courte, the xx of May, 1555. A lettrre to Sir Roger Cholmeley to set at libertye Katheryne Assheley, who hath of long tyme remained in his custodie.'[33]

Sir Roger Cholmeley, illegitimate son of Sir Richard Cholmeley, Lieutenant of the Tower of London, was a lawyer who had served under Henry VIII and Edward VI. He had been Lord Chief Justice of the Court of King's Bench from 1552 until King Edward's death. He was imprisoned following Northumberland's coup, but having been reluctant to support Edward's Device for the Throne, he was soon released.

It is not clear when Cholmeley took Kate into custody.[34] On her way from Ashridge, Elizabeth's party had rested overnight on 15 February 1554 at Cholmeley's residence in Highgate. It is possible Kate was detained during Elizabeth's stay, or it may have been later when Elizabeth's party reached Whitehall. It is likely that after initial questioning, Kate was held under house arrest either at Cholmeley's mansion in the Old Bailey, in the parish of St Martin's, Ludgate, or at his country house at Highgate. By the sixteenth century, the road through Highgate became the favoured route from London to the North. Convenient for the city, wealthy Londoners like Cholmeley began to build country houses along the roadside.[35]

If Kate was held at Highgate, her conditions were relatively pleasant, with gardens where she might walk with Cholmeley's wife, Christian, under scrutiny of her gaoler. Cholmeley would have been instructed to use his sharp legal mind to extract a confessions that would implicate Elizabeth in the plot. However, in the early days of Kate's detention, he directed his attention to prosecuting Sir Nicholas Throckmorton, accused of involvement in the rebellion. To his horror, Cholmeley failed to gain a conviction, the jury finding Throckmorton's arguments persuasive. The queen was not amused and had the jury sent to the Fleet for a while, but Throckmorton, who remained in the Tower until the following March, had survived.

Although he dutifully followed Mary's instructions and, as prosecutor he sent many Protestants to gruesome deaths in the flames, Elizabeth held no grudge against Cholmeley after her accession. She may have rested at his Highgate house before the Lord Mayor of London welcomed her as queen at the foot of Highgate Hill on 23 November 1558.[36]

Kate had said goodbye to her husband before the posse of council members arrived to bring Elizabeth to London. John left the country, increasing suspicions of his involvement in the plot. Thomas Hobey met him in August in Padua.[37] He had three of Joan and Anthony Denny's sons with him. Garrett suggests the boys may have been involved in the plot.[38] However, since they were born after the Dennys married in 1538, they were only teenagers, and it is unlikely they played a large part. John Cheke was another who left England to join a trickle of exiles that soon become a flood. Edward's former tutor had been a secretary to the council at the time of Northumberland's fall, and initially supported Jane. He therefore spent some time in the Tower on Mary's accession. Released in September 1553, by April 1554 he was overseas.

Soon after their arrest, Mary gave the wives of Gawen Carew and Arthur Champernowne permission to take income from their estates while they remained in custody.[39] On 14 June, Sir Gawen was granted leave to make a short visit to Devon to sort out his affairs, but returned to custody.[40]

Sir Peter Carew was already on the other side of the English Channel. On arrival in France in the spring he set up his headquarters in Rouen and for a time pursued a fanciful plan to land rebels on the Isle of Wight. Having received little encouragement from the French king, he left France for Italy, while also humbly suing Mary for a pardon. In Venice he narrowly escaped death at the hands of Mary's ambassador, but by September, Mary had given Peter's wife, Margaret, permission to write to him and send him supplies.[41]

Kate was almost certainly not with Elizabeth during her darkest days in the Tower of London, wondering if she was to share her mother's fate. Nor was she there when, in May, a partial reprieve came. Sir Henry Beddingfield arrived at the Tower with a hundred men to escort Elizabeth to Woodstock in Oxfordshire. Kate was already under house arrest, held by Sir Roger Cholmeley, and was not one of the group of Elizabeth's faithful servants waiting to glimpse her when she landed on the north bank of the Thames as her ferry approached from Richmond.[42]

Had she been with Elizabeth, Kate might have smiled to see the boys of Eton College, where her nephew Humphrey Gilbert studied, run out to cheer Elizabeth on her way. She could have congratulated the five men who rushed to the church to ring the bells in Aston Rowant, where Kate had spent some of her childhood. The bellringers were 'clapped in ward' for their excessive enthusiasm.[43]

Nor was Kate among the few ladies who shared Elizabeth's cramped conditions at Woodstock Palace. Lodged in four rooms in the gatehouse, Elizabeth was allowed only a few servants, not of her choosing. Her life at Woodstock was not wonderful, but at least it was not the Tower. She had survived.

Although refused a place in the gatehouse at Woodstock, Thomas Parry, Elizabeth's cofferer, persuaded her gaoler, Beddingfield, to allow him to visit Elizabeth so that he could assist her on matters regarding her household and estates. He even paid Beddingfield's wages from Elizabeth's coffers.[44] The arrangement did not please Mary. After Parry found a room at the nearby Bull Inn, he did exactly what Mary feared. He established for Elizabeth a clandestine means of communication with the outside world and may even have kept Kate in touch.

Mary ordered that Edward Courtenay, also under suspicion because of the Wyatt plot, remain under house arrest at Fotheringhay. Courtenay's mother Gertrude, was cast out of court and lived in relative obscurity, likely in one of the dower houses associated with the Courtenay family estates.

Mary married Philip II of Spain in Winchester Cathedral on 25 July 1554, with a great show of pageantry. She proceeded with her religious policies at speed, including sweeping away one of the most significant changes enacted under Edward VI: the law allowing priests to marry. Kate's uncle, George Carew, and Archdeacon John Pollard had both taken advantage of the new freedom. As married priests, if they did not separate from their wives they faced dismissal from their posts. George, it seems, refused to put aside his wife Anne, and was deprived of his deanery and all his church preferments in April 1554. Anne Harvey may have retired to her father's estates in Devon, where George must have continued to visit her, since their family continued to grow. A second son, George, was born on 29 May 1555, and daughters followed.[45] Despite his marriage, by some miracle, Kate's Uncle George secured an appointment as Archdeacon of Exeter in May 1556, and collected a raft of new livings during Mary's reign. This has led to his being called a Nicodemite, since he seems to have concealed his true religion.[46] Elizabeth Champernowne's husband, John Pollard, deprived of his archdeaconry in April 1554, took a little longer to secure a new appointment. He did not become Archdeacon of Totnes until 1558.

Meanwhile, Sir Arthur Champernowne and Sir Gawen Carew were finally released on 18 January 1555, and went back to Devon.

So far parliament had resisted Mary's attempts to reconcile England to Rome. However, in the autumn, Cardinal Reginald Pole, the exiled grandson of George Duke of Clarence, a man with Plantagenet blood who had been a thorn in Henry VIII's side, came home. He presided over the reestablishment of the Catholic Church in England and the persecution of Protestants.

In the autumn Mary believed she was pregnant and was overjoyed at the prospect. However, that did not dampen her religious zeal. She was determined to expunge what she saw as heresy. Anyone who persisted in publicly proclaiming their Protestant beliefs fell foul of reinstated heresy laws that carried a brutal punishment: burning at the stake. The burnings started on 4 February 1555 with the execution of John Rogers, a clergyman and Bible translator.

Months passed and Mary exhibited all the signs of pregnancy, yet by April Ambassador Renaud was concerned. He pointed out to King Philip the dangers should the queen not give birth to a healthy heir. Philip feared Mary, Queen of Scots, wife of Francis, the Dauphin of France, might make a claim, as Henry VII's granddaughter. Philip could tolerate Elizabeth as a Protestant queen rather than allow the French to gain a foothold through the Scots queen. This thought prompted Philip to establish friendlier terms with Elizabeth. So, Mary recalled Elizabeth to court. According to Foxe, she left a lasting reminder of her imprisonment at Woodstock – words scratched on a window pane: 'Much suspected of me, Nothing proved can be. Quoth Elizabeth, prisoner.'[47]

The council agreed that it was unjust to hold others taken into custody after the rebellion any longer, and they were set at liberty. Edward Courtenay left Fotheringhay to travel overseas. His mother, Gertrude, was recalled to court in the summer of 1555.

However, Sir Peter Carew was not among those pardoned. He may have returned surreptitiously to his father-in-law's estates in Lincolnshire in the spring of 1555 but was soon back on the Continent, while his wife worked tirelessly on his behalf.

On 20 April 1555 a passport was issued for Sir Arthur Champernowne, Sir Amyas Paulet and Sir William Courtenay to travel to Calais for four months. Arthur also served as MP for Plympton in that year.

Reunited at Hatfield

As summer 1555 slipped towards autumn, Queen Mary had to admit she was not pregnant. Her husband left England in September to travel to the Netherlands, where he joined his father, Emperor Charles V, who was preparing to abdicate. Feeling depressed and dispirited, Mary permitted her sister to depart the court, and Elizabeth returned to her people at Hatfield. Her reunion with Kate was a moment for both to cherish. John was back in England in time to be elected as MP for St Albans in 1555, and to vote against the government in the parliament of that year. Thomas Parry resumed his duties; Elizabeth reassembled her ladies, including Dorothy Broadbelt, Elizabeth Markham and Elizabeth Norwich, and she resumed her studies with her Italian tutor Giovanni Castiglione. Roger Ascham had married a year earlier and was serving as Latin secretary to Queen Mary. Whenever he could secure time off from his duties he visited Hatfield. In a letter of 14 September to German educator and reformer Johannes Sturm, Ascham wrote that he and Elizabeth were comparing the opposing orations of Aeschines and Demosthenes. These would have stretched her knowledge and given good preparation in convincing oratory. This may indicate that Elizabeth saw a realistic prospect she would rule.[48] Perhaps Ascham also enjoyed friendly fireside conversations with Kate and John as the autumn nights drew in.[49]

It was probably in October 1555 that Kate introduced her nephew Humphrey Gilbert to Elizabeth.[50] She may have visited her family in Devon to celebrate her release, bringing Humphrey back with her. A precociously intelligent youth, it seems he made a good impression. Humphrey's brothers John and Adrian are also thought to have met Elizabeth. Kate may also have brought another relative into Elizabeth's household at around this time. Her 16-year-old second cousin, Frances Newton was established as a chamberer before 1558. (Frances's mother Margaret, née Poyntz, was Elizabeth Huddesfield's daughter.)

While Kate was enjoying a return to the normality of life at Hatfield, Peter Carew, who had spent the summer in Strasbourg, went to Antwerp. His wife Margaret travelled to Brussels on 27 October and pleaded with King Philip, asking him to permit her husband to return home.[51] King Philip hoped to persuade Mary to support his army in the Netherlands with English soldiers. Conscious of his need for good fighting men he wrote to Mary suggesting she pardon Sir Peter Carew. In November, while waiting for Mary's answer, Peter met Edward Courtenay in Brussels. The pardon duly arrived, but it had conditions.

The 'Dudley' Conspiracy

Elizabeth remained at Hatfield for Christmas 1555, with people she could trust, a welcome relief after a frightening and stressful time. However, the peaceful interlude did not last. Discontent about Queen Mary's marriage continued to grow amid rumours that she planned a coronation for Philip, while the burnings continued. Among the Protestants sent to the flames were bishops Nicholas Ridley and Hugh Latimer, burned at the stake on 16 October in Oxford. Elizabeth's godfather, Archbishop Cranmer, followed them the following March. Mary made a public exhibition of Cranmer who, under severe duress, had forsaken his Protestant faith. However, he defied the queen in his last moments by withdrawing his previous recantation.

Against that background, despite the failure of the Wyatt plot, a fresh conspiracy took root. Once again, it rested on a marriage between Courtenay and Elizabeth. Sir Henry Dudley was one of the prime movers in a hare-brained scheme to depose Mary and put Elizabeth on the throne.

Dudley, a distant relative of John Dudley, Duke of Northumberland, had been dispossessed because of his part in the Jane Grey coup, and had run up considerable debts. It may have been the pressure of debt rather than principle that drove him into treason. Dudley had the backing of his father-in-law Christopher Ashton, who had become the fourth husband of Scottish noblewoman, Catherine Gordon prior to her death in 1537; she, at one time, had been married to Perkin Warbeck. Ashton was a larger-than-life adventurer, who had a habit of causing trouble.[52]

Dudley drew in a long list of co-conspirators, including his brother-in-law, Sir Henry Killigrew, John Throckmorton, Sir Anthony Kingston and Richard Uvedale, who had command of Yarmouth Castle on the Isle of Wight. However, unlike the 1554 conspiracy, he failed to attract any of the higher nobility. The plan was for Dudley to lead an invasion from France, bringing with him soldiers and weapons, funding the enterprise by robbing the exchequer of £50,000 (a staggering sum, over £13,735,000 today), in Spanish silver bars.[53]

With Uvedale's help, Dudley crossed to France to seek aid from Henry II, but the French king had just signed a truce with Philip of Spain, so had no interest in being involved. Many people knew about the plan, and inevitably details leaked out. Early in March, word of the plot reached the ears of Reginald Pole. Thus betrayed, on 4 April and while still in France, Dudley was proclaimed a traitor.

Elizabeth had been the magnet for another plot to oust her sister, and the trail led to Kate and her inner circle. Mary ordered investigations and became so concerned about the threat her sister posed that she even revived the idea of marrying Elizabeth to Philip of Spain's 10-year-old son, Don Carlos, and sending her to Spain.

On 29 April, Sir William Courtenay, a relative of the Earl of Devon, and several others, some of them Peter Carew's Wyatt rebellion co-conspirators, were taken to the Tower. Kate's brother Arthur had visited Calais with William Courtenay, and his involvement with the earlier uprising put him under suspicion. After questioning, on 14 May Arthur was ordered to pay £1,000 (roughly £234,000 today) as recognisance, and report to the council regularly in person. However, on 7 July he was discharged and allowed home.[54]

In a surprising development, the Venetian ambassador reported it was Peter Carew who revealed details of the Dudley conspiracy.[55] On 17 May, Peter and Sir John Cheke were arrested on their way from Brussels to Antwerp.

Cheke, King Edward's former tutor, was the author of many anti-Catholic, anti-Mary and Philip pamphlets and writings, that were widely circulated in England and fuelled the fears of ordinary people. Even though he had tipped off the authorities about the Dudley plot, they also arrested Peter. The likelihood is that his arrest was a 'smokescreen' hiding the true story; delivering John Cheke into the authorities' hands had been the price of his pardon. To cover up his involvement, particularly to his Protestant friends, Peter remained in the Tower for several months, as did Cheke. In July, their wives visited them. Another condition of Sir Peter's release was the repayment of long-standing debts to the Crown. He faced no trial and by the end of the year, Peter was free.

Accounts of Peter's role in Cheke's arrest are convoluted and confused. Hooker, who worked for Peter and paints him in a favourable light, tells it a little differently. However, Garrett gives a convincing account of Peter's guilt.[56] It is not clear whether Kate or Elizabeth knew about Peter's actions, but it is noticeable that when she came to the throne Elizabeth rewarded Peter with lower-profile appointments than other Wyatt conspirators.

With the harrowing experience of his friend Archbishop Cranmer at the forefront of his mind, Cheke wrote to the queen expressing his willingness to obey her laws. Forced to make a public recantation in front of Mary I, he was released and regained his lands. Afterwards, he was ashamed and regretted his cowardice. Cheke died just over a year later, on 13 September 1557.

With Dudley's intent uncovered, Elizabeth immediately fell under suspicion. Enquiries led to Francis Verney, a servant who Thomas Parry had used to deliver messages to Elizabeth from the Bull Inn, in Woodstock. Under questioning he revealed his links to others, including Ashton and Lord Bray, Elizabeth's neighbour at Hatfield and Ashridge. Verney was charged with treason, tried, convicted and sentenced to death, but eventually received a pardon. Lord Bray spent about a year in the Tower of London while his mother and wife worked to secure his release.

Searchers found books and pamphlets against Queen Mary's religion and government at Somerset House, Elizabeth's London residence. They traced the seditious materials to the rooms occupied by Kate, and Castiglione. The Italian had been questioned in the Tower during two previous investigations.

At the end of May, soon after Peter Carew's arrest, two royal agents descended on Elizabeth's house, and arrested Kate, Castiglione and three more of Elizabeth's servants.

Writing on 2 June, Giovanni Michiel, the Venetian ambassador, reported that Kate was taken to the Tower and interrogated, and added darkly that she and the other servants had confessed all and: 'may probably not quit the place alive'.[57]

Denying knowledge of any conspiracy beyond what was 'commonly reported of a plot to seize the queen's treasure', contrary to the ambassador's opinion, Kate gave nothing away.[58] Castiglione, similarly questioned, gave a spirited response, so full of domestic details it is a masterclass in obfuscation. Asked when he came to London and what he did there, he replied first that he could not remember it well but afterwards produced an account of a day full of frivolous details and innocent meetings:

> For he had been to a milliner's shop, to a book-binder's, 'to a friend of mine called Mrs. Watson in Mark Lane, to look how she did'; he had 'spent the night in the house of Mistress Burnell'; he had gone next day to buy lute strings, etc. Even when all was told he must add that he had bought black lace to edge a cloak, sarcenet in Cheap, points, two pairs of sleeves and two dozen buttons.[59]

Kate was transferred to the Fleet Prison, which more often housed those accused of civil rather than criminal offences; mainly debtors and those who had committed minor misdemeanours. However, during Mary's reign, increasingly it also held dissenters against Mary's religious polices. Although considered more comfortable than some other London prisons, three months in the Fleet would not have been a pleasant experience. Prisoners had to pay for their board and lodging. We must hope John Astley could afford to pay for tolerable conditions and decent food for Kate. John may have been concerned that he too would be implicated and may have left the country again around this time.[60]

That her servants held seditious writings did not prove Elizabeth's complicity in Dudley's scheme, but it's hard to imagine she was completely unaware. Whether or not she was involved, Philip ordered the investigations to be dropped.

Queen Mary sent a ring to Elizabeth and, in an astonishing volte-face, professed her friendship and wish to comfort her sister in the loss of her servants. However, her conciliatory words reflected instructions from Philip, not her own inclination. Knowing how close Elizabeth was to her childhood governess, Mary could not resist delivering what she believed was a crushing blow. Perhaps Mary acted partly in spite. However, by insisting on Kate's dismissal, Mary also revealed she saw Kate as a significant threat. Kate's close bond with Elizabeth, together with her known Protestant contacts, made her too dangerous to be allowed near the queen's sister.

A widowed gentlewoman whose identity remains unknown replaced Kate, and Sir Thomas Pope arrived at Hatfield to oversee Elizabeth's household.

Although reluctant at first, the witty and cultured Sir Thomas soon settled in, and Elizabeth found him a much more pleasant governor than Beddingfield, who had kept her imprisoned at Woodstock. It helped that she already knew him, since he had served in her household at Ashridge in 1554. This time Elizabeth did not make a fuss about Kate's removal.

A rather feeble attempt to reinvigorate the failed plot proved to be the last attempt to overthrow Queen Mary. Cleobury, a schoolmaster from Yaxley in Sussex, failed to convince anyone when he impersonated Edward Courtenay and declared Elizabeth to be queen and her 'beloved bedfellow' king.[61] In September, the young Earl of Devon who might have been King of England, died in Padua, thus snuffing out the plotters' last hopes.

Another Separation

In October, the Venetian ambassador reported that Kate was released:

> The governess of the Lady Elizabeth has also been set at liberty, but deprived not only of her office as governess, but forbidden ever again to go to her ladyship; the knight [Sir Thomas Pope], who was placed as keeper in her residence, being also removed.[62]

Forbidden to rejoin Elizabeth, Kate's whereabouts during the autumn and winter of 1556, through 1557 and most of 1558 are uncertain. She may have retreated to John's moated manor house at Melton Constable in Norfolk, or visited her relatives in Devon. It may have been during this time that she assisted with family matters, such as leases and properties. A letter from Sir Walter Raleigh to his nephew, the second Sir John Gilbert, on 11 November 1601 regarding Brixham Rectory, mentions that his 'Aunt Ashley' knew all about the lease.[63]

There is no evidence to suggest Kate was in Exeter when her sister, Katherine Raleigh, visited Agnes Prest, a poor Cornishwoman burned at the stake on 15 August 1557, for refusing to accept Queen Mary's religion.[64]

On 5 May 1557, probably in London, Kate witnessed the will of her brother-in-law, Archdeacon John Pollard, which named her and her uncle, George Carew, now Archdeacon of Exeter Cathedral, as executors.[65]

Kate may have visited Margaret Newton at Barre's Court in Gloucestershire or East Harptree, in Somerset, and educated Margaret's daughters in court etiquette. It's possible she had a long-term plan to establish Frances Newton as her own successor, bringing Frances's younger sister, Nazareth, to court when Frances was promoted.[66] As Baroness Cobham, Frances would eventually become one of Elizabeth's most trusted ladies.

The queen invited Elizabeth to court for Christmas 1556. She probably missed Kate's wise counsel when Mary and Philip tried to force her into a marriage with the Duke of Savoy, a match she was determined to avoid. Infuriated by Elizabeth's refusal. Mary sent her back to Hatfield after only a few days.

In March 1557 Philip returned to England, hoping to persuade his wife to send English troops to bolster his army in the Netherlands. On 7 June, Queen Mary gave way to her husband's demands and England, as an ally of Spain, declared war on France. To Mary's intense distress, having achieved his aim, Philip left England in early July.

In a strange irony, like many other English noblemen Sir Peter Carew – who had been so strong against the Spanish marriage – fought on the Imperial side against the French. Kate's brother, Sir Arthur Champernowne, joined the Earl of Lincoln's contingent alongside the Spanish at the Battle of Saint Quentin – a resounding victory for the Imperial forces. After the decisive victory, Philip failed to pursue his advantage, withdrawing to the Spanish Netherlands to the north. On 1 January 1558, the French responded to the loss of Saint Quentin by seizing Calais during an unexpected winter offensive.

Losing England's final foothold in France was a devastating loss for Queen Mary. After Philip's visit she had once again experienced symptoms of pregnancy: no menstrual bleeding, swollen breasts and a swelling abdomen. It was a second 'phantom pregnancy'. By the spring of 1558, when she had been expecting to welcome a child, most people could see that Mary was dying. The succession of the Protestant Princess Elizabeth could not be far off.

Confident in the future status of his family because of his sister's relationship with Elizabeth, Arthur Champernowne (Plate 10) began upgrading Dartington Hall in Devon. He had gained the magnificent fourteenth-century manor through a complicated property deal, involving part-exchange for Polsloe Priory. John Holland, half-brother of King Richard II, had built his great hall at Dartington to be fit to entertain royalty. Arthur was going up in the world.

Gertrude Courtenay, whose son might have been king, continued to serve Mary until she died on 15 September 1558. She asked for a traditional Catholic burial mass, and is buried at Wimborne, Dorset.

As Mary weakened throughout 1558, Elizabeth's position improved. The trees in Hatfield Park blazed with autumnal colours and courtiers thronged the dusty road.

Chapter 15

Chief Gentlewoman of the Privy Chamber

1558–1560

Mary Tudor, gave up her earthly struggles as a bright autumn dawn broke over London on 17 November 1558. The woman who had fought so hard for her crown died sadly disappointed and disillusioned, leaving a country that was divided and heavily in debt.

According to tradition, Elizabeth was sitting under an old oak tree in the park at Hatfield, reading a book, when she received the news of Queen Mary's death. It is said Elizabeth sank to her knees and cried out in Latin, quoting from Psalm 118: 'This is the Lord's doing: it is marvellous in our eyes.'

Tradition also has it that Lord Robert Dudley rode at once to Hatfield on a snow-white horse. If so, he was but one of many who hurried to congratulate England's new queen. We can only imagine the pride and relief Kate felt when she heard the news on that November day.

Elizabeth had known William Cecil, for years. In 1548, she signed herself 'your friend Elizabeth' when endorsing a letter Kate had written to him when he was still Edward Seymour's secretary.[1] Cecil, who had first entered Elizabeth's service as surveyor of her properties in 1550, was already at Hatfield. She immediately appointed him her Secretary of State, the start of a remarkable partnership that lasted for forty years. With Cecil, she set about remodelling the court and government, although she wisely kept some of her sister's advisers on a slimmed-down Privy Council for a while.[2]

Among the first appointments, Dr George Carew became Dean of the Chapel Royal, replacing the papist, Thomas Thirlby.[3] He also became registrar of the Garter and Master of the Savoy. Despite his having married – Elizabeth privately disliked clerical marriage, although she did not forbid it[4] – Elizabeth knew and trusted George. She could rely in him to do precisely as she wished in terms of religion. He was Kate's uncle, and had been one of those reportedly in favour of Thomas Seymour's suit at the December 1548 meeting attended by Kate in London. In the prominent role of Dean of the Chapel Royal, George oversaw the royal chaplains and often attended court. Reinstated as Dean of Bristol, later also serving as Dean of Exeter, George Carew became one of Elizabeth's closest advisers on ecclesiastical policy.[5] It appears George was already serving as Elizabeth's chaplain, before her accession. During their long separation George may have kept Kate in touch with Elizabeth.

Elizabeth rewarded many who had served her well. There were appointments for men like James Croftes and Nicholas Throckmorton, who had risked all during the Wyatt rebellion, suggesting that she had supported their aims, even though she was careful not to leave evidence of involvement. Robert Dudley became Master of the Horse, a position that meant he was frequently in attendance on the queen. Elizabeth also remembered her faithful friends from Hatfield days. Newly knighted, Sir Thomas Parry became Treasurer of Elizabeth's household and a Privy Councillor, working closely with William Cecil; Roger Ascham became her Latin secretary; Kate's husband, John, became Master of the Jewel House; Blanche Parry, a Gentlewoman of the Bedchamber and Keeper of the Queen's Books. But chief among them all was the prestigious position Elizabeth earmarked for Kate Astley.

Elizabeth made Kate Chief Gentlewoman of the Privy Chamber, the highest position available to a non-titled woman. As Charlotte Merton points out, even at the time there was some confusion about titles given to women of the Privy Chamber.[6] Ladies with titles were usually called 'Lady', while those without titles, such as Kate and Blanche Parry, were called 'Gentlewomen'.[7] There was some overlap in the duties of ladies, gentlewomen and the maids of honour, who were unmarried. Ladies tended to be ceremonial escorts at state events or public processions, whereas maids escorted the queen day to day in her gardens, palaces and parks; Gentlewomen of the Privy Chamber saw to the queen's needs in her most personal and private world assisted by chamberers. Elizabeth was more concerned about the qualities of the individual than the job title.

Kate carved out a new and powerful role for herself. At the Tudor Court, the Presence Chamber was a formal, public room for ceremonial audiences and official functions, while the Privy Chamber was a more intimate suite of rooms that made up the monarch's private lodgings, and included the royal bedchamber. Under male monarchs, two sets of men had immense influence: those who served on the Privy Council and those who served in the Privy Chamber. During Henry VIII's reign, the Privy Council developed from a fluid group of advisers into a more formal body. The Privy Chamber, where men like Anthony Denny had direct access to the king, also operated as a crucial political space for male courtiers.

Under Elizabeth the Privy Council was, as it had been in her father's time, a formal body of powerful men who met every day to advise her on domestic and foreign policy and to manage government administration. For both Mary and Elizabeth, their gender significantly shaped the Privy Chamber, making it a primarily female space for personal attendants.

In the past, historians have considered the women of the Privy Chamber to have had limited political involvement.[8] Kate attended Elizabeth at the close stool, as Anthony Denny did for Henry VIII when he served as Chief Gentleman of the Stool. However, she was not also Keeper of the Privy Purse or the dry stamp, as Anthony was. This has been taken to indicate she was restricted to domestic and personal duties. More recently scholars have reconsidered that view.[9]

Elizabeth's Privy Chamber was not only an intimate and personal world staffed by her ladies, but also played a significant part in her political life. Business often took place there within a small circle of Elizabeth's most trusted courtiers and ladies. As Chief Gentlewoman of the Privy Chamber, Kate established her role as gatekeeper and confidante, as well as overseeing the queen's personal attendants. She had near-constant access to Elizabeth, and as a trusted adviser who had served faithfully for many years, could discuss both personal and state matters. Kate's influence was by no means restricted to the domestic sphere.

Other members of the Kate's inner circle also featured in the round of new appointments. Sir Gawen Carew was dispatched on 3 December with Sir Nicholas Throckmorton to recover some items of Cardinal Pole's plate, and place them in the Jewel House. On 31 December Sir Gawen became Master of the Henchmen. This was a minor role, overseeing personal attendants, squires and pages, but required his presence at court.

There was as yet no formal appointment for Sir Peter Carew, but Elizabeth sent him to speak on her behalf with Count de Feria on 28 December. Elizabeth wanted to sound out the count – who served as Philip II's ambassador to England and was a close adviser – about Philip of Spain's likely reaction, should she make changes to the church. She also wanted to test whether Philip would stand by his alliance with England. Peter seems a strange choice for a delicate matter of this nature, and we might wonder if Kate exerted some influence and put his name forward. Yet Philip knew Peter, so perhaps Elizabeth saw him as a useful messenger. And sending him might underline that Philip might not always have the skills of men like Peter at his disposal.[10]

In the coming years, Sir Peter undertook other diplomatic and military missions and was in charge of ships in the English Channel to attack 'pirates', but did not find a permanent place at court.

Elizabeth's accession was greeted with celebrations throughout the country. After holding her first meeting of the new Privy Council at Hatfield, she made her way to the capital. Christophe d'Assonleville, a diplomatic representative for Philip II of Spain wrote that on 23 November:

> The Queen, clad in a gown of purple and crimson velvet and riding on a white hackney, came to Lord North's house whilst preparations were being made at the Tower. In front of the house were great numbers of people congratulating and welcoming her and making the greatest possible show of elation and joy; the Queen for her part showed both by words and actions how pleasing this was to her.[11]

How delighted Kate must have been to see her mistress so welcomed after all the trials they had endured together.

After a brief stay at the Tower, Elizabeth moved to Whitehall Palace, where Kate and John joined the crowd of courtiers and ladies to celebrate Elizabeth's first Christmas as queen. Amid the lavish festivities on Christmas Day 1558, Elizabeth gave a strong hint about her views on religion. The Archbishop of Canterbury usually held a mass on Christmas morning for the monarch. However, in 1558 there was a vacancy since Reginald Pole had died on the same day as Queen Mary. Owen Oglethorpe, Bishop of Carlisle, stood in, but when he held the bread and wine up to the heavens to be transformed, Elizabeth was furious. She ordered him to cease and desist. When he ignored her and continued with the service in the old way, the queen rose and left the chapel, followed by her retinue.[12]

Robert Dudley oversaw all the yuletide entertainment during that first Christmas. An early sign of Elizabeth's regard for her Master of the Horse came on 29 December when she granted him his father's former lands at Kew.

On New Year's Day 1559 Elizabeth received gifts as sovereign, and Kate began a pattern which held good almost until her death. Each New Year Kate presented the queen with items of clothing, almost certainly embroidered by her own hand. On this occasion, she gave a partlet and a pair of ruffs wrought in black silk.[13] In return, as the queen's most valued companion, each year she received costly items of plate or jewellery. This time the queen gave her a gold tankard and a gold cross. Similarly, John Astley received valuable gifts such as gold cups, and he also held the official role of Master of the Jewel House at the gift exchanges. Dean of the Chapel Royal, Archdeacon Carew, gave gold sovereigns and received a gilt cup. Lord Robert Dudley, Master of the Queen's Horses, gave the queen a chain set with a pearl.[14] Rare and costly, although becoming more available as new trade routes opened up, pearls held significant symbolic meaning, representing purity, chastity and a connection to the divine. Dudley's more intimate gift rather stands out among all the silk purses full of sovereigns and the embroidered handkerchiefs.

Frances Newton was already well established in her position at court. She was named as custodian of a long list of gifts presumed to the queen on New Year's Day 1559. For example, miniature painter Levina Teerlinc, gave 'the Quenis picture finly painted upon a Card with the Quene by Mistress Newton.'[15]

Plans were in hand for Elizabeth's coronation, and the astrologer Dr John Dee had declared that the stars and planets would be in their most favourable positions for the start of the new monarch's reign on 15 January. Henry Machyn recorded in his diary that during Christmas week scaffolds and platforms were already going up along the route, ready for the pageants and proclamations.[16]

Kate was given purple velvet and scarlet tinsel fabrics to wear on coronation eve, and her husband and Sir Gawen Carew were among those receiving livery. Elizabeth wore the same robes as her sister Mary had at her coronation, but she added a new slim-fitting bodice. She looked magnificent in a gown of cloth of gold, with her hair loose about her shoulders, topped by a gold circlet. We can imagine how proud Kate felt, seeing her charge finally take her rightful place on the world stage.

The magnificent procession passed through cheering crowds to Westminster Abbey, where Bishop Oglethorpe placed the crown on Elizabeth's head. None of Queen Mary's other Catholic Bishops was prepared do it, so the task fell to Oglethorpe. To prevent him raising the host, as he had at Christmas, some historians suggest that George Carew, Dean of the Chapel Royal, had the honour of taking the coronation mass behind a screen.[17] George may have clandestinely included concessions to her own conscience and particular wishes. At this time Elizabeth seems to have had a preference for the form of worship laid out in the 1549 prayer book, rather than the more radical 1552 version.[18]

Following the ceremony, there were feasts and tournaments. Sir Arthur Champernowne was among the knights listed to compete in the jousts planned to take place over two days.[19] However, according to an Italian resident in London named Schifoya, the first joust was postponed. He wrote, 'on this day, the 16th [January] these English personages had prepared a joust, but it was postponed until the next day, her Majesty being rather tired'.[20]

Elizabeth was preoccupied with finding a religious settlement during the first months of her reign. In trying to steer a middle course, to please both sides, she risked being attacked by both.

Religion was not the only challenge facing the new queen. England was up against powerful rivals like France and Spain, and she had to navigate foreign policy while reviving a stagnant economy. Elizabeth lacked experienced and loyal advisers, and faced the widespread belief that a female ruler was inherently weak. The question of the queen's marriage soon surfaced.

Everyone expected Elizabeth to marry; it was unthinkable she could rule alone, and she must provide an heir. However, she was in no hurry to choose a husband. She had already voiced her misgivings several times, saying she preferred spinsterhood. Some historians cite the Thomas Seymour affair as the cause of her reluctance to marry, while others believe the example of her father's wives appalled her and put her off marrying. The negative example of her sister's marriage to Philip, which split the nation and diminished Mary's authority, almost certainly influenced her thinking.

Elizabeth's careful reply to a parliamentary petition on 9 February urging her to marry did little to satisfy those who felt that, for the good of the country, she must take a husband. Sir Peter Carew did himself no favours by supporting the bill.[21]

As one of the most eligible women in Europe, Elizabeth could have her pick of a list of European bridegrooms. In 1559 the prime contenders were Philip of Spain, Emperor Ferdinand I, who wanted to arrange a marriage with his son Archduke Charles, and Gustav I, who had been negotiating for some years for a marriage with his son, Eric of Sweden. French princes and others later entered the lists, hoping to secure her hand.

Over the coming months a succession of delegations and ambassadors sought audiences to promote the attractions of marriage with their masters. The international marriage market had not served Henry VIII and Anne of Cleves well, and Elizabeth was understandably cautious of marrying a man she had not met. But no foreign prince wanted to risk travelling to England only to be rejected.[22] She was also acutely conscious of the danger of ceding power to a foreign prince and being drawn into another country's wars, as Mary had.

Elizabeth flirted with the envoys, seemingly enjoying the game of pitting them against each other. She skilfully feigned interest in each proposal, but never committed. She kept Philip of Spain's ambassador, the Count de Feria, dangling for as long as she could. It was wise not to dismiss Philip while peace talks between Spain and France were ongoing. But there was never any chance of her staying within the Catholic Church, and in March 1559 she gave Philip a firm refusal, clearing the ground for others.

Many in England preferred a marriage with an Englishman and floated the names of several noblemen, including Henry Fitzalan, Earl of Arundel, and Sir William Pickering. The one man she might have accepted was not on the list. Robert Dudley was already married.

William Cecil had never really approved of Kate; in their new roles they often clashed about access to the queen as Kate sought to establish her status and influence. Yet on Robert Dudley, Kate and the queen's Secretary of State were in complete agreement. They were both increasingly concerned to see Elizabeth granting her Master of the Horse, a married man, unprecedented favours.

Robert, the younger of the two surviving sons of the disgraced Duke of Northumberland, had known Elizabeth since they were children. They were both prisoners in the Tower of London in 1554, although it is doubtful they saw much of each other. Robert was lucky to have survived his father's efforts to gain power; had he not wed Amy Robsart, the daughter of a Norfolk squire while in his teens, it might have been he, not his brother Guildford, who was married to Jane Grey. He probably met Amy when he accompanied his father to Norfolk to put down Kett's Rebellion in 1549. It seems Robert and Amy married for love, Amy visited him while he was in the Tower, suggesting they were close. However, their youthful passion waned. It was not unusual for wives not to accompany courtiers at court, and long periods of separation did not seem to bother Dudley. He didn't neglect Amy entirely, visiting her now and then and bringing her gifts, but she lived in the country, far from the royal court.

Robert was tall by the standards of the day, with dark good looks and long, shapely legs. Like Thomas Seymour, he excelled at marshal sports like jousting; later that year in November 1559, he and Lord Hunsden took on all comers. Handsome, sophisticated and well-dressed, Robert Dudley shared Elizabeth's sense of humour and her love of dancing and hunting. Elizabeth was a skilled horsewoman, prompting Bishop Álvaro de la Quadra, the Spanish prelate and diplomat who served as Spain's ambassador to England, to comment to de Feria in February 1560: 'The Queen rides out every day into the country on a Neapolitan courser or a gennet to exercise for this war … She makes a brave show and bears herself gallantly.'[23]

As Master of the Horse, Dudley had lodgings at court. It was not long before people noticed Elizabeth enjoyed his company rather more than was seemly. The gossips whispered she even visited him in his chamber. Writing to King Philip while visiting England in April 1559, the Count de Feria reported that:

> during the last few days Lord Robert has come so much into favour that he does what he likes with affairs and it is even said that her Majesty visits him in his chamber day and night. People talk of this so freely that they go so far as to say that his wife has a malady in one of her breasts and that the Queen is only waiting for her to die so that she can marry Lord Robert.[24]

Dudley was not concerned about gossip; his star was rising fast. On St George's Day, 23 April, Elizabeth installed him into the Order of the Garter, a significant mark of royal favour. He was ever-present, dancing attendance on the queen, and even advising her on policy matters. Whenever another suitor seemed to make headway, Dudley turned up his attentions. For example, at the end of May, not long after Baron Breuner, the ambassador sent to negotiate a match with Archduke Charles, reported optimistically about the prospects for his master, Lord Robert Dudley put on a rather public display. He arranged a supper for the queen and others in tents in St James's Park, where everyone could see him dancing attendance on the queen.[25]

On 19 June, Ambassador de la Quadra cast doubt on Breuner's optimism in a letter to Philip of Spain writing: 'She makes her intimates think she is favourable to the Archduke's affair, and her women all believe such to be the case, but there is really no more in it than there was the first day.'[26]

Through one of her ladies, Robert's sister Mary, Lady Sydney, Elizabeth had discreetly indicated her serious intention to marry the archduke and that he should immediately come to England. Lord Robert himself and Sir Thomas Parry also gave the ambassador assurances. However, Elizabeth later told him that Mary did not speak for her, and cooled the negotiations. Not surprisingly, Mary felt betrayed.[27]

De la Quadra could see through Elizabeth's ploys. Towards the end of June he reported that the queen had lodgings prepared at Greenwich for Sir William Pickering, another potential suitor 'with whom she had long conversations lately. She has told Baron Breuner "that she would die a thousand deaths rather than marry one of her subjects".'[28]

Elizabeth had some fourteen palaces at her disposal, but in the summer months she usually visited the homes of noblemen and gentry, who had to bear the costs of accommodating the entire royal court. The entire court travelled with the queen wherever she went. Nobles, higher gentry and the Privy Council, along with their servants and other members of the royal household, sometimes as many as 1,000 people, accompanied Elizabeth on progress. In her position as Chief Gentlewoman of the Privy Chamber, Kate played an important part.

When the queen left Greenwich to go on progress in Kent and Surrey, Robert Dudley, of course, went with her. At Cobham Hall, William Brooke – who had inherited his father's title in September 1558 – entertained the queen 'with sumptuous fare and many delights of rare invention', and had installed a banqueting house made especially for the queen's visit.[29] William's first marriage to Dorothy Neville was not a success, and the couple eventually separated. So it is unlikely that Dorothy, who died on 22 September 1559, was at Cobham Hall when the queen's party visited. If young Frances Newton was in attendance, she may have met Lord Cobham, her future husband. It is tempting to wonder what role Kate played in arranging the match.

Kate still saw it as her responsibility to act as Elizabeth's mentor and protector. Listening to what people were saying about the queen was part of her job description. Writers have occasionally portrayed Kate negatively, by labelling her a 'gossip', but it was actually crucial for her to stay informed. While the queen and her entourage journeyed on, visiting Eltham, Croydon, Beddington and Nonsuch, Kate was dismayed to hear the talk circulating in taverns and inns, among servants and nobles alike. Rumours had even spread beyond England to the court of Emperor Ferdinand in Vienna. The emperor demanded Ambassador Breuner launch an investigation, since he could not have his son courting a 'loose woman'.

Kate bustled about her duties, tight-lipped and angry. Perhaps she whispered to Elizabeth when no one else could hear, urging her to be more careful. She may have reminded her how long it had taken to repair her reputation last time scandalous gossip had circulated about her.

But as they travelled from one country house to another, Robert Dudley was always at Elizabeth's side. No one could mistake the chemistry between them. Away from the confines of the London Palaces, Elizabeth and Dudley may have felt free to take more risks, alarming Kate. Or perhaps Kate was indignant when Baron Breuner's agent, François Borth, questioned Elizabeth's serving women. Perhaps Kate even felt pushed aside as Robert Dudley became Elizabeth's closest confidante and policy adviser. Whatever it was that tipped her over the edge, in early August Kate's patience ran out, probably at Nonsuch Palace. She astonished all the other ladies by going on her knees before Elizabeth, and demanding that she marry. Kate not only dared to challenge Elizabeth directly, but she did so in full public view with the ambassador looking on.

Baron Breuner described the scene he had witnessed when he wrote to Emperor Ferdinand:

> Her most intimate Lady of the Bedchamber, Catherine Ashley, some days ago fell at her Majesty's feet and … implored her in God's name to marry and put an end to all these disreputable rumours, telling her Majesty that her behaviour towards the said Master of the Horse occasioned much evil-speaking; for she showed herself so affectionate to him that her Majesty's honour and dignity would be sullied, and her subjects would in time become discontented. Her Majesty would thus be the cause of much bloodshed in this realm … Rather than that this should happen she would have strangled her Majesty in the cradle.[30]

Strong words, wrenched from the depths of Kate's heart! Elizabeth's first response was her standard line; she knew Kate had her best interests at heart, and she was quite willing to marry in order to console her and please her subjects. But she reminded Kate that she had no wish to change her state, and needed to consider marriage carefully.

As we might imagine, Kate was sceptical, entreating Elizabeth again: 'for the love of God, where she had so many and worthy offers to resolve upon one, lest God punish her, call her away from this world before her time'.

Kate had pricked Elizabeth's conscience, for according to Baron Breuner, Elizabeth's next response was more defensive:

> Her Majesty rejoined that she hoped that God who had freed her from the violence of her enemies and suffered her to rise to her exalted dignity, would continue to preserve her and the realm and would dispose according to His Divine Will, whether she were alive or dead. But as regards the question that they in their talk coupled her with her Master of the Horse, she hoped she had given no one just cause to associate her with her Equerry or any other man in the world. But in this world she had had so much trouble and so little joy. If she showed herself gracious to her Master of the Horse, he had deserved it for his honourable nature and dealings.
>
> She had also never understood how any person could be displeased, seeing that she was always surrounded by ladies of the bedchamber and Maids of honour, who at all times could see if there was anything dishonourable between her and her Master of the Horse.
>
> … If she had ever had the will or had found pleasure In such a dishonourable life, from which may God preserve her, she did not know of anyone who could forbid her; but she trusted in God that nobody would ever live to see her so commit herself.

This exchange gives an interesting insight into the relationship between Kate and Elizabeth. Elizabeth's responses sound rather like a teenager's refrain to an angry parent – it's not fair; I deserve to have fun; anyway nothing happened, and if it did no one can stop me!

Kate was the only one who dared to tackle Elizabeth face to face. That Elizabeth didn't dismiss her speaks volumes about their strong bond and Elizabeth's respect for Kate.

Kate spat out some harsh words, even hinting she'd have preferred to strangle Elizabeth in her cradle rather than see her end up like this. That was probably simply an expression of Kate's frustration, rather than signifying she had actually cared for Elizabeth when a baby. Blanche Parry, said she had rocked baby Elizabeth in the cradle in her self-composed epitaph at St Faith's Church in Bacton, Herefordshire. There is no similar record for Kate. Her 1536 letter to Cromwell hints at a new position.

Notwithstanding that, Kate had been with Elizabeth for a very long time, and she was disappointed and worried by her relationship with Dudley.

In the same dispatch Baron Breuner commented: 'This Master of the Horse is, I hear, married to a fine lady… Nevertheless since the Queen was crowned he has never been away from court. Moreover they dwell in the same house and this it is which feeds suspicion'.[31]

The incident shocked Elizabeth. True to form when facing an emotional crisis, later that month the queen fell ill, experiencing several fevers. Breuner reported on 23 August that he found the queen somewhat dejected, saying she was,

> daily pestered with petitions from her subjects desiring her for her honour's sake and for the welfare of her Kingdom and for other reasons to change her mind and to marry… she would rather be dead than that her realm should suffer harm or loss through her. She was prepared to marry even the vilest man in her Kingdom rather than give people occasion to speak ill of her.

Breuner's spy told him Elizabeth's ladies said she had been quite melancholy, alone in her room of nights and had not slept half an hour … in the mornings she was pale and weak. The queen cut short her progress: Guildford and Windsor missed out on visits in 1559.

The marriage question was clearly praying on Elizabeth's mind. She had plenty of suitors to choose from – according to Neale, by October 1559 there were ten or twelve competing for her favour.[32] Yet her attachment to Dudley remained strong, and she bestowed many honours on him, including making him Lieutenant of Windsor Castle and Windsor Great Park in November of that year.[33]

The rumour mill, once cranked up, went on turning. In early December Baron Breuner was preparing to leave England, reporting that Elizabeth showed a marked preference for 'his enemy' Dudley above all others. He'd heard from many people that Dudley was trying to do away with his wife by poison.[34] A sinister rumour was already in the air when Amy Robsart moved to Cumnor Place in December 1559, reported to be suffering from a 'malady of her breast'.

Sir Thomas Parry, Kate's former co-prisoner during the Seymour investigation, was also meddling, saying he could further the baron's cause. However, Breuner rightly felt him untrustworthy.[35] Robert Dudley divided opinions, and Parry was firmly in Dudley's camp, considered one of the strongest advocates for the queen to marry her Master of the Horse. When Parry died on 14 December 1560, he was said to have died of shame for having promoted a marriage between Lord Robert Dudley and the queen.

Sir Nicholas Throckmorton, however, was not a fan. Sir Nicholas, who was the English ambassador to France, wrote to the queen and Cecil in December 1559, to tell them about the scandalous tales circulating there.

Throckmorton's letters were so diplomatically indiscreet that Cecil wrote to him on 15 January 1560, warning of the likely consequences of speaking out.

Cecil's frustration is obvious in his letter to Throckmorton: 'What hir Majesty will determine to do only God I think knoweth, and in her, his will be fulfilled.'[36]

On 25 February 1560 Kate's possible protégé, Frances Newton, married William Brooke, Lord Cobham, in a lavish ceremony at Whitehall Palace. The ceremony was followed by jousts, feasts and dancing.[37]

Kate was likely in attendance on 11 April 1560 when the queen kept the traditional Maundy Thursday ceremonies at Whitehall Palace. With Dr Bill, her almoner, Elizabeth distributed money to twenty-six poor women – 20s (around £303) in a red purse and 26d (£27) in a white purse and in the afternoon, twenty gowns to twenty women. She even gave away her best gown to one lucky woman, and she washed their feet. The miniature painting of an Elizabethan Maundy Ceremony, attributed to Levina Teerlinc (Plate 11), might depict this very 1560 ceremony, although the year is uncertain. If the painting dates from the early 1560s, then the figure holding the queen's train is most likely Kate. If it is from 1565, however, she may have been too ill to attend, and Blanche Parry may be the one holding the train.[38]

On the same afternoon during the 1560 ceremony, the queen gave 2d (£1.94) each to a crowd numbering more than 1,000 people in St James's Park. The queen often used the park for jousting, fetes and festivals. On 27 May, Elizabeth made John and Kate jointly keepers of St James's Palace. Henry VIII had commissioned the red-brick palace on the site of a leper hospital and used it as a hunting lodge in his newly enclosed deer park. It offered a peaceful escape from the busy court, while still being close to the much larger Whitehall Palace. The palace sometimes hosted visiting dignitaries, and being appointed keeper was a prestigious position, showing Elizabeth's high regard for Kate and her husband.

On 9 April 1560 an irritated Ambassador de la Quadra reported that the queen missed an important meeting because she was indisposed, but went to watch Lord Robert playing tennis. Whether it was watching bear baiting at Spitalfields or taking part in tournaments, riding in the park, or dancing, Robert Dudley was always there. At the end of July he entertained the queen and others at a lavish banquet at his riverside house at Kew. Later that year, during the summer progress, he wrote to the Earl of Sussex, praising the queen as a great huntress. It is no wonder the gossips were still busy. In August, Mother Dowe of Brentwood found herself in prison after she declared the queen was with child by Lord Robert Dudley.

Kate must have been on the brink of another outburst of disapproval. But then, on 8 September 1560, servants returned from Abingdon Fair to find 28-year-old Amy Robsart, Dudley's wife, dead at the foot of the stairs at Cumnor Place, Oxfordshire. The queen immediately sent Dudley to Kew while an enquiry was held.

Although William Cecil professed friendship for Dudley and offered his support, in reality he saw Amy's death as good news. Kate may also have felt relieved. It was unthinkable that the Queen of England could marry a suspected murderer, and even if he were innocent, the whiff of scandal was damaging to Elizabeth's international standing. Dudley must be out of the running.

The official ruling was accidental death; Amy had fallen and broken her neck. Yet whispers persisted, both locally and internationally, questioning Dudley's role in the event. In October, in one of his less than temperate letters, Throckmorton told the Marquess of Northampton that the young Queen of Scots had commented: 'The Queen of England is going to marry her Master of Horse, who has killed his wife to make room.'

Kate knew Elizabeth better than anyone. She was not convinced Elizabeth had entirely given him up. According to Violet Wilson, some time after Amy's death, when Kate boldly asked Elizabeth if she intended to marry Lord Robert. Elizabeth replied: 'Dost thou think me so unlike myself; and so forgetful of majesty, as to prefer my servant, whom I myself have advanced, before the greatest Princes of the Christian world.'[39] So, duty might come first, but there was no sign of her accepting any other marriage proposal.

Kate was by now established as a formidable presence among the queen's ladies. Lady Jane Seymour, Somerset's daughter, contrived to arrange the secret wedding of her brother, Lord Hertford, and Lady Katherine Grey, (Jane Grey's sister, who could not lawfully marry without the queen's consent). Wilson tells us Jane warned the newly married pair they should not tarry much longer, 'lest Mrs. Ashley, should ask inconvenient questions'.[40]

Kate ruled the Privy Chamber with an iron grip, and she was increasingly seen as an important courtier. Because she had so much influence with the queen, people often asked her for advice. On 10 December 1560, for example, Thomas Bentham, the recently appointed Bishop of Coventry and Lichfield, asked her about a suitable New Year's gift.[41]

Emboldened by her status, as Christmas approached, Kate was considering direct action in the high-stakes world of Elizabethan politics.

Chapter 16

Meddling in the Marriage Game

1561–1562

Kate certainly felt the queen should marry, and of all the potential bridegrooms, she preferred Eric of Sweden. Sweden was a Protestant nation, and an alliance with the newly Protestant England had political attractions. Negotiations with Sweden for Elizabeth's hand in marriage had been going on for several years. In 1560, Eric sent his brother John, Duke of Finland, to make his case, but Elizabeth was unimpressed. She wrote to Eric in February 1560 making it clear she could not return his professed love, and telling him not to come to England.[1] Eric had inherited the throne of Sweden when his father died on 29 September 1560. Although previously rejected, Kate judged the King of Sweden could still have a chance, but only if he came in person to woo Elizabeth.

One of those who had heard Kate was the best contact for news about the queen's marriage intentions was a man named Dymock. A former gentleman usher to Henry VIII, Dymock had set himself up as a London merchant trading with Sweden. About a month before Christmas 1560, he sought Kate out. According to his later statement, Dymock asked if she thought the queen was going to marry Dudley. Kate, he said, declared that she thought the queen was free of any man living, and would not have the Lord Robert. Kate saw an opportunity in Dymock's approach, and asked him to return on the next day to talk with her husband.

When he met John in the park after dinner next day, Dymock explained his plan to take jewels, and patterns of jewels on parchment to Sweden. He asked again about the queen's marriage intentions. John told him that queen would rather not marry, but he wished the Prince of Sweden had come. He asked to see the jewels, which Dymock brought to him next day. Dymock wanted a passport for them, two men, and £100 (£23,000), but John said he wanted first to show the queen the jewels to know whether she would buy any.

Elizabeth was interested in a jewel with a large ruby and pearl pendant, and Dymock claimed she jokingly said the King of Sweden might buy it for her. Elizabeth, according to Dymock, commented that he, Dymock, was an old man to be planning long journeys, and granted him a passport. Dymock interpreted the queen's actions as showing favour to King Eric's suit. It certainly appears she knew all about his planned visit to King Eric's court.

On Christmas Eve John asked Dymock if the King of Sweden could speak Italian and advised him to buy a little book called the *Courtisan*, which was written in French.[2] Dymock presented the book to King Eric when he met him in Sweden.

On 2 January 1561 Dymock dined with John, and later spoke with Sir William Pickering. Pickering told him he hoped Dymock could persuade the king to come to England. When Dymock left for Sweden on 14 January it was not only to sell the jewels, but also to encourage the King of Sweden to come to England.

However, either in his remarks to Dymock or at some other time, John had been too outspoken. On 21 January the queen ordered him to keep to his chamber, and soon after dismissed him from the court.

The rumour went round that she dismissed John 'for displeasure of my Lord Robert'.[3] The rivalry between Dudley and Eric was the talk of the court. Ambassador de la Quadra wrote gleefully about it:

> Things have reached such a pitch that her Chamberlain has left her, and Axele of the Privy Chamber is in prison for having babbled '...Cecil is he who most opposed the business, but he has given way in exchange for the offices held by Treasurer Parry, who died recently of sheer grief'.[4]

Cecil had succeeded Sir Thomas Parry as Master of the Court of Wards.

John wrote an apologetic letter to Lord Robert from Melton in Norfolk. It seems he had failed to wait on Lord Robert at Christmas, and offered the feeble excuse that he was 'half drowned in debt', but also hinted at 'some other changes your lordship partly knowest'.[5]

Kate sent an outraged letter to Dudley, saying she had asked permission to leave the court and had done so. Her letter appears written in haste. Kate was clearly upset. She wrote that she was wretched because the queen had told her she would never forgive John. Kate intended to go to her own country and 'dwell with my poor kin and pray for her Grace daily. I have a sister widow will be glad of us both for although I would rather choose death than go from her, yet such is my bond of friendship as of marriage. I must follow.'

Kate leapt to her husband's defence. John, she said, had served Elizabeth well, and meant no harm. She ended with a heartfelt plea: 'You can be a witness to this and could he now be judged he had any intent to dishonour her? No! No! My lord forgive me and bear with my folly for I cannot well tell what I write.'[6]

This letter is the best evidence we have that Kate and John shared a loving relationship.

Dudley, who must have complained to the queen, may have stitched John up having got wind of the plan to induce the Swedish king to make an appearance. In January 1561, Dudley was trying desperately to recover his position with Elizabeth after Amy's death, and did not welcome the Swedish king's arrival on the scene. (Many years later, in 1579, Dudley tried to frustrate Elizabeth's marriage with Francis, Duke of Anjou.)

Kate and John were caught in the crossfire as Elizabeth's complex relationship with Dudley played out. There can be no doubt that Elizabeth had feelings for her handsome Master of the Horse, but she would not allow him, or any man, to have the upper hand. In August 1565 she is reputed to have said 'I will have but one mistress here and no master', during an intense argument with Dudley.[7] It is possible that the queen initially encouraged the Astleys to think she was seriously considering the Swedish king, but then, as she did with Mary Sydney and Archduke Charles, denied it. Robert Dudley was also keenly aware that Kate disapproved of him, and likely held her partly responsible for Elizabeth's evasions.

By taking the extreme and quite extraordinary measure of leaving the court, Kate made sure the queen knew how offended she was at John's dismissal. The widow she mentioned was her sister Elizabeth, whose husband, Archdeacon John Pollard, died in the spring of 1560.[8] (Walter Raleigh Senior and Roger Budockside were still living, and her other sisters were themselves dead.) After the archdeacon died, Elizabeth Cole/Pollard went back to her first husband's home, The Slade, near Cornwood, Devon. It's probable that Kate stayed there during John's six-week exile. It is not clear why she did not join him in Norfolk, and it is possible he too went to Devon.

Elizabeth missed Kate, and whether Dudley liked it or not, she reinstated both John and Kate after six weeks, However, the affair was not over. On 24 May, Cecil wrote to Sir Nicholas Throckmorton with news of Dymock, who, on his return from Sweden, was arrested and sent to Fleet Prison, accused of pretending to sell jewels while in fact 'provoking' the King of Sweden to come to England. Cecil adds: 'I am sorry to think that this matter will extend to two whom I love well, Sir William Pickering and Mr John Astley.'[9]

In July, the queen set off on a progress in Essex. There was a lot of talk that summer about whether the King of Sweden intended to visit England to renew his suit.

Kate often acted as a go-between for people wishing to see the queen. For example, the Duchess of Suffolk's accounts for August show a payment 'To Mistress Ashley's man at the court … which let my master into the Privy Garden, the Queen being there, 3s 4d [around £39].'[10]

It is not clear exactly when or where this took place.

By early September John was at Enfield, where he was keeper of the palace, preparing for the queen's arrival. She stayed for several days, during which news came that King Eric had indeed set off, but had been driven back by storms. On 22 September, the queen and her retinue moved to St James's Palace, where John and Kate were the keepers. John Sommers, a secretary to Throckmorton, recently returned from France, reported that they still expected the King of Sweden. However, King Eric never arrived, although two of his ships, carrying horses and treasure, did survive the perilous journey. Eventually, King Eric abandoned his visit to England and headed for home.

At New Year 1562 Kate gave Elizabeth twelve handkerchiefs edged with gold and silver and, clearly back in favour, received in return two gilt bowls and a salt with a cover (salts were highly prized and often ornately decorated).

Throughout the spring, people were still talking about the queen's marriage. Even Roger Ascham, who was Latin secretary to Elizabeth and spent a lot of studying time with her, wrote to his Johannes Sturm in Strasbourg on 11 April, saying no one knew what to think, as 'for of her own nature, without the advice of anyone, she is so entirely averse and abstinent from marriage'.

Ascham described the queen's achievements: purifying religion, making peace with Scotland and France, restoring the coinage, building up the navy. After fulsome praise for her talent and learning, he concluded: 'besides all this, my most munificent mistress ... If she would only marry, she would leave no room for higher commendation'.[11]

In June 1562, on behalf of the queen, Kate delivered £30 (£7,000) to Elizabeth St Loe, (later known as Bess of Hardwick) of Gloucestershire, a Gentlewoman of the Privy Chamber. Katherine Grey had confided in Bess about her secret marriage, and asked for help to smooth things over with the queen. Although Bess refused, the queen still suspected her involvement and sent her to the Tower in August 1561. She regained her freedom in April.

According to Natalie Mears, Robert Dudley was not satisfied with the outcome of the enquiry into Dymock's activities and by early July he was agitating for his arrest.[12]

Preoccupied with matters in France and Scotland, the queen did not go on progress in the summer of 1562. On 22 July, Kate was meddling in the affairs of Eric of Sweden once more. Cecil intercepted a letter written by Kate and Dorothy Broadbelt, a Gentlewoman of the Bedchamber who had served alongside Kate for many years, to Nicolas Guildenstern, formerly Swedish ambassador to England. They wrote warmly, assuring him the King of Sweden would be most welcome in England.[13]

Dymock and a man named Goldborn, a servant of the King of Sweden, were examined for their part in encouraging the King of Sweden to renew his suit in person. And on 4 August they were committed to the Tower. Under suspicion of involvement Kate was commanded to keep to her chamber. Cecil took Dorothy into his custody, while the examinations continued. The crux of the matter was that Dymock was not an accredited diplomat, but he had involved himself in a diplomatic mission to encourage the King of Sweden's suit. Mears also suggests that the attempt to advance a marriage with Eric of Sweden was linked to efforts to secure an increase of English support for the French Huguenots.[14] Kate's brother Sir Arthur Champernowne was a notable supporter of the Huguenot cause, and we might speculate that he had encouraged Kate to intervene. After several weeks of confinement Elizabeth allowed Kate and Dorothy to return to court.

The Astleys' involvement in the King of Sweden's suit may not have been successful, but Kate continued to exercise political influence. Nobles and courtiers went through her to ask for favours, and she was also a vital a source of information for the queen. An Italian newsletter of the time said: 'Mistress Asheley had such influence with the queen that it seemed she were patroness of all England.'[15]

There had been sporadic outbreaks of smallpox during the summer; one who succumbed was the Countess of Bedford, who died at Woburn Abbey on 27 August. By October, some female courtiers had already contracted the disease, but most had survived. At Hampton Court Palace, Elizabeth was weighing up how to deal with the return to Scotland of her cousin Mary, Queen of Scots. When Elizabeth started to run a fever and experienced chills, Kate and the other women ran her a hot bath, hoping to ease her symptoms. Elizabeth's condition worsened, and she had headaches and a sore throat as well as the fever. As yet, there were no telltale blisters, the hallmark of smallpox.

It was several days before the marks erupted on her skin, first as small spots, then developing into blisters which eventually scabbed over. Smallpox often left its victims scarred for life, but the queen's doctors were far more concerned about whether the queen could survive. There was no cure for smallpox; around 30 per cent of those who caught it died.

Everyone was desperately concerned about what might happen in terms of the succession, should Elizabeth die. The country would split between people who supported the Catholic Scots queen, and those who supported Lady Katherine Grey, who remained disgraced because of her secret marriage to Somerset's son.

More pus-filled spots erupted, and Elizabeth did not improve. Thinking herself on her deathbed, surrounded by her councillors, no doubt to Kate's and to William Cecil's horror, she demanded that the council make Robert Dudley Lord Protector of England, with an income of £20,000 (£4.6 million) a year. She also took a solemn oath that her relationship with Dudley had never been improper – a claim rather undermined when she later awarded Dudley's groom, a man named Tamworth who slept in Dudley's room and knew all of his (secret) movements, an annuity of £500 (well over £100,000). Luckily, after ten days, the queen slowly recovered and suffered only minor blemishes on her face. These she covered with what became her trademark white lead makeup. During her illness Elizabeth's doctors had wrapped her in red cloth, a Japanese treatment thought to prevent serious skin scarring.

Sir Thomas Smith, England's ambassador to France, wrote to Sir William Cecil on 9 November, saying of the smallpox:

> in England it took aged folks and ladies. The Duchess of Suffolk had it first, the Countess of Bedford died of it, and divers ladies of 40, 50 and 55 years of age have died of it. This disease is best acquainted with Duchesses, Marchionesses, and Countesses, so it is no marvel that at last the Queen should have it. Where they use no physic nor strive with it they escape best. The Queen bathed herself before they came out, which put her in great danger.[16]

The records do not specify which of Elizabeth's women looked after her, but it is inconceivable that Kate was not at her bedside. However, she seems to have escaped the disease. Mary Dudley, Lady Sydney, was not so lucky; she survived the illness, but it scarred her face dreadfully.

After this frightening episode, Elizabeth could no longer deny her close relationship with Dudley. She appointed him to the Privy Council, a great honour, and he remained one of her closest confidants for the rest of his life.

Chapter 17

The End of a Life of Faithful Service

1563–1565

From this time onward, Kate fades from the scene. At New Year 1563 she presented the queen with a caule (cap) and night-rail (a loose-fitting informal gown) wrought with black silk. We do not hear of her again until next New Year, when she gave the queen a smock worked with black silk with a square collar.

Kate was over 60, and she may have been suffering bouts of ill health. During the spring of 1564, she was certainly dosing herself with a range of herbal and other remedies. Mathews quotes from the only surviving set of detailed accounts of payments to the queen's apothecary, John Hemingway, for 'one half yere endyed at mydsomer last in ye sixth yere of her most graycous raigne'.[1]

The account is for January–June 1564 and includes details of the many items Hemingway supplied for Kate during that six-month period, besides her 'accustomed pils', Hemingway provided the following for 'Mystres Asheley':

- camomile flowers, rose leaves, oil of roses, almond milk and vinegar;
- pills and lotions;
- plasters[2] – hot or cold pastes spread on parchment, covered in silk and an outer covering and applied to affected areas;
- pectoral powders – probably to treat aches and pains like rheumatism; bitter electuary – a type of medicinal preparation which combined bitter herbs with honey to make it more palatable, in a paste or syrup;
- Venice turpentine – historically taken internally for conditions like intestinal parasites and as a purgative, also for throat conditions and colds, or applied to the skin to treat abrasions or wounds. While turpentine is still used for treating horses' hooves, modern medicine strongly warns against its internal consumption.

Kate may also have had a sweet tooth since Hemingway also supplied her with 'anisede cumfytts, whyte sugar candy and whyte lozenges'(Hemingway suggests these were for children in the house).

Kate's bill for six months amounted to 30s 2d (more than £500), around 7 per cent of the queen's total expenditure with Hemingway in that period. The lengthy list of expensive ingredients and remedies might suggest that Kate was concerned about her health. Unfortunately, without the accounts for earlier years, it is not possible to know if this was unusual for Kate, or to pinpoint exactly what her ailments were.

It is likely that her health was indeed failing in the summer of 1564 as, unlike her husband, it seems Kate did not accompany the queen on progress. On 26 July 1564 it appears the royal entourage set off from Whitehall Palace without Kate. After visiting William Cecil, probably at his house at Cheshunt, they went to Enfield. Then, via Hertford Castle, the party headed for Cambridge, where they stayed for five days from 5 to 10 August. Cecil, despite suffering with a sore leg, arrived at the master's chambers of St John's College on 4 August. He was presented with 'two pair of gloves, a marchpane, and two sugar-loaves'. Court officers ensured sufficient supplies of beer, ale, and wine were available, and prepared the queen's lodging, verifying no one had recently died of the plague. The queen arrived on the following day, to be welcomed with gifts:

> at one Mr Ray's, alderman, because the Duke is Steward to the town, and gave unto his Grace two pair of gloves, a marchpane and a sugar-loaf. And from thence to the Earl of Sussex and presented him with a pair of gloves.[3]

The town dignitaries and scholars from the colleges put on lavish entertainments for the queen and court. Kate was not there to see her husband John receive an honorary degree as Master of Arts from the university. Because she knew many Cambridge men and was herself well-educated, missing the plays, lectures and debates on philosophy and divinity was especially disappointing. She also missed the opportunity to visit her niece Honora, Joan and Anthony Denny's youngest daughter, when the party went on to Kimbolton Castle. Honora lived there with her husband, Thomas Wingfield.

The court was away until early September; after Cambridge visiting other properties in Northamptonshire, Buckinghamshire and Hertfordshire. During that summer, Kate may have remained at Whitehall Palace, or stayed at another of the queen's properties, or moved to her own rooms at Somerset House until the queen returned. Wherever she was, she ate well. On 13 September, Katherine Astley, Chief Gentlewoman of the Privy Chamber, received a payment from the Privy Purse 'for her table in the Queen's absence in the progress time the 6th year, £100'.[4]

Kate's food bill amounted to £100, (around £24,000 today).[5] It is a measure of her enduring affection for Kate that the queen was prepared to spend such sums to keep her table well-furnished.

Kate's name does not appear in the record again until the New Year's gift exchange. The court spent the Christmas season of 1564 at Whitehall Palace. As Keeper of the Queen's Jewels and Plate, it was John's job to take custody of all gifts of silver and gold plate. On this occasion, Kate gave the queen 'a square stool of walnut, the seat covered with yellow silk knottes of Venice silver and green silk fringed with silver and silk'.[6] In previous years, Kate may well have worked the needlework on her gifts for the queen herself. However, it seems less likely that she had done so for this, her last New Year's gift. This might suggest her health was failing. In return, Kate received sets of bowls and spoons and a gilt cup, costly gifts for Elizabeth's valued companion.

It remains unclear whether Kate attended court throughout the spring of 1565, when the queen moved between her various palaces. On 12 April the queen performed the customary Maundy service at Whitehall Palace, distributing alms to thirty-one poor women, who 'each received 20 shillings in a red purse and 31d in a white purse'.

According to de Silva, the Spanish ambassador in a letter to King Philip she did so 'with great dignity and decorum, dressed in black as usual'.[7] We do not know if Kate was in attendance.

It's often asserted that Kate recovered from a short illness at some time in the spring or early summer of 1565. However, source material to support this statement is elusive. Others close to the queen were ill in the early summer of that year. Katherine Knollys (née Carey), the queen's cousin, suffered a brief spell of illness,[8] prompting Elizabeth to send her physician, Dr Huick, to attend her. With so many women named Katherine at court, it is possible that names have been confused. Fortunately, Lady Knollys made a swift recovery and was well enough to attend her son's wedding on 16 July.

Moving the court was a frequent upheaval, enabling the regular cleansing and airing of the royal palaces. The River Thames connected Greenwich, Westminster, Whitehall, Richmond and Hampton Court, while Eltham and Nonsuch were only 4 miles away from it. Each palace had its own landing stage. Whenever it was possible, they travelled and transported heavy baggage by river. The local church bells rang on the morning of departure to signal the court's removal.

In early July 1565, it was time to move from Greenwich to the fresher air of Richmond. A few miles upstream, Richmond, would be safer from contagion until the court set off on the usual summer progress.

Affairs of state likely preoccupied the queen as she prepared to leave Greenwich Palace that July morning. She may have missed Kate's good counsel as she considered the question of Mary Queen of Scots' marriage to Lord Darnley, or the continued speculation about her own marriage.[9]

On 14 July 1565 the bellringers of St Botolph's Aldgate were paid fourpence for ringing when the queen went from Greenwich to Westminster to take up residence at Whitehall Palace for a few days, on her way to Richmond.[10]

After two days at Whitehall Palace, Elizabeth went to Durham House on the Strand for the marriage of Katherine (Carey) and Francis Knollys' eldest son, Henry. His bride was one of Elizabeth's maids of honour, Margaret Cave, daughter of Sir Ambrose Cave, a Privy Councillor, and Chancellor of the Duchy of Lancaster. Since Elizabeth's accession, Durham House had been the residence of the Spanish ambassador. Robert Dudley used the palatial building in the Strand between 1565 and 1568 until he found a more permanent home at Leicester House. Later still, it became the home of Kate's nephew, Sir Walter Raleigh. Durham House, one of six large, noble houses with extensive gardens along the River Thames near the Strand, stood next to Somerset House, Elizabeth's former London home, where Kate and other royal servants still kept rooms. By 1565 the sprawling palace built by Edward Seymour was used only occasionally for meetings of the queen's council.

Work had been in hand since April to refurbish the main buildings at Durham House, which lay on the waterfront, approached through a gatehouse, courtyard and gardens. The noise from workers employed to pave the road outside Durham House in preparation for the wedding celebrations probably carried to Somerset House, where the main buildings were close to the Strand, with gardens behind, sloping away towards the river. Kate did not attend the wedding, but the strains of merriment from the jousting, the masques, the supper and dancing, which went on until 1.30am, may have reached her ears. Evidence concerning the place of Kate's burial suggests that it may have been at Somerset House where she lay, gravely ill.

On 17 July the bellringers of St Martin-in-the-Fields were paid 8d 'For ringing at the remove of the Queen from Westminster to Richmond'.[11]

It is sometimes suggested that Kate and Elizabeth were already at Richmond Palace on 17 July, and that is where Elizabeth visited her faithful confidante and sat at her bedside. Kate, who was in her sixties, died the following day, 18 July.[12] Ambassador Zwetkovitch writes: 'Some few days ago a lady of the name of Ashley died here.' However, he dispatched that letter from London, not Richmond. The ambassador did not arrive at Richmond until 22 July and the queen did not see him until 23 July. On 23 July, the Duchess of Parma's trade commissioners went to Richmond to take their leave, and de Silva wrote to Philip II:

> I went to Richmond with the Commissioners from the States of Flanders who went thither to take leave of the Queen on their departure. After they had done so and kissed her hand – which she

> gave very liberally – the Queen took me aside and said she had been much grieved by the death of the lady [Katherine Astley] … who brought her up.[13]

The bells of St Martin's rang for the court's removal on 17 July. Elizabeth visited Kate on the morning of 17 July before setting off for Richmond. The entry in Folgerpedia reads: '17 July, Tues. visit to Katherine Astley, **Westminster** [author's emphasis]. The Queen's visit was on the day before Mrs Astley's death.'[14]

Elizabeth may not have realised how ill Kate was when she visited her bedside, perhaps leaving in hopes that Kate would make a full recovery. Kate died on 18 July, and was buried on the same day.

An entry in the parish register for St Mary le Strand church for the month of July 1565 reads: 'Katherine Ashley was buried on the xiix daie of this month.'[15]

Kate had rooms at Somerset House during Elizabeth's residency before her accession. After ascending the throne Elizabeth kept part of Somerset House for her own use and assigned other parts as 'grace and favour' apartments for her retainers and officials. Somerset House was within the parish of St Mary le Strand. It is also possible she remained at Whitehall Palace, but at Somerset House, in her extreme illness, she would have been away from all the noise and upheaval of court removals.

There is a complication in locating Kate's exact burial place. Edward Seymour, Lord Protector Somerset, demolished the church of St Mary le Strand and its graveyard to build his Elizabethan mansion. He promised a replacement church, but never built it. The parishioners initially worshipped in nearby St Clement Danes, and from 1558 the congregation moved to the Savoy Chapel. The parish register records the weddings and burials carried out there, the chapel being known as St Mary le Savoy. John of Gaunt built the Savoy Palace in the fourteenth century, but rioters plundered and burned it in 1381 during the Peasants' Revolt. It remained semi-derelict until the early sixteenth century when King Henry VII ordered the construction a foundation to be known as 'Hospital of Henry, late King of England of the Savoy'. Although building started before the king's death, the hospital, a charitable foundation to provide 'a night's lodging for 100 pour and nedie men',[16] was completed in the early years of his son's reign. In 1565, it comprised an extensive complex of buildings, including a great dormitory, longer than Westminster Hall, and three chapels dedicated to St John the Baptist, St Catherine and Our Lady. There was also a graveyard.

Only one chapel survives in 2026 – the same chapel that the parishioners of St Mary le Strand used as their home church at the time of Kate's death. Known as The King's Chapel of the Savoy, it is a private chapel of the monarch in the right of the Duchy of Lancaster and the Chapel of the Royal Victorian

Order. Dwarfed by modern office developments, the chapel stands in the former graveyard, which has long been a public park since burials were banned in central London. Previously laid out in a plain square with a path around the edge of a lawn, it was renewed and replanted with an oval lawn and benches in 2002 for Queen Elizabeth II's Golden Jubilee. The inscription on the front of the St Mary le Strand parish register shows Kate's burial must have been nearby. It reads;

> Register of the names and surnames of all persons,
> men, women and children as have been
> married, buried and christened since the
> year of our lord 1588 within this parish of St Mary le Strand
> at Savoy, with the tymes
> of their several marriages, deaths and christenings,
> newly recorded this present year 1599 Gilbert
> Tyncombe and John Halsall
> being then Church Wardens

Few of those who seek a moment of peace in this 'pocket park' amid the bustle of modern-day London, realise that nearby lies the last resting place of the woman who was perhaps closer to the first Queen Elizabeth than any other. Plate 12 shows the author at the King's Chapel of the Savoy.

A cemetery beneath the chapel of Somerset House became the burial place of Catholic supporters during the reign of Queen Henrietta Maria. There is a certain irony that this was near to where Kate, a staunch Protestant, called a 'heretic' by the Spanish ambassador, lay at the Savoy.

The parish register shows Kate's burial occurred on the day of her death, presumably without ceremony. It was not unusual for a burial to follow so soon after death, particularly in the height of summer in London. What is perhaps a little surprising is that the queen did not insist on a state funeral for the woman she held so dear, nor is there any evidence of a memorial to Katherine Astley. Many years later, when Blanche Parry died after fifty-six years' service, Queen Elizabeth made sure she had a magnificent funeral. Blanche died, aged 82, on 12 February 1590, and on the evening of 27 February, Queen Elizabeth ordered a funeral fit for a baroness.[17] Blanche had herself set aside £300 (around £50,000 today) for a procession, service and interment, but it was the queen herself who footed the bill.

The queen did not usually attend funerals. Kate's uncle, George Carew, who had an official position as Master of the Savoy, could conceivably have arranged her burial and even conducted the service.[18] Frances, Baroness Cobham, or Gawen's wife, Lady Carew, may have been there.

Perhaps it was Kate's own wish to slip quietly away, without undue pomp or ceremony, or perhaps her husband John preferred little fuss. No memorial exists to this remarkable woman today. If there ever was one it has gone. There were many memorials within the Savoy Chapel dating back to the 1520s but a devastating fire gutted the chapel in 1864, destroying most of the fittings. In his 1878 account, the Reverend Loftie says: 'of the monuments which blocked up the chancel and were dotted here and there all over the walls, almost all have perished'.[19]

When he republished Stow's Survey of London in 1720, Strype listed around forty inscriptions from memorials of the chapel, but Kate's name is not among them.[20]

Chapter 18

Legacy

Although clearly overwhelmed in the first few days after Kate's death, Elizabeth soon picked up the reins of government and was back in action, hunting with the French ambassador less than a week later.[1] Kate had taught her well, and would not have wanted her to neglect her duties as queen while in mourning. Kate's greatest and most enduring legacy was her star pupil, Elizabeth. She had laid the foundations that enabled Elizabeth to rule for forty-five years.

Her legacy as Chief Gentlewoman of the Privy Chamber

Kate left an enduring legacy by developing the political role of the women of the Privy Chamber. She set a precedent that would endure throughout Elizabeth's reign.

At the top of a new female hierarchy Kate controlled access to the queen, acted as her 'eyes and ears', and remained her most intimate confidante. The young queen's position was not secure and during the vital first years of her reign Kate played a key role in keeping her informed about how her policies were being received. From her appointment in 1558, Kate acted as gatekeeper and influential advocate, as well as a conduit for information to and from the queen. A year after Kate's death, Hugh Fitzwilliam wrote to the queen saying: 'Now that Mrs Ashley is gone he has no friend to make his moan to.'[2]

After Kate's death, Blanche Parry took her place. Whereas Kate's relationship with William Cecil was sometimes stormy, Blanche was related to him and the pair often worked in tandem. Blanche continued to serve as Elizabeth's Chief Gentlewoman until her death in 1590.

Her legacy to the Inner Circle

As a married woman, Kate did not leave a will. However, she left her family a lasting legacy. Kate's high standing in Queen Elizabeth's memory secured advancement and preferment for many of her kin in the years to come.

John Astley

Kate's husband moved on quickly. On 13 October 1565, now in his fifties, he married the considerably younger Margaret Lenton, alias Grey, illegitimate daughter of Lord Thomas Grey, who had been executed in 1555 following his involvement in the Wyatt plot. In January 1549, Thomas Grey had been the one to persuade Thomas Seymour to hand himself in.

Margaret was perhaps an unexpected choice. To quote Charlotte Merton in the *Oxford Dictionary of National Biography*:

> An ambitious man would have been wise to make an equally judicious match within the golden circle of families closest to the queen but instead his choice fell on Margaret Lenton (d. in or after 1596), an illegitimate daughter of Lord Thomas Grey.[3]

John may have felt some sense of obligation to Margaret, whose father had been a fellow protagonist in the most dangerous of times, and had ultimately lost his life. It was not a politically advantageous second marriage, but John was clearly keen to start a family and have sons to follow him. This perhaps reveals how much he had given up by marrying Kate, knowing that she was beyond childbearing age. Margaret, who was born around 1550, gave him a son in 1568, and the queen stood godmother.[4] Two more sons and three daughters followed.

In the same year as his son's birth, the queen granted John a 'lease in reversion' of the castle and manor of Allington, near Maidstone. He did not live there, preferring his other estate at Maidstone, but received the right to a long-term lease after the existing lease expired or ended, essentially securing future possession and income from the Crown (who owned it) for himself or his heirs. It is interesting to note that Allington was previously Thomas Wyatt's home. This may have been a coded message thanking John for his service during the rebellion, after which he spent several years abroad.

Throughout their married life, John had been somewhat in Kate's shadow. After her death, while continuing to serve as Master of the Jewel House, he spent more time in Kent, where he became an authority on horse breeding and riding. In 1584, he published perhaps his most enduring personal achievement, *The Art of Riding*, which describes the doctrine of the Italian riding schools as he and the Gentleman Pensioners understood it. John amassed estates in Dorset, Kent and Middlesex and represented Maidstone in the parliaments of 29 October 1586 and 4 February 1588–1589.[5]

By the 1590s John's health was failing and in August of 1595 a new patent was issued, granting the Mastership of the Jewel House jointly to him and to Edward

Carey, Groom of the Privy Chamber. John died on 1 August 1596 and was buried at All Saints Church, Maidstone, on 5 August. In his will be left the 'great house' at Maidstone to his widow, and ordered that she should not cut down trees on his estates. He also made charitable bequests to the poor people of Maidstone.

Kate's family

Sir Arthur Champernowne (1524–1578), Kate's younger brother, served as Vice Admiral of the Fleet of the West under Elizabeth. He and his wife Mary (Norreys, Carew) (d.1570) had a large family at Dartington Hall in Devon. Like many of the seafaring men of the West he trod a fine line between privateering and piracy. A staunch Protestant, Arthur supported the Huguenots, who were being persecuted in the French Wars of Religion. In 1568 he funded an expedition in their support, led by his nephew **Henry Champernowne of Modbury**. The queen gave Henry permission to take a troop of a hundred Englishmen, including a group of Champernowne cousins (a young Walter Raleigh among them) to France, where they fought valiantly. Henry Champernowne died in La Rochelle in 1570, probably of illness. Henry's son **Sir Richard** inherited Modbury and served as Deputy Lieutenant of Devon. Arthur's son, Gawen, married Lady Gabrielle Roberda Montgomery, daughter of the Comte de Montgomery, a Huguenot general.[6] The Champernownes remained at Dartington Hall until 1925. Arthur's grandson, **Captain Francis Champernowne** (1614–*c*.1686/1687) was influential in the early colonisation of New England, particularly Maine.

Three of Kate's sisters were still living at the time of her death: **Elizabeth**, **Katherine** and **Frances**. (The date of the death of Joan the elder is unknown and often confused with that of her younger sister, Lady Denny.)

Elizabeth was widowed for a second time when Archdeacon John Pollard died in 1560 and lived quietly at The Slade, Near Cornwood, Devon, the home of her son, **Philip Cole**, until her death in 1574.

Katherine the younger and her second husband, Walter Raleigh Senior, moved from the farm at East Budleigh in the early 1560s. They spent their remaining years in a house 'close by the Palace Gate', near Exeter Cathedral. Walter Senior died in 1581 and was buried in St Mary Major's church. Katherine Raleigh made her will in April 1594, and died soon after. An iron cross on Cathedral Green, Exeter, marks the site of St Mary Major's church, which was demolished by the Victorians who built a new church, which in turn was demolished in 1970.[7]

We remember Kate's nephew, **Sir Walter Raleigh** (*c*.1552/54–1618) as a soldier, poet, writer and courtier. His relationship to Kate helped young Walter to climb high in Elizebeth's favour. Having fallen from grace by marrying without permission in 1592, he embarked on a voyage to South America in 1594, and was active in the continuing conflict with Spain during the late 1590s. Under Elizabeth's successor, Walter was accused of treason and spent thirteen years in the Tower of London before his last desperate expedition to Guiana ended in failure and the death of his eldest son. After a show trial he was executed on 29 October 1618 in Old Palace Yard, Westminster, on the orders of King James I. Walter's brother, **Carew** (*c.*1550–1625) joined his half-brother Humphrey Gilbert's first failed expedition in 1578, and was Gentleman of the Horse to Sir John Thynne of Longleat, later marrying Thynne's widow. Carew Raleigh became a politician and served as a naval commander during the Spanish Armada threat. Queen Elizabeth recognised Carew with a knighthood in 1601.

Frances, Kate's youngest sister is mentioned in Elizabeth Pollard alias Cole's will, made in 1567, and may have been alive when the will was proved in 1574, but her date of death is unknown. Her son, **Philip Budockside** died in La Rochelle with Henry Champernowne in 1570. One of Frances's daughters, Winnifred, married William Gorges, who served in Elizabeth's Gentlemen Pensioners and was Deputy of Ireland, where he was knighted in 1579. William became Constable of the Tower of London. He was related to Sir Ferdinando Gorges, who participated in Essex's rebellion against the queen in 1601, but escaped punishment by testifying against the main conspirators. In 1622 Sir Ferdinando Gorges founded the Province of Maine in North America.

In 1565, Kate's uncle, Dean **George Carew** was serving as Dean of the Chapel Royal at Windsor, as well as Archdeacon of Exeter, appointments he held until his death on 1 June 1583. He was buried at St Giles-in-the-Fields, London. On 27 February, Ash Wednesday, 1566, he preached at Greenwich, his only known sermon at court. On 1 September of the same year, his eldest son, Peter, made an oration to the queen in Latin, with two Greek verses, which the queen liked her so well she asked him to repeat it.[8] **Sir Peter Carew the younger** died in 1580 fighting for the queen in Ireland. Dean George's second son, also named **George** (29 May 1555–27 March 1629), soldier and antiquary, became **1st Earl of Totnes**, served the queen with distinction in Ireland and gathered a large collection of materials relating to Irish history and pedigrees, including the genealogical records held at Lambeth Palace Library. In 1580 Carew married Joyce Clopton. They had a daughter. Sophia, born 1610 who served as a maid of honour at court and married Walter Stewart, son of Walter Stewart, 1st Lord Blantyre. Her daughter Frances became Duchess of Richmond and famously caught the eye of King Charles II. George, Earl of Totnes also had illegitimate son, Sir Thomas Stafford, a courtier and MP, who served under his father in Munster. Joyce's family were from Stratford-upon-Avon and owned several properties there, including New Place, which they sold in 1567. Thirty years later, William Shakespeare bought New Place. George Carew, 1st Earl of Totnes, was high steward of Stratford in 1610 and would probably have known Shakespeare. George died in 1629 and is buried in Holy Trinity Church, Stratford-upon-Avon.

Sir Gawen Carew likely went to Richmond with the queen in July 1565, as he was Master of the Henchmen from 1559–1565. His role involved managing the personal staff and maintaining the queen's appearance and security within her household. He often had to accompany the queen in processions and at other public events. After Kate's death Sir Gawen was concerned mainly with Devon affairs, but his third wife, **Elizabeth Norwich**, remained at court as one of Elizabeth's longest serving ladies.[9] Elizabeth Norwich, daughter of Sir John Norwich, had been in attendance on Elizabeth since around 1547. When she married Sir Gawen the queen gave her a gown of purple velvet (purple is a very high status colour) with sleeves of cloth of gold, a measure of the regard Elizabeth had for her and also for Kate's family connections.[10] She continued to serve after Sir Gawen's death on 25 March 1585, and was the Lady Carew listed as one of the Ladies of the Bedchamber in 1587. Sir Gawen Carew lived to be over 80. By the will which he made on 11 October 1582 he asked to be buried in Exeter Cathedral, where a monument was later erected.

Sir Peter Carew retired to his estates in Devon after 1560. He served the queen on various commissions of enquiry, often paired with his cousin, Sir Arthur Champernowne, was involved in efforts to suppress piracy and was MP for Exeter in 1566. Sir Peter found it hard to live within his means, and debts may be one of the reasons he left court. Although there is no clear evidence that he fell out of favour with the queen, she may have remembered the part he played in events before the death of Sir John Cheke. He left England for Ireland in 1568 and spent years trying to recover what he believed was his Irish inheritance. He died there in November 1575, and was buried at Waterford. John Hooker's somewhat partial account of his life is rich in detail.[11]

Kate introduced all her **Gilbert** nephews at court and they thrived under Elizabeth. The queen bestowed a knighthood on the eldest, **Sir John Gilbert**, (1536–1596) in 1570. John served as Deputy Lieutenant of Devon and played a prominent part in the defence against the Spanish Armada. He operated the Gilbert family shipping business and invested in the exploratory voyages to the Americas of his brother, Sir Humphrey. On 1 January 1570, Sir Henry Sidney, the Lord Deputy of Ireland, knighted **Sir Humphrey Gilbert** for his service during the brutal and deeply troubling suppression of an uprising in Munster. Sir Humphrey went on to serve as a soldier in the Netherlands and also wrote a treatise on the search for the North West Passage, and a blueprint for an academy for young gentlemen. He went down with his ship, the *Squirrel* in 1583 when returning from his second voyage to claim Newfoundland for the English Crown. His eldest son, the second Sir John Gilbert, a soldier and sea captain, inherited the Gilbert estates after his uncle's death in 1596. His brother, Raleigh Gilbert was 2nd President of the short-lived Popham Colony, founded in Maine in 1606. **Adrian Gilbert**, the only one of the three brothers who never achieved a knighthood, was a popular figure at Elizabeth's court. A garden designer and a chemist, Adrian had an interest in silver mines in North Devon and invested in his brothers' enterprises.

The Denny children also thrived. **Henry Denny** (d.24 March 1574) became Dean of Chester. His son, **Edward**, (d.12 February 1600) was a parliamentarian and courtier and became 1st Earl of Norwich. He was a soldier, privateer and adventurer and joined the colonising expedition led by Humphrey Gilbert. He served in Ireland with Raleigh, and commanded a naval expedition to the Azores in 1591, before returning to Ireland. His wife, **Margaret**, née Edgecumbe, was serving as a maid of honour to Elizabeth in 1582.

Frances, Baroness Cobham

Although still nominally a chamberer, after her marriage Frances, Baroness Cobham, was already becoming close to the queen. Frances's sister replaced her as chamberer in 1564, and there are indications that as Kate's health deteriorated it was Frances who began to 'fill her shoes'.[12] It is clear from the costly gifts Frances received at the New Year Exchange in 1565 that even before Kate's death she was a highly valued member of Elizabeth's court.[13] She would eventually become a Lady of the Privy Chamber. Frances followed Kate's lead in political activity, and forged close ties with figures like Bess of Hardwick and the Cecils. Her daughter Elizabeth, born 1562, married Robert Cecil who, after his father's death, became the queen's chief minister. A charming portrait of the Cobhams and six children by the Master of the Countess of Warwick hangs at Longleat House.[14]

Kate's legacy to Devon

In the sixteenth century Devon was not a rural backwater. Through the export of wool from the backs of the sheep that thrived on the lush grazing on Devon hills, and minerals like tin from the moors, Devon had been a crucial engine house of the English economy for generations. A long coastline and sheltered harbours allowed merchants to send ships out from Devon ports, to return with commodities England needed, like salt and wine. When the merchants' ships encountered the Barbary pirates, they armed them to protect their cargoes.

This created the conditions that led to the birth of fine Devon sailors, soldiers and explorers within a network of families related by marriage that held sway in the West. Devon ports guarded the channel approaches and were vital to the strategic defence of the nation, as proved to be the case in 1588 during the attack by the forces of King Philip of Spain. Whoever sat on the throne far away in Whitehall, Windsor or Greenwich needed to keep the men of Devon on side. Because of Elizabeth's fondness for her, many of Kate's Devon relatives came to notice and found preferment. We might wonder whether these Devon men could have achieved such fame or held positions so close to the Crown, had it not been for the bond between Elizabeth and her Lady Mistress.

Conclusion

Was Katherine Champernowne/Astley the gossiping nanny of fiction and on-screen portrayals? Was she an indiscreet and foolish middle-aged woman, who herself became infatuated with the charming chancer, Thomas Seymour? Should we write off 'Kat Ashley' as a childless woman of poor judgement who had a sentimental attachment to Elizabeth Tudor? Or was she a formidably educated, fiercely loyal and determined woman who, through her contacts and force of character, exercised considerable political influence? The answer probably lies somewhere in between. Analysing her life anew against the historical record, in the context of the values and societal norms of her own time, allows a nuanced character to emerge. This Kate Astley is more believable as the woman Elizabeth cherished as her closest companion for nearly thirty years.

Unfortunately the historical record tells us little about Kate's early life. Many questions remain unanswered. However, by exploring her background and placing her among her 'inner circle', we can consider a range of plausible possibilities, the most likely being that Kate acquired her excellent education among her powerful Courtenay or Poyntz relatives. They were also well placed to introduce her at court.

In 1536 Thomas Cromwell recommended Kate as one of 3-year-old Elizabeth's gentlewomen. Later she would lay the foundations for the education of the king's youngest daughter. Cromwell rarely acted without purpose. But was it only Kate's proficiency in languages and Latin that prompted him to choose her in 1536? There must surely have been a political element in his calculations when he selected Kate for the post.

Kate mingled with some of the finest scholars of the day. Roger Ascham summed up her contribution to Elizabeth's upbringing:

> Hartie Commendations and healthe in Him that is the author of all Health, my **Gentle Mrs Astley**. Would God my wit wist [knew] what words would express the thanks you have deserved of all true English hearts for that noble imp by your labour and

> wisdom now flourishing in all her goodly godliness and the fruit whereof doth even now redound to Her Grace's high honour and profit. I wish Her Grace to come to that end in perfection with likelihood of her wit and painfulness in her study … which your **diligent overseeing** [author's emphasis] doth most constantly promise.[1]

Kate instilled in Elizabeth a lifelong love of learning, and set her moral compass. As Elizabeth herself recognised: 'she brought me up in learning and honesty'.

Perhaps with the stereotypical model of a Victorian governess in mind, the focus has often been on Kate's personal qualities as a teacher. She has been described as kind, jolly, fun-loving, and unconventional in her approach. However, supporting evidence in contemporary accounts and documents is elusive. On the contrary, Ascham hinted that Kate set an exacting curriculum and had high expectations of her charge when he cautioned her against pushing Elizabeth too hard. Recognising her pupil's intellectual potential Kate happily made way for other tutors who could stretch Elizabeth to her full capabilities. William Grindal, Elizabeth's tutor spoke highly of Kate.

As a royal governess, Kate had to be much more than a teacher. She must also be Elizabeth's mentor and protectress. Many aspects of the traditional view of Kate's character rely on her own words and those of Thomas Parry, Elizabeth's cofferer, extracted under duress during investigations into Elizabeth's potential complicity in Thomas Seymour's ambitious and treasonous plans. Taken at face value, Kate's own words show that she failed as Elizabeth's protectress. However, given the power imbalance between her and Thomas Seymour, Kate did everything she could. She was brave enough to call Seymour out, but in reality, she could have little influence over such a powerful man while she and her charge lived under his roof.

On the basis of her deposition, Kate has been judged as negligent; her conversations with Parry have branded her a foolish gossip. There is another plausible explanation. Sir Robert Tyrwhitt, who was charged to investigate, recognised that Elizabeth's defence was orchestrated, commented: 'they all sing one song'.[2] It is possible that Elizabeth, Denny, Kate and Parry colluded in a well devised plan to shield Elizabeth from all accusations of treasonous intent to marry Thomas Seymour. That is not to say the events Kate describes did not happen. Rather they were presented in a way that set Thomas Seymour in a bad light. Taking her share of the blame and distracting attention by sharing the salacious details of Thomas Seymour's attentions Kate successfully deflected attention away from Elizabeth. Anthony Denny, whose influence during Elizabeth's younger years has been largely overlooked, was close to Protector

Seymour, and likely knew that Thomas Seymour was already beyond help. Kate's confessions threw Thomas under the proverbial bus, but also implicated her. If it was indeed a deliberate strategy it carried a high level of risk for Kate. She bravely endured harsh conditions in the Tower of London, in fear of her life, yet said nothing to implicate Elizabeth.

Kate's apparent support for Seymour after Catherine Parr's death also draws heavy criticism, and has invited suggestions she herself was besotted with him. However, after his wife's death, Seymour was free to marry, and was one of the most eligible men in the country. Kate was not the only one to consider a match between Elizabeth and Thomas Seymour desirable. If she erred, it was in continuing to press his cause when his dangerous plans to defy his brother and the king's council were being openly discussed on the streets of London.

Kate's connections to those at the heart of plots during Queen Mary's reign drew suspicion not only on her, but also on Elizabeth. Kate endured further lengthy periods of imprisonment and house arrest. Yet she gave nothing away to implicate her mistress. In 1556, Queen Mary clearly saw Kate as a continuing threat and forbade her return to Elizabeth's service.

Members of Kate's inner circle became strong advocates of religious reform. Although labelled a heretic by ambassadors, there is little evidence to suggest that Kate was as fervent a supporter of reform as her sister Joan, Lady Denny. Kate likely adopted a more flexible, pragmatic approach, like her uncle, George Carew, Elizabeth's Dean of the Chapel Royal. Kate's close association with her Uncle George bears further scrutiny. Rather than naming one of his male relatives, Sir Philip made Kate an executrix of his will, along with that same George Carew. Similarly, Archdeacon Pollard left the administration of his affairs in Kate and George's hands. Kate was also trusted to manage family matters in Devon, as seen in Sir Walter Raleigh's letter concerning Brixham Rectory. All of this points to Kate being a sensible and trustworthy administrator.

When she became queen, Elizabeth made Kate her Chief Gentlewoman of the Privy Chamber. Kate made the role her own, developing significant political influence. Her powerful position was recognised when she was referred to by an Italian commentator as 'the patroness of all England'.[3]

During the crisis caused by Elizabeth's relationship with Robert Dudley, Kate was the only one brave enough to tackle the queen. It speaks volumes that Elizabeth did not chastise her. Later Kate took direct action when she advocated for Elizabeth's marriage to Eric of Sweden, attracting Dudley's anger. Incensed at what she saw as unfair treatment of her husband, Kate even removed herself from court, until Elizabeth recalled her.

Kate Astley was fiercely loyal, impulsive, forthright, and determined. Robert Dudley was wary of her. William Cecil disapproved of her. She occasionally disagreed with her husband, yet she leapt to John's defence when Elizabeth dismissed him, demonstrating their loving relationship.

The woman Roger Ascham addressed as 'Gentle Mrs Astley', became known as the 'patroness of all of England'. She showed that Gentlewomen of the Privy Chamber could have political clout.

Elizabeth always spoke of Kate Astley with respect and affection. She never forgot the closest companion of her young life. It is often suggested that Kate stood in place of a mother to Elizabeth. Their relationship was, however, more complicated than that of parent and child. The adult Elizabeth had authority over Kate in a way no child ordinarily has over a parent. Yet still they remained close. Elizabeth and Kate shared a unique bond of mutual respect and love forged and strengthened through adversity; a bond that would endure for nearly thirty years. Katherine Champernowne, later the wife of John Astley, lived and died in the service of Elizabeth Tudor. She deserves further consideration.

Appendix

Sir Robert Tyrwhitt's Confusing Letter

Letter from Sir Robert Tyrwhitt to Edward Seymour, Duke of Somerset, dated 31 January 1549[1]

The letters exchanged between Sir Robert Tyrwhitt and Protector Seymour offer a valuable insight into Tyrwhitt's questioning of Elizabeth. Historians have interpreted Sir Robert's letter of 31 January 1549 in different ways.[2] This may be partly due to the illegible nature of Sir Robert's handwriting.[3] However, the content of this letter is crucial for a full evaluation of Kate Astley's decisions and conduct. Here, you will find a comprehensive transcript and additional analysis.

Transcript with original spellings and punctuation

> Plesyth yt yowr Grace to be advertysed that I hav resavedyowr letters the xxix of thys Instant and hayth declared your com[m]e[n]dacyo[n]swt your Instrucyons to my ladys Grace wych she resavyth very kyndly but further thene shehayth all redy wryttyn to your Grace she will In no weyce aknowlege as yet, but sayeth as yt comyth to her rem[em]brance frome tyme to tyme she wyll wrytt to your Grace.
>
> She doyth nowe confesse to me and never be for that she comandyt her cofferer to tell mestrys Aschlay the sayme tayll he told her towchinge the maryage of her and my lorde admyrall and sayd to hyme she wold heyr no sych thynge but that Kaytt Aschley shall knowe yt seynge she was put by the Kyngs Majesty her father to be her mestrys and he dyd promys her so to do, and by caws Asclhley dyd say nothing o her of yt this nyght,

she asked the cofferer the next day wether he had told Aschlay of yt or not and he sayd ye hene she demandyt of hyme what ansuer she mayd he sayd she wold nether mell nor spek in the matter unless she had mor atoryte her Grace wyll In no weyce confesse that ether befor or after that Cayt Aschlay spake To her towchynge the maryage betwyx her and my lorde admyrall wych I thynke nothynge mor untrewe and do well parsave that she wyll no mor ackews mestrys Aschlay thene she wyll her owne selffe and at thys present cane abyd no body that doyth dyscomend her doyngs, and sayth they shall all fayr the wours for ther so sayngs.

And for her repayr to se the Kyngs majesty she mych desyeryth.

She doyth confesse the puttyinge away of her palett awt of her bed chambr was be caws her chambr was so lettyll at Chelsay but the confessyone of iiij of her gentyllwomene ys that first Aschlay dyd put owt my lady of Troy who lay ther contenewaly be for that tyme wych ys a bout iiiyers paste, and after she put owt mestrys Pary who sucsaded her place so she could not abyd to hav no body lay thr but onnly her selff after she cayme to the J[]oyne[?], and she beyng absent, mestrys Norwege her mayd lay with her Grace.

Yf your Grace dyd knowe all my parswasyons wyth her all manerof ways, weynge her honor and scerrtay one way, and the danger to the contrary, yo[u]r Grace wold not a lettyll marvell that she wyll no mor cough owt matter thene she dowth, but the love she hayth to Aschlay ys to be wondered at wych next[?] neds be for eyllbut yf mestrys Aschlay wold opyne eny of theys thyngs wychshe ys fully replenychyt wythe all, that she myght se som[] e part of yt, thene I wold have good hope to mak hercoughe owt the huoll, and th[i]s I comyt your Grace to the leving god, frome Hatfyld the xxxi of Janeuary.

yo[u]r Graces humble to co[mm]and
Robert Tyrwhyt

Transcript with somewhat modernised language and punctuation

Pleaseth it your Grace to be advertised that I have received your letters the 29th of this month and have declared your commendations and instructions to my Lady's Grace [Elizabeth], which she received very kindly, but further she has already written to your Grace. She will no way acknowledge as yet, but says that as it comes to her remembrance from time to time she will write to your Grace.

She confessed to me … that she commanded her cofferer [Thomas Parry] to tell Mistress Astley the same tale he told touching the marriage of her and my lord admiral. She said to him she would hear no such thing but that Kate Astley knew of it. She says the King's Majesty her father appointed Kate to be her mistress and he did promise her so to do. Because Astley said nothing to her of it this night, she asked the cofferer the next day whether he had told Astley of it or not. He said he had and she demanded to know what answer she [Kate] made. He [Thomas Parry] said she [Kate] would neither tell nor speak in the matter unless she had more authority.

Her Grace will in no wise confess that, either before or after that, Kate Astley spoke to her touching the marriage between her and my lord admiral, which I think nothing more untrue. I do so well perceive that she will no more accuse Mistress Astley than she will her own self. At this present she can abide no body that criticises her [Kate's] doings, saying they will fare the worse for saying so.

And as for her [Elizabeth's] repair to see the Kings majesty, she much desires it.

She [Elizabeth] confesses she put her pallet out of her bed chamber because the room was so little at Chelsea. But the confession of four of her gentlewomen is that first Astley put out my Lady of Troy who lay there continuously for that time which is about three years past. And after that she [Kate] put out Mistress Parry who succeeded her [Lady Troy's] place so she [Kate] could abide no body to lay there only her self after she came to the [?this word is indistinct] and she being absent Mistress Norwcge [Elizabeth Norwich, who would later marry Gawen Carew] her [Kate's] maid lay with her Grace.

If your Grace did know all my persuasions with her all manner of ways, weighing her honour and secrecy one way, and the danger of the contrary, your grace would not a little marvel that she will no more cough out natter the she does. The love she bears to Kate Astley is to be wondered at which next needs to be for [?ill]. If Mistress Astley would open any of these things which she knows, then I would hope to make her [Elizabeth] cough out the whole.

Analysis

Sir Robert's main aim is to find out if Kate spoke to Elizabeth about marrying Thomas Seymour. He also wants to know if Thomas Parry, the cofferer, informed Kate about his conversation with Elizabeth. However, Elizabeth will not be drawn. She staunchly supports Kate, declaring that anyone who dares to criticise Kate will regret it. What's also interesting is that Elizabeth clarifies that prior to his death her father made Kate her Lady Mistress.

Sir Robert turns his attention to the puzzling question of Elizabeth's sleeping arrangements, for which some critics have deemed Kate to be negligent. According to Sir Robert, four gentlewomen told him that Kate first removed Lady Troy from her customary place on the pallet next to Elizabeth's bed. The reference to 'three years past' causes confusion. Does Sir Robert mean 'three years ago' or 'for the last three years'? No other source documents supply the exact date of Lady Troy's retirement. She assumed Lady Bryan's position in Elizabeth's bedchamber from 1537 and continued to do so. By 1549, Lady Troy, who was in her sixties, had been sleeping beside Elizabeth for much longer than three years. Rather, the mention of 'three years past' suggests that Lady Troy left three years ago, in 1546, i.e. not long after Kate's marriage to John Astley. Given that Elizabeth confirms King Henry VIII appointed Kate as her Lady Mistress before his death, that is entirely plausible.

Kate later, perhaps upon their arrival at Chelsea, demanded that she alone should sleep in Elizabeth's chamber. On the rare occasions she was absent, her maid, Elizabeth Norwich, would take her place. She dismissed Blanche Parry from her sleeping position, but there is no evidence of discord between Kate and Blanche Parry. Perhaps Kate removed Blanche because she was worried about Admiral Seymour's attentions. Aware that as Lady Mistress it was her duty to safeguard Elizabeth's reputation, Kate might have believed she must be there herself. Kate and Elizabeth shared a strong bond; Elizabeth's words to Tyrwhitt confirm it. It's also possible that during this confusing time, Elizabeth would rather have Kate by her side.

The room at Chelsea was not large enough to accommodate additional sleeping pallets. But this doesn't necessarily mean Elizabeth was by herself. In the sixteenth century, people of the same sex often shared beds for warmth and comfort, and for security. It would not be at all unusual for Kate or Elizabeth Norwich to have shared Elizabeth's bed. As Anna Whitelock says, 'Elizabeth was never alone, and **in or adjacent to** her bed [author's emphasis] she also had a sleeping companion – a trusted bedfellow – with whom she might gossip, share dreams and seek counsel.'[4] Kate's deposition, taken later at the Tower of London, included her confirmation that she shared a bed with Elizabeth at Hanworth when Seymour and his wife tickled Elizabeth in her bed. Kate stated, 'and this examinate lay with her Grace.'[5] The same arrangements could have been in place at Chelsea.

Abbreviations

BL	British Library
CP	Cecil Papers Hatfield House
CSPS	Calendar State Papers, Spain, 1485–1558
CSP Sim	Calendar of State Papers, Spain (Simancas), 1558–1567
CSPV	Calendar State Papers, Venice
CSPR	Calendar of State Papers Relating to English Affairs in the Vatican Archives, Volume 1, 1558–1571
CSP D	Calendar of State Papers Domestic: Edward VI, Mary and Elizabeth, 1547–1580
CSP F Eliz	Calendar of State Papers Foreign: Elizabeth, Volume 1, 1558–1559
DNB	*Dictionary of National Biography*
EEB	Early English Books, 1641–1700
HHA	Hatfield House Archives
IPM	Inquisition Post Mortem
KK	Kressen Kernow, Cornwall Record Office
L&P	Letters and Papers, Foreign and Domestic, Henry VIII
LPA	Lambeth Palace Archives
ODNB	*Oxford Dictionary of National Biography*
SWHT	South West Heritage Trust (The Devon and Somerset Archives)
TNA	The National Archives

Endnotes

Author's Note

1. Leland, J., *The Itinerary of John Leland in or about the years 1535–1543*, p.217.
2. His claim rested on his grandmother having been one of the daughters of William Blount, Lord Mountjoy.
3. Williams, J.R., *Summary of the Champernowne family records,* SWHT65/16/1/2a-b.
4. Champernowne, C.E., *The Champernowne Family,* SWHT 2522Z/1.
5. TNA SP10/6/ff.16-15v; Starkey, D., *Elizabeth, The Struggle for the Throne,* p.77.
6. Norton, E., *The Temptation of Elizabeth Tudor*, p.70.
7. SWHT 1855A/PB/1, Lease for 60 years, Sidmouth, 1559, Tithes of Fish. Tithes of fish were leased by the manor of Sidmouth to 'Walter Rawlegh the elder' 'Carow Ralegh' and 'Walter Ralegh the younger' in a deed dated 10 September 1559. In 1578, the same persons passed over their interest in the fish-titles in another deed, which contains their signatures. This time the father writes his name as 'Ralegh', his elder son Carew as 'Caro Rawlyh', while young Walter calls himself 'Rauleygh'.
8. Stebbing, W., *Sir Walter Raleigh A Biography,* pp.30–31.
9. HPA: CP 150/89. The confession of the Lady Elizabeth.

Introduction

1. Folger, *The Elizabethan Court Day by Day,* 1565, p.29.
2. Marcus, Mueller and Rose, *Elizabeth Collected Works,* pp.33–4.
3. Online Etymological Dictionary https://www.etymonline.com/
4. Strickland, A., *The Life of Queen Elizabeth*, p.5.
5. Richardson, R.E., *Mistress Blanche,* p.44, quoting Sir Robert Tyrwhitt's letter to Lord Protector Somerset, 31 January 1549.
6. Starkey, D., *Elizabeth, The Struggle for the Throne*, p.26.
7. Howell, Bea., *A Galaxy of Governesses,* p.26.
8. Strickland, A., *The Life of Queen Elizabeth.* p.10.
9. Ibid.
10. Neale, J.E., *Queen Elizabeth I,* pp.30–31.
11. Jordan, W.K., *Edward VI: The Young King*, pp.43–45.
12. Ashdown, D.M., *Ladies in Waiting*, p.55.
13. Sitwell, Dame E., *Fanfare for Elizabeth,* [Kindle Edition].
14. BBC TV, *Blackadder* – a series of four period comedies which first aired on BBC 1 between 1983 and 1989.

15. Plowden, A., *The Young Elizabeth,* p.101.
16. Tallis, N., *Young Elizabeth*, p.148.
17. Bohun, Edmund, *The Character of Queen Elizabeth*, p.3.
18. Mumby, F.A., *The Girlhood of Queen Elizabeth*, p.37. Mumby has little to say about Kate beyond reproducing her depositions.
19. LPL MS 318, George Carew Earl of Totnes, Collection of Genealogies, late sixteenth century.
20. Ibid, ff.165v – Kate's name is spelt 'Catherina'.
21. *The English Baronetage*, p.65.
22. Borman, T., *Elizabeth's Women the Hidden Story of the Virgin Queen*, p.62.
    Starkey, p.25.
    Tallis, N., p.78.
    Merton, C., ODNB.

Who's Who in Kate's World

1. Many variant spellings of this name occur in the record, including Butshed, Budockshyde, Budockshead, Budockshed, and Buttockside.

Chapter 1

1. Williams, J.R., *Summary of the Champernowne family records.*
2. Champernowne, C.E., *History of the Champernowne Family*, SWHT 2522Z/1.
3. Ibid.
4. In 1545 in his will Sir Philip Champernowne left Dodbrooke for the use of his wife.
5. TNA PROB11/5/117.
6. Charles Dynham's brother, Lord Dynham served as Treasurer of England and one of the few men to have served as councillor to King Edward IV, Richard III and Henry VII, and was trusted by all of them.
7. Champernowne, C.E., *History of the Champernowne Family*, p.53.
8. Suggestions that Joan Champernowne Denny and Kate were Sir John's daughters do not bear scrutiny against the record.
9. The peerage records William Courtenay as High Sheriff in 1483.
10. Miss Champernowne cites a confusing reference supplied by the Brereton family, which mentions a 'Richard Champernowne' fighting for Henry VII at Bosworth. This is unproven.
11. The three Courtenay brothers, each successively Earl of Devon, were all killed or executed during the Wars of the Roses. Thomas Courtenay, the 6th Earl was beheaded after the Battle of Towton in 1461. Henry died in 1466 and John, the 15th Earl, died fighting for the Lancastrian side at the Battle of Tewkesbury in 1471.
12. Hodder, S.J., *The York Princesses*, p.99.
13. Anonymous, *The Receyt of the Ladie Katerine,* Kipling, G. (ed.), Early Oxford University Press, for the English Text Society, 1990, p.5. 'with all goodlie manner and haste [they] sped themselves … to repaire to that noble princesse'.
14. John Champernowne had a connection to Lord Broke through the Dynhams, John Dynham having married Lord Broke's daughter.

15. Creighton, C., *A History of Epidemics in Britain*, p.284.
16. Champernowne, C.E., p.53. Also in Williams, J.F., p.18.
17. Prince, J., *The Worthies of Devon.* Prince, vicar of Berry Pomeroy, compiled a list of the Worthies of Devon which was first published in 1701. Miss Champernowne quotes from an early version.
18. Rogers, W.H. Hamilton, *The Ancient Sepulchral Effigies and Monumental and Memorial Sculpture of Devon*, p.15.
19. According to Hamilton Rogers, John Champernowne's second wife was Jane West. However, it was Sir John's widow who remarried John West. Miss Champernowne quotes a case in the Early Chancery Proceedings instituted by Philip Champernowne 1514, claiming delivery of properties which had come into the possession of 'Margaret, now the wife of John West'. She later married a third time, to John Fortescue.
20. Philip's son John would marry Lord Mountjoy's daughter Catherine in 1538. Another of Mountjoy's daughters, Gertrude, would marry Philips relative, Henry Courtenay, son of William Courtenay and Katherine Plantagenet, and became Marchioness of Exeter.
21. Privy purse expenses of Elizabeth of York: wardrobe accounts of Edward the Fourth, p.xxvi.
22. In the mid-fifteenth century a branch of the Carew family was established at Beddington, Surrey. In 1480, Sir Edmund's father, mortgaged the ancestral home at Carew Castle in Wales, and Mohun's Ottery in Devon, inherited from the Mohuns in the thirteenth century, became the base of the senior line. Other branches would divide in the late fifteenth and early sixteenth century, forming the Antony and Haccombe branches. Sir Nicholas Carew, who would become one of the close companions of the young King Henry VIII, was of the Beddington branch, and was therefore distantly related to Sir Edmund.
23. Jennet was the daughter and heiress of John Bosome of Dittisham in Devon, and widow of Sir Baldwin de Fulford of Great Fulford House, near Dunsford, also in Devon.
24. Katherine Courtenay (of the Powderham branch) sister to Sir Philip Courtenay of Molland, and therefore great-aunt by marriage to Kate's grandfather, Sir John Champernowne. She had been widowed twice before she married William Huddesfield. A monumental brass of Huddesfield and his second wife survives in Shillingford St George Church, Devon. Kate's grandmother and her sister are also depicted on the brass.
25. Robert Poyntz was Catherine of Aragon's chancellor and his second son, John served as her 'sewer' attending her during meals, organising the seating and serving of guests; a position of trust and proximity to the queen. Robert died in 1520 and is buried in the magnificent chapel he installed in Gaunt's Chapel in Bristol (now known as the Lord Mayor's Chapel, or St Mark's Church). The arms of Catherine of Aragon are prominently displayed on the fan-vaulted ceiling, beside those of Henry VIII and Poyntz. Robert's grandson, Anthony and Elizabeth's son, Nicholas, built a new wing at Acton Court in Gloucestershire for a visit by Henry VIII and Anne Boleyn in 1535.
26. The Fitzwilliam Museum, Cambridge, MS 48, f.86. The Carew Poyntz Book of Hours eventually passed through the female line into the Poyntz family.

27. Kressen Kernow (Cornwall Record Office) AR/37/24 - 29. They were to be married 'by 16th January next'.
28. LPL MS 318 George Carew Earl of Totnes, Collection of Genealogies, late sixteenth century, ff.68v-69r.
29. TNA C 142/21/86.

Chapter 2

1. TNA C 142/21/86.
2. In 1538, acting as Henry VIII's 'Vicegerent in Spirituals', Thomas Cromwell mandated that all parishes in England begin keeping registers to record baptisms, marriages, and burials.
3. Norton, E., *Jane Seymour, Henry VIII's True Love,* p.11.
4. TNA WARD 7/2/77, E 150/187/11, C 142/73/43. A deed of 1543 quoted in the IPM mentions Katherine, eldest daughter of the said Philip. This cannot be the other Katherine, mother of Sir Walter Raleigh, as she was at that time the wife of Otho Gilbert and would have been named as such.
5. Vivian, *Visitation of Devon 1620*, p.59.
6. LPA MS 318, ff.119v – Denny; 120r-121r – Raleigh; 165r-193r, Astley; 192r-193r – Gamage.
7. Duffy, E., *The Voices of Morebath– Reformation and Rebellion in an English Village,* p.14. In 1534 the branch of Timewell family living at Wood had three unmarried sons, all called John, identified by the priest as John major, John minor and John minimus.
8. SWHT PEARSE/Box/2/4/1/6. Will of Christopher Chudleigh, probate granted 5 November 1570.
9. Vivian, *Visitation of Devon 1620*, p.59.
10. TNA C 142/73/43, IPM Sir Philip Champernowne.
11. TNA PROB 11/56/233.
12. Harris, B.J., *English Aristocratic Women, 1450–1550*, p.242.
13. PROB 11/19/388. In his will Robert Poyntz of Iron Acton, (d.1520) left his daughter, Margaret 'for her advancement in marriage 300 marks sterling and also 50 marks sterling for her apparel, to be paid to her at her marriage by the advice of my brother Thomas Poyntz, of my son Anthony Poyntz, and of my executors. If she refuse to be so ordered she shall have only 100 marks.' After listing other bequests in the will he seems to have relented a little, adding '50 marks for my daughter Margaret, besides what I have bequeathed.' After his death, Margaret married Sir John St Loe, Constable of Portbury and of Thornbury Castle.
14. Starkey, D., *Elizabeth, The Struggle for the Throne*, p.25.
15. Snell, L.S., *The Suppression of the Religious Houses of Devon and Cornwall*, p.139. Anne Carew was sub-prioress at dissolution in 1539 she was awarded a pension of today 5.6s 8d per annum (around £2,500). The prioress, Eleanor Syndnam, received £30 per annum (roughly £12,500). Elizabeth (Isabel) Carew at Cannonsleigh Priory, £5 per annum (around £2,000 today).
16. Guy, J., *The Children of Henry VIII*, p.44. Latin was part of the princess's curriculum and her lessons to be shared with other girls.

17. Champernowne, C.E., *The Champernowne Family*, p.89.
Embroidered purse, National Trust Collection, Seaton Delaval Hall, Northumberland, NT 1276904.
Although the purse bears Wolsey's arms, a connection to Kate could not be proved.
18. Oliver. G., *Ecclesiastical Antiquities of Devon*, Vol. 2, p.130.
19. TNA C 4/53/53. Philip Chambernon v John West and Margaret, late the wife of John Chambernon: replication.
20. Philip was not chosen on this occasion, but would serve as sheriff in 1527.
21. L&P *Henry VIII*, Vol. 3, 1519–1523, 1250–1265, Grants in April no 26.
22. Hodder, S.J., *The York Princesses*, p.102.
23. Weir, A., *Henry VIII, King and Court*, p.136.
However, see also L&P *Henry VIII*. Nicholas Wykes, husband of Anthony Poyntz's sister Elizabeth is also named in the list to be appointed to serve the young prince. The date of their marriage is uncertain, some sources suggesting as early as 1506, which would seem to rule Anthony Poyntz's sister out, as she would be referred to by her married name in 1511.
Elizabeth Poyntz may have been the wet nurse rather than the person in charge of the nursery. Most aristocratic women did not breast feed. However, the scholar Erasmus, encouraged it, saying a mother who doesn't breastfeed only deserves to be called 'half-mother' by her offspring. It is possible that Elizabeth Poyntz, heeded his advice. She had a child of the correct age.
24. Robert Poyntz's granddaughter, another Margaret, married Sir John Newton, and 8 sons and 12 daughters appear on Sir John's tomb at St Laurence Church, East Harptree, Somerset. Margaret was the daughter of Elizabeth Huddesfield, Kate's great-aunt, and her daughter, Frances, later Baroness Cobham served in Queen Elizabeth's Privy Chamber.
25. Westcott, M., 'Katherine Courtenay Countess of Devon' in *Tudor and Stuart Devon: The Common Estate and Government*, pp.13–38.
26. L&P *Henry VIII*, Vol. 3, 1519–1523, 1250–1265, Grants in April no 26.
27. Leland, J., *The Itinerary of John Leland in or About the Years 1535–1543,* p.217.
28. L&P *Henry VIII*, Vol. 3, 1519–1523, 3282.
29. Wagner, J., *The Devon Gentleman: A Life of Sir Peter Carew,* p.21. In 1512 Sir John Carew was the joint commander, alongside Sir Thomas Knyvett, of the English warship *Regent* during the Battle of St Mathieu against the French. Both men lost their lives.
30. TNA C 1/1502/27, C 1/412/8.
Documents (somewhat damaged) in The National Archives show that Sir Edmund owed a substantial sum to John Gilbert of Compton in Devon, whose nephew and heir would marry Kate's sister, Katherine the younger.
31. Hall, E., *Hall's Chronicle*, p.538.
32. Wagner M.J., *The Devon Gentleman: A Life of Sir Peter Carew,* p.143, refers to obligations found in the records of the Treasurer of the chamber showing that Philip and Thomas Carew had bound themselves for the debt amounting to £1,400 owed to King Henry VIII in 1510.
33. L&P *Henry VIII*, Vol. 2, 1517–1518, 981–4.
34. Ibid, Vol. 4, 1524–1530, 6792.

35. Margaret, daughter of Sir William Skipwith of Kettleby and South Ormsby, Lincolnshire. In 1538 she was rumoured to be Henry VIII's mistress. She married first George, Lord Talboys, and then, on 20 February 1547, the same day as Edward VI's coronation, she married Sir Peter Carew.
36. SWHT 4088M/E/2/1/1 December 1552, by warrant, signed by Edward VI. Includes Sir George Carew for a benevolence of £100 (roughly £28,000) (pardoned).
37. *Alumni Oxonienses* 1500–1714, George Carew Broadgates Hall, supplicated for B.A. 1522 (3rd son of Edmund, Lord Carew).
38. Macleane, D., *A History of Pembroke College Oxford, Anciently Broadgates Hall*, p.117.
39. It is difficult to be certain if the George mentioned is the younger or elder George Carew. Since the elder George had already attended Broadgates College and may have travelled abroad, it is likely the younger.
40. L&P *Henry VIII*, Vol. 4, 1525–1530, 1792.
41. Hooker, alias Vowell, J., *The Life and Times of Sir Peter Carew, Knight,* pp.4–6.
42. Banting, D.R., *Life and Times of George Carew, Vice Admiral of the Mary Rose*, p.9.
43. Cooper, J.P.D., *ODNB,* 'Henry Courtenay, Marquess of Exeter'.
44. L&P *Henry VIII,* Vol. 3, 1519-1523, 703 and 704.
45. Page, W., *Some Notes on Hatfield, St Albans and Hertfordshire, Architectural and Archaeological Society Transitions*, Vol. 1, Part IV, 1901–1902.
46. Gertrude Courtenay indicated that she had lost children in infancy when she consulted Elizabeth Barton in 1532.
47. Cooper, J.P.D., ODNB, 'Henry Courtenay, Marquess of Exeter' includes reference to a confession at the Savoy Chapel.
48. Banting, D.R., *Life and Times of George Carew, Vice Admiral of the Mary Rose,* p.10.
49. Westcott, M.R., ODNB, 'Katherine Courtenay, Countess of Devon'.
50. Bowle, J.E., *Henry VIII,* p.217.
51. Baring-Gould, Rev. S., *A Book of the West; Being an Introduction to Devon and Cornwall*, p.344.
52. Hooker, H., 'A host of Holborne', 14 March 2023, blog post in Music recommendations by Helen Hooker, recorder player, conductor and educator.
53. Knox-Lawton, J. and Lee, S., *DNB*, Sir Walter Raleigh, 1885–1900, Vol. 47.
54. Lobe, M.D., *A History of the County of Oxford*, Vol. 8, Lewknor and Pyrton Hundreds; 'Parishes: Aston Rowant', pp.16-43.
55. TNA WARD 7/2/77, C 142/73/43, E 150/187/11, Sir Philip's Inquisition Post Mortem, taken at Tiverton in November 1545, records that on 2 November 1528, Henry Courtenay, Marquess of Exeter and his wife Gertrude settled lands in Goodrington, Stancombe Danny, and Brixham in Devon on Sir Philip Champernowne, his wife Katherine and his heirs.
56. Champernowne, C.E., *History of the Champernowne Family*, p.54.
57. Brewer, J.N., *A Topographical and Historical Description of the County of Oxford*, Aston Rowant.
58. Weir, A., 'Ladies in Waiting', Article, *H for History.*
59. Martienssen, A., *Queen Katherine Parr*, p.67.
60. Batley, R., *The Lord Protector and His Wives,* p.36.
61. Siddons, M,P., *Visitations by the Heralds in Wales,* Harleian Society.

William Fellow's heraldic visitation of South Wales and Herefordshire conducted in 1531 states 'Robert Gamage married Jane, daughter to Sir Phillip Chamber [*sic*] of Devon, and had issue Margaret.'

Chapter 3

1. Cooper, J.P.D.,ODNB, 'Henry Courtenay, Marquess of Exeter'.
2. Pierce, H., *Edward IV's Fatal Legacy,* p.112. After an investigation Kendall was sent to the Tower. A man named as Peter Corryngton publicly declared he had heard Kendall's servant declare that the marquess was heir apparent, and 'in case the King should die or marry should be King.' The affair was raised again as part of the 'Exeter Conspiracy' proceedings. Kendall was executed in 1539,
3. Miller, H., *Henry VIII and the English Nobility*, p.65.
   In 1534 the Marquis of Exeter was awarded damages of £3,000 (over £1 million today), against Peter Corryngton.
4. Pierce, H., *Edward IV's Fatal Legacy,* p.108, (citing Chapuys's letter, suggesting Anne Boleyn demanded Gertrude be dismissed).
5. BishopofLondonMarriageLicences,Vol.I,1520-1610,licencedated28January1531.
6. Bryson, S., *The Brandon Men in the Shadow of Kings,* p.229.
7. TNA PROB 11/24/42. Will of Sir John Shilston.
8. Wagner, J., *The Devon Gentleman: A Life of Sir Peter Carew,* p.32.
9. McElroy, A., *Mary Tudor Queen of France*, p.136.
10. Parry, C.J., Britain, Knights of the Realm and Commonwealth Index. George Carew, the younger, was knighted in June/July 1536. The index includes another George Carew as receiving a knighthood in 1527, which begs the question whether Sir Philip's brother-in-law, the elder George Carew might have received a knighthood before he went into the church. By 1532, George the elder may already have taken holy orders – it was common to address a priest as 'Sir'.
11. Duffy, *Voices of Morebath,* p.14.
12. Rose Troup, F., *The Western Rebellion of 1549,* p.26.
13. Everett, M., *The Rise of Thomas Cromwell*, p.249.
14. Hoskins, W.G., *Devon*, p.134.
15. Neame, A., *The Holy Maid of Kent*, p.173.
16. Hall, E., *Hall's Chronicle*, p.790.
17. Ibid, p.794.
18. Ironically, in view of his later separation for the Church of Rome, Henry VIII had argued so vehemently against Luther that Pope Leo conferred on him the title 'Defender of the Faith' still used by English royalty in the twenty-first century.
19. Soberton, S.B., *The Forgotten Tudor Women: Gertrude Courtenay* [Kindle edn].
20. Hall, E., *Hall's Chronicle,* p.801 lists.
21. L&P *Henry VIII,* Vol. 6, 1533, 635. Letter from Ambassador Chapuys to Charles V, 16 June 1533.
22. Neame, A., *The Holy Maid of Kent*, p.184. Listed as clients of Father Hugh Rich, Sir John (later changed to George) Carey (misspelling of Carew), brothers. Mrs Catherine Champer. His brother and sister-in-law. This likely what prompted for Sir Philip's letter referred to on page XXx.

Chapter 4

1. Williams, F.E., *The Champernowne Family Records,* Part 3, p.19.
2. Some sources have suggested erroneously that the woman who served Elizabeth and married John Astley was actually Kate's mother.
3. Von Klarwill, V., *Queen Elizabeth and Some Foreigners: Being a Series of Hitherto Unpublished Letters From the Archives of the Hapsburg Family,* pp.113–115.
4. Margaret Pole, was appointed Mary 's Lady Mistress when Mary was the much loved daughter of the king and queen.
5. L&P *Henry VIII*, Vol. 3, 1519–1523, 361.
6. Margaret Bryan was the maternal aunt of Anne Boleyn and Katheryn Howard and a member of the wider circle of kin and dependents around the Howard family. Through her daughter, Elizabeth, she was the great-grandmother of Elizabeth Throckmorton, Lady Raleigh, wife Kate's nephew, Sir Walter Raleigh, and chief lady-in-waiting to Queen Elizabeth I.
7. Strickland, A., *Elizabeth*, [Kindle edn].
8. Morgannwg, Lewis, Glamorgan Bard writing between 1520 and 1565.
   Quoted by Richardson, *Mistress Blanche*, pp.41–42. Details of Lady Troy 's position 'in charge of queens' are given in an elegy composed by Glamorgan Bard, Lewys Morgannwg.
9. Richardson, R.E., *Mistress Blanche*, p.41.
10. Ibid, p.37.
11. Blanche Parry herself wrote an epitaph which is inscribed on a monument in St Faith's church, Bacton, Herefordshire, saying that she was the queen's servant, 'whose cradle saw I rocked', from Elizabeth's birth in 1533. From the age of 25 or 26, Blanche hardly left Elizabeth, staying with her until her own death fifty-six years later.
12. Tallis, N., *Young Elizabeth*, p.25.
13. Neame, A., *The Holy Maid of Kent*, p.171.
14. L&P *Henry VIII*, Vol. 6, 1533,1468.
15. Not the younger Sir George Carew but his and Kate's uncle, George Carew (priest).
16. L&P *Henry VIII*, Vol. 6, November 1533, 1464.
17. Simon, J., *Education and Society in Tudor England,* pp.95, 205.
18. Sil, N.P., *Sir Anthony Denny: A Tudor Servant in Office*.
19. Norton, E., *The Temptation of Elizabeth Tudor*, p.9.
20. Hooker, alias Vowell, J., *The Life and Times of Sir Peter Carew*, p.14.
21. L&P *Henry VIII*,Vol.10, January–June 1536, 296.
22. Duffy, E., *The Voices of Morebath*, p.88.
23. TNA, *Star Chamber Proceedings Henry VIII,* STAC 2/2/106 ff.267-272.
24. L&P *Henry VIII,* Vol. 9, August-December 1536, 699.
25. L&P *Henry VIII,* Vol. 8, January–July 1535, 802.
26. Collinson, P., *Elizabeth I (Very Interesting People)*, [Kindle edn].
27. Tallis, N., *Young Elizabeth*, p.44.
   See also Cal SP Foreign, Elizabeth, Vol. 1, 1303. In 1559 in a letter to Queen Elizabeth Alexander Alesius (Ales), a Scottish theologian and Protestant reformer

residing in London in 1536, provided a first-hand, deeply sympathetic account of Anne Boleyn's final days.

28. Tallis, N., *Young Elizabeth*, pp.49, and 54.
Borman, *Anne Boleyn and Elizabeth I,* [Kindle edn].
29. Norton, E., *The Temptation of Elizabeth Tudor*, p.10.
30. After Anne Boleyn's execution, Henry promoted Bryan to Chief Gentleman of the Privy Chamber.

Chapter 5

1. L&P *Henry VIII*, January-June 1536, Vol. 10, 1187.
2. L&P *Henry VIII*, 1534, Vol. 7,171. (Chapuys to Charles V).
3. L&P *Henry VIII*, 1534 Vol. 7, 1095.
4. L&P *Henry VIII*, Vol.10, January–June 1536, 968.
5. L&P *Henry VIII*, Vol. 11, July-December 1536, 203.
Rails – nightdresses, Bodystychets – corsets, Begens – nightcaps.
6. Loke, W., Account of materials furnished for the use of Anne Boleyn and Princess Elizabeth 1535–1536.
7. Borman, T., *Anne Boleyn and Elizabeth: The Mother and Daughter Who Changed History,* [Kindle edn].
8. L&P *Henry VIII*, Vol. 10, January-June 1536, 913. The queen's reckoning, beginning in December 1536.
9. Tallis, N., *Young Elizabeth*, pp.49 and 54.
Borman, *Anne Boleyn and Elizabeth I*, [Kindle edn].
10. Plowden, A., *The Young Elizabeth*, p.61.
11. L&P *Henry VIII*, Vol. 11, July–December 1536 – the exact date of appointments is unclear.
12. Starkey, D., *Elizabeth, The Struggle for the Throne*, p.24.
13. L&P *Henry VIII*, Vol. 11, 203.
14. In 1538, Sir John Shelton was granted ownership of the 800-year-old Carrow Abbey in Norwich. He died 21 December 1539 aged 62 and is buried at St Mary's Church, Shelton, Norfolk. His wife Anne died on 8 January 1556 in Norwich.
15. L&P *Henry VIII*, Vol. 11, July–December 1536, 639.
16. Carew, R., *Survey of Cornwall.*
17. Borman, T., *Elizabeth's Women*, p.64.
18. Some sources refer to Kate's brother as 'Sir John'. However, evidence that he was ever knighted is elusive. He held a relatively junior position as squire in 1540. His cousin, Peter Carew was not knighted until1545, after he had acquitted himself well as a soldier and at sea. It's unlikely John Champernowne, who died before he had the chance to achieve military glory, ever received the honour of knighthood.
19. L&P *Henry VIII*, Vol. 11, No. 1417. Grants in December, No. 17. Gawin Carewe. Licence to import 500 tons of Gascon wine and Toulouse wood. Richmond. No date of delivery.
20. L&P *Henry VIII*, July–September 1536, 519. Grants in September, No. 12.

21. Sil, N.P., *Anthony Denny: A Tudor Servant in Office*, published by: Renaissance and Reformation, a peer-reviewed quarterly journal, New Series, Vol. 8, August 1984, pp.190–201.
22. Gates was married to Anthony Denny's sister, Mary.
23. BBC TV, *Yes Minister* – a British political satire written by Anthony Jay and Jonathan Lyn. The series ran from 1986 to 1988. The sequel, *Yes, Prime Minister*, continued with the same cast.
24. Hamil, K.A., *The Humanist Studies of Princess Elizabeth, 1538-1558,* MA Thesis, University of Alberta, 1917, p.36, citing Loades, D., *Elizabeth I,* p.41.
25. In her letter, Kate mentions other letters from Cromwell and that her friends tell her he speaks well of her to the king.
26. On 2 July, Cromwell became Lord Privy Seal, replacing Thomas Boleyn and on 8 July, the king elevated him to the peerage, making him the 1st Baron Cromwell of Wimbledon.
27. L&P *Henry VIII*, Vol. 11, October 1536, 670.
28. TNA PROB/11/27. SWHT Tapley-Soper Collection – transcript of the will of John Gilbert died 1539.
29. Emerson, K.L., *A Who's Who of Tudor Women*. The Jane Broadbelt listed in 1536, may be the same woman as Dorothy Broadbelt who is later a chamberer for Elizabeth. Alternatively Jane and Dorothy might be sisters. The name is sometimes spelt Bradbelt.
30. L&P *Henry VIII*, January–June 1536, Vol. 10, 1187.
31. McElroy, A., *Mary Tudor Queen of France,* p.55.
32. Elizabeth Kildare was born in Maynooth, County Kildare, Leinster, Ireland in 1527.
33. Borman, T., *Elizabeth's Women*, pp.62 and 58.
34. Tallis, N., *Young Elizabeth.*
35. Richardson, R.E., *Mistress Blanche*, p.42.
36. Howell, Bea, *A Galaxy of Governesses,* p.25.
37. It is possible Kate gained experience by teaching her younger siblings, or in some other household. For example, if she served in the Courtenay household she may have had a hand in the early upbringing of Edward Courtenay.
38. Borman, T., *Elizabeth's Women*, p.65.
39. Robert Aske was the son of Sir Robert Aske of Aughton and Elizabeth Clifford, the daughter of the 9th Baron de Clifford. Jane Seymour was his third cousin.
40. Cooper, J.P.D., ODNB, 'Henry Courtenay, Marquess of Exeter'.
41. L&P *Henry VIII*, June-December 1537, Vol. 12, Part 2, 228. (Cromwell to Sir Thos. Wyatt, confirming Aske's fate).
42. Tallis, N., *Young Elizabeth*, p.67.

Chapter 6

1. L&P *Henry VIII*, June-December 1537, Vol. 12, Part 2, 911.
2. Ibid, 894.
3. Ibid, 911.
4. Richardson, R.E., *Mistress Blanche*, p.46.
5. L&P *Henry VIII*, June/July 1539, Vol. 16, 655.

6. Bruce, J., *Correspondence of Matthew Parker*, p.ix.
7. *Accounts of Princess Elizabeth 1551–1552*, Smythe, P.C.S. (Viscount Strangford) (ed.). Blanche Parry was reimbursed for 'horsemeat' in Elizabeth's household accounts in suggesting she kept a horse.
8. Madden, F., *Privy Purse Expenses of the Princess Mary*, p.lxxxiv. Mary made payments to both her own minstrels and those of her brother on several occasions.
9. McElroy, A., *Educating the Tudors,* pp.28, 38 and 43.
10. Quinn, D.B., *The Voyages and Colonising Enterprises of Sir Humphrey Gilbert,* Vol. 1.
11. LPA FI/V vf. 176v Muniment book.
12. L&P *Henry VIII,* January–June 1538, Vol. 13, Part 1, 384. (Grants in February No. 47).
13. LPA MS 318, ff.119v – Denny: another girl, Katherine, is shown as 'died young'.
14. SWHT parish register for St Budeaux records baptism of son, John, on 2 August 1541.
15. TNA C142/73/43.
16. Pierce, H., *Edward IV's Fatal Legacy*, pp.134–135 and 155.
17. Katherine, the younger, had at least eight, possibly nine children with two very different husbands, Sir John, Sir Humphrey, Adrian, Otho (died in infancy), Katherine (and possibly another girl, Elizabeth) from her first marriage to Otho Gilbert and Margaret, Carew and Sir Walter Raleigh from her second marriage to Walter Raleigh Senior.
18. Thomasine's elder brother Archdeacon John Pollard later married Kate's sister Elizabeth. Another Pollard brother, Richard, had an influential position at the Court of Augmentations, while Kate's Aunt Dorothy Carew's second husband was Hugh, another of Sir Lewis's many sons.
19. Banting, D.R., *The Life and Times of Sir George Carew*, p.13. George's brother-in-law, Richard Pollard represented Lord Lisle in negotiations that went on for over a year. By the time a settlement was reached George had sold his lease on the priory.
20. L&P *Henry VIII,* Vol. 13, Part 2, August-December 1538, 980. It is not clear why Sir Philip went the Duke of Norfolk rather than Cromwell.
21. L&P *Henry VIII*, Vol. 15, January to August 1540, 404 and 435. (Grants in March No. 87).
22. Edward Courtenay remained a prisoner in the Tower of London until released by Queen Mary in 1553.
23. L&P *Henry VIII*, Vol. 16, September 1540 to December 1541, 580. (Grants in February No. 76).
24. Snell, L.S., *The Suppression of the Religious Foundations of Devon and Cornwall,* p.164.
25. This suggests that Sir Philip remained in favour after Courtenay's fall.
26. Sources differ on the timing and staffing of the prince's establishment at Hampton Court Palace.
27. L&P *Henry VIII*, August–December 1539, Vol. 14, Part 2, 697. (Thos. Wriothesley to Cromwell).
28. Plowden, A., *The Young Elizabeth*, p.69.

Chapter 7

1. Hall, E., *Hall's Chronicle*, p.838 and Turpynn, R., *Chronicle of Calais*, p.168.
2. Turpynn R., *Chronicle of Calais*, pp.72–179.
3. Garrett, C.H., *The Marian Exiles*, p.15, quoting an article by Lord Hastings published in the *Eastern Daily Press*, 15 August 1936. However, LPA MS 316, George Carew, Earl of Totnes, Collection of Genealogies, f.165v-166r shows first wife Anne Boughton, no issue; second wife Anne Wood, mother of John the Elder (d.1558); third Wife Anne Cruse, mother of 1, John the younger, and 2, Thomas, who will eventually marry Mary Denny, Sir Anthony and Joan's daughter.
4. Marcus, Mueller and Rose, *Elizabeth Collected Works*, p33.
5. L&P *Henry VIII*, August–December 1539, Vol. 14, Part 2, 638.
6. Ibid, 572.
7. John Champernowne may also have served among the fifty Gentlemen Pensioners before his death. The only known list – included in Regia Insignia – was compiled after his death. Gawen Carew, Thomas Astley, Peter Carew, Sir George Carew, and George Pollard (another of the large Pollard family) are known to have served as Pensioners.
8. Regia Insignia, *An Account of the King's Honourable Band of Gentlemen Pensioners,* p.3. The Honourable Band of Gentlemen Pensioners was revived on Christmas Eve 1539 as an elite bodyguard for the king.
9. McElroy, E., *Educating the Tudors,* Chapter 3, pp.27-45, compares the education of all of Henry VIII's children.
10. L&P *Henry VIII*, January to August 1540.Vol. 15, 602.
11. 'History of Parliament' online. Members John Astley, cites this without source reference.
12. The exact words of Gawen's deposition are not recorded. He and his wife were at court in 1542.
13. Tallis, N., *Young Elizabeth,* p.88.
14. TNA T SP 1/40 (207).
15. Guy, J., *Children of Henry VIII*, p.111.
16. Strickland, A., *The Life of Queen Elizabeth*, p.13.
17. Carew, R., *Survey of Cornwall,* p.178.
    It is no known whether it was after the episode Carew describes brought John Champernowne the lease of St German's Priory in south-east Cornwall, In 1540 he held it at a rent of £6 15s per annum (roughly £3,000 today). After John died his widow purchased the estate from the Crown for £434 (around £180,000 today). She later remarried and made the estate over to her son Henry Champernowne of Modbury.
18. Hooker, alias Vowell, J., *The Life and Times of Sir Peter Carew*, pp.15-22.
19. Wagner, J., *The Devon Gentleman: A Life of Sir Peter Carew*, p.58.
20. L&P *Henry VIII*, Vol.16, 306. (Grants in December 30b). Sir George Carewe, king's servant, and Mary his wife, Polls Priory and manor, Devon. 1 February.
21. Portrait of Mary Wotton, the second wife of Sir Henry Guildford, comptroller of the royal household under King Henry VIII, 1527, after Holbein Metropolitan Museum of Art.

22. TNA C 1/961/3.
23. It is not known whether John Lympanye had any connection with the West Country family of the same name. A burial record exists for a John Lympanye 23 June 1557, St Margarets, Westminster – it is not known if this is the same man.

Chapter 8

1. L&P *Henry VIII,* January–July 1543,Vol. 18, Part I, 873.
2. Guy, J., *The Children of Henry VIII,* p.103.
3. Norton, E., *Catherine Parr,* p.74.
4. Guy, J., *The Children of Henry VIII,* p.10.
5. Norton, E., *Catherine Parr*, p.102.
6. James, S.E., *Catherine Parr: Henry VIII's Last Love,* p.122.
7. Mueller, J.M., *Katherine Parr: Complete Works and Correspondence,* p.369.
8. Guy, J., *The Children of Henry VIII,* p.101.
9. Simon, J., *Education and Society in Tudor England,* p.205.
10. Starkey, D., *Elizabeth, The Struggle for the Throne*, p.78.
11. Strype, J., *The Life of the Learned John Cheke, Kt.*, p.168.
12. L&P *Henry VIII*, Vol. 19, Part 1, January–July 1544, 780. They were to be served five courses and the voyde – a 'voyde' or 'void', was a course comprising sweetmeats and drinks, served after the main meal and before the guests departed.
13. Chronicle of Edward VI.
14. Tallis, N., *Young Elizabeth*, p.96.
15. McElroy, A., *Educating the Tudors,* pp.43-44.
    Guy, J., *The Children of Henry VIII*, p.99.
16. Vives, J.L., *The Education (or Instruction) of a Christian Woman.*
17. L&P *Henry VIII*, May 1543, 57.9.
18. L&P *Henry VIII,* Vol. 18, Part 2, 345, and 352.
19. Hooker, alias Vowell, J., *The Life and Times of Sir Peter Carew,* pp.24–25.
20. Parry, C.J., Britain, Knights of the Realm and Commonwealth Index, Anthony Denny, dubbed at Boulogne, 30 September 1544.
21. L&P *Henry VIII,* Vol. 19, Part 2, 502.
22. Ascham, R., *The Whole Works of Roger Ascham*, Vol. I, Part I, pp.85–87. Although undated, this letter is filed in the 1545 sequence by Giles. It must have been written after Kate Astley's marriage. Ascham commends himself to Lady Troy, suggesting she remained in some capacity in Elizabeth's household.
23. Richardson, R.E., *Mistress Blanche*, p.43. Lady Troy remained at least nominally in post until around 1547, and then received a pension until her death which was likely in 1557.
24. Tallis, N., *Young Elizabeth*, p.95.
25. Ascham, R., *Whole Works*, Vol. I, Part I, p.86. In 1545, Roger Ascham mentioned the favour Kate had shown to Grindal.
26. The original manuscript survives and is currently held in the Bodleian Library, Oxford, MS, Cherry 36.

Chapter 9

1. LPA MS 318 f.119. The Denny family tree shows Katherine, (died young); Henry; Anne; Mary; Douglas; Edward; Anthony. But does not include Charles. Garrett, C.H., *The Marian Exiles*. Garrett gives Charles as the third son. Some sources confuse Anthony Denny's brothers and sisters and their offspring, and include them as Anthony and Joan's children.
2. Norton, E., *Catherine Parr*, p.125.
3. Hooker, alias Vowell, J., *The Life and Times of Sir Peter Carew*, p.32.
4. *Hall's Chronicle*, p.863.
5. L&P *Henry VIII*, August–December 1545, Vol. 20, Part 2, 994. Peter was found in possession of controversial books and kept in custody of the Lord Privy Seal and the Chancellor. He was set at liberty on 13 December.
6. TNA C142/73/45; E 150/187/11 and WARD 7/2/17. Champernowne, C.E., *History of the Champernowne Family,* p.60. Transcription of IPM dated 4 November 1545, gives his date of death as 2 August 1545.
7. Calendar of Patent Rolls Philip and Mary, Vol. III, No. 511, p.499, 2 June 1557, 'Licence, for 33s. 4d., to Katherine Champernon, widow, late the wife of Philip Champernon, knight, and to Arthur Champernon, knight, to grant lands in Webbenton in Loddeswell, co. Devon, late of Studley priory …' The date of death of Sir Philip Champernowne's wife has not been confirmed.
8. TNA E 150/187/11.
9. Richardson R.E., *Mistress Blanche*, p.46.
10. Ascham, R., *The Whole Works of Roger Ascham*, Vol. I, Part I, pp.85–87. Although undated, this letter is filed in the 1545 sequence by Giles. It must have been written after Kate Astley's marriage. Ascham commends himself to Lady Troy, suggesting she remained in some capacity in Elizabeth's household.
11. Borman, *Elizabeth's Women,* p.65.
12. Richardson R.E., *Mistress Blanche*, p.46.
13. Cited in History of Parliament online for John Astley, without source reference.
14. Ascham, R., *The Whole Works of Roger Ascham,* Vol. I, Part I, p.77, 1545 to Princess Elizabeth.
15. Ascham, R., *The Whole Works of Roger Ascham*, Vol. I, Part I, pp.85–87.
16. Ryan, L.V., *Life of Roger Ascham*, p.104.
17. British Library, Royal MS 7D X.
18. Plowden, A., *The Young Elizabeth*, p.80.
19. Champernowne, C.E., *The Champernowne Family,* p.79.
20. L&P *Henry VIII,* Vol. 21, Part 1, 1181. Joan, Lady Denny, is mentioned at point 5. This account was printed by John Bale with a preface and running commentary 'at Marpurg in the land of Hessen, 16 die Januarii, anno 1547.' Bale states that he received it 'in copy by certain Dutch merchants coming from thence, which had been at their burning and beholden the tyrannous violence there showed.'
21. Norton, E., *Catherine Parr*, p.150.
22. L&P *Henry VIII,* Vol. 21, Part 2, 1235. A list of those given rewards 'towards their furnitures in their journey into France.'
23. L&P *Henry VIII*, Vol. 21, Part 2, 199, No. 28.

24. L&P *Henry VIII*, September 1546–January 1547, Vol. 21 Part 2, 555, depositions 4 and 5.
25. In 1538 and again in 1543, Mary's name had been linked with Thomas Seymour's but nothing came of the proposal that they marry.
26. Foxe, J., *Actes and Monuments*, Vol 7, p.387.
27. Starkey, D., *Elizabeth, The Struggle for the Throne*, p.59.
28. In January 1560, Elizabeth I appointed John Astley and Kat Astley keepers of Elsyng, with the adjacent manor of Worcesters, the New Park, and its game.
29. Norton, E., 'The Lost Elsyng Palace', *Tudor Places Magazine*, Issue 18, pp.12, 17.
30. He would later write a treatise on horsemanship, *The Art of Riding*.
31. Hayward, J., *The Life and Raigne of King Edward the Sixth,* p.4.
32. Edward VI, King of England, Chronicle, p.4.

Chapter 10

1. L&P Henry VIII, January–July 1543, Vol. 18, Part II, 473.
   Seymour's appointment as ambassador to the Habsburg court in Brussels in 1543 may have been designed to get him out of the way so that the king could marry Catherine Parr, who had fallen in love with Thomas.
2. Hall, E., *Hall's Chronicle*, p.858.
3. Hayward, J., *The Life and Raigne of King Edward the Sixth,* p.81.
4. Starkey, D., *Elizabeth, The Struggle for the Throne,* p.66.
5. Eriksen, C., *The First Elizabeth*, p.66.
6. Norton, E., *The Temptation of Elizabeth Tudor*, p.21.
7. Tallis, N, *Young Elizabeth,* p.122.
8. Norton, E., *The Temptation of Elizabeth Tudor*, p.39.
9. CSP Spain, Vol. 9, 1547-1549, 10 February 1547.
10. Sil, N.P., *Sir Anthony Denny,* p.7. Sir William Herbert's first wife was Anne Parr. He had served alongside Denny in King Henry's Privy chamber.
11. St Claire Byrne, M., Lisle Letters 3 January 1538, Vol. V, p.13.
12. Hooker, alias Vowell, J., *The Life and Times of Sir Peter Carew,* pp.44–46.
13. Dabby, B., *Loyal to the Crown; The Extraordinary Life of Sir Roger Cholmeley*, p.55. Cholmeley had risen under Cromwell, but survived his downfall. He was one of the senior judges who sat on the commission to consider the cases of the Earl of Surrey and his father. Following the Wyatt rebellion, he was chief prosecutor in the trial of Sir Nicholas Throckmorton and kept Kate in custody.
14. Norton, *The Temptation of Elizabeth Tudor,* p.40.
15. Ibid, citing 'Articles Against Thomas Seymour,' (Cobbett), which include his request to the council in January 1547.
16. Leti, G., *La Comediante Politica or La Vie d'Elizabeth Reine d'Angleterre*. The exchange of letters between Seymour and Elizabeth included in Leti's seventeenth-century biography cannot be found in any archive, and their authenticity is disputed. Leti also included a letter supposedly written by a 3-year-old Elizabeth to Jane Seymour which is clearly false. She could not possibly have written it at that age; it refers to Anthony and Joan Denny at Cheshunt before they were married or living there: the wording mirrors closely a later letter to Catherine Parr.

However, the Seymour letters do not seem out of character, and fit broadly with other events and descriptions of the time. A translation of Elizabeth's purported reply can be found in Green, M.M.E., *Letters of Royal and Illustrious Ladies of Great Britain,* pp.191–192.

17. This line of argument depends on the veracity of Leti's transcribed letters. If they are a fabrication we have to search for another explanation for Kate's words, which were later reported by Elizabeth in her 'confession' HHA, Cecil Papers, CP150/89. Elizabeth is careful not to specify the date on which Kate spoke those words.
18. Rose Troup, F.J., *The Western Rebellion*, p.105.
    Youings, J., *The South-Western Rebellion* of 1549.
19. In 1549, a pro-government author wrote a manuscript tract entitled 'An answer to the articles of the commoners of Devonshire and Cornwall', in response to the Prayer Book Rebellion Philip Nichols is thought to be the author, though it is also suggested Nicholas Udall may have been responsible. The month's mind is cited by Rose Troup in '*The Western Rebellion of 1549*', and by Whiting in '*The Blind Devotion of the People*'. Joyce Youings, in '*The South Western Rebellion of 1549*' says Nichols dedicated his response to Sir Peter Carew.
20. Tallis, N., *Young Elizabeth*, p.126, from Mueller, Katherine Parr.
21. Norton, E., *The Temptation of Elizabeth Tudor,* p.44, citing Catherine Parr's accounts. TNA E15/340, f.22v and TNA E101/424/12, f.80, which detail expenses at St James.
22. Norton, E., *The Temptation of Elizabeth Tudor*, p.44.
    HHA Cecil papers, CP 150/85, CP 1.66; the confession of Katherine Ashley.
23. *A History of the County of Middlesex*, Vol. 12, pp.14–26.
24. TNA SP 10/6, ff.16–17v; Sir Robert's handwriting is very difficult to decipher.
25. Richardson, R.E., *Mistress Blanche*, p.55. Richardson citing Tyrwhitt's letter of 31 January 1549.
26. Shanette, H., *Elizabeth I's Ladies, Gentlewomen and Maids,* p.30.
27. Norton, E., *The Temptation of Elizabeth Tudor*, p.95.
28. Merton, C.I., *The Women Who Served Queen Mary and Queen Elizabeth; Gentlewomen and Maids of the Privy Chamber 1553–1603*, p.85.
29. HHA Cecil Papers, CP 150/85.
    Transcription in Haynes, State Papers, p.99. Confession of Kateryn Aschyly.
30. Batley, R., *The Lord Protector and His Wives*, p.92.
31. Norton, E., *The Temptation of Elizabeth Tudor*, p.83.
32. HHA Cecil Papers, CP 150/79, CP 1.58; the confession of Thomas Parry.
    Transcription in Haynes, State Papers, pp.95–97.
33. Wood, M.A.E., *Letters of Royal and Illustrious Ladies of Great Britain,* pp.369–172.
34. HHA Cecil Papers, CP 150/85.
    Transcription in Haynes, State Papers, p.99. Confession of Kateryn Aschyly.
35. Haynes, State Papers, p.100.
36. Ibid, p.99.
37. Ibid.
38. Ibid.
39. Ibid.
40. Mumby, F.A., *The Girlhood of Queen Elizabeth.*

41. Neale, J.E., *Queen Elizabeth I*, p.29.
42. Haynes, State Papers, p.99.
43. Ibid.
44. Ascham, R., *The Whole Works of Roger Ascham*, Vol. I, Part II, p.158.
45. Muller, J.A., *The Letters of Stephen Gardiner,* p.396.
46. HHA Cecil Papers, CP 150/79, CP1/62. The Confessions of Thomas Parry.

Chapter 11

1. Fuller, E., *History of the University of Cambridge and of Waltham Abbey*, p.208.
2. Denny, H., *East Herts Archaeological Society Transactions*, Vol. 2, Part 3, 1904. Foxe, *Book of Martyrs*, second edition tells us that Katherine Raleigh kept vigil with Exeter Martyr Agnes Prest in August 1557. Agnes is a rare example of Protestant persecution in Devon during Queen Mary's reign. Joan died in 1553, so could not have joined Katherine Raleigh when she visited Agnes.
3. Ascham, R., *Whole Works, A Report on Germany*, pp.3–4, letter to John Astley 14 October 1552.
4. Clifford, H., *The Life of Jane Dormer, Duchess of Feria,* p.86.
5. Norton, E., *The Temptation of Elizabeth Tudor*, p.179, quoting Elizabeth Tyrwhitt's account of Catherine Parr's state of mind and behaviour, *Katherine Parr: Complete Works and Correspondence*, p.177.
6. Marcus, Mueller and Rose, *Elizabeth I, Collected Works*, No. 13.
7. Haynes, State Papers, p.99
8. Batley, R., *The Lord Protector and His Wives,* p.106.
9. Haynes, State Papers, p.64.
10. Haynes, State Papers, p.100. Confession of Kateryn Aschyly.
11. Haynes, State Papers, p.89. Letter from Tyrwhitt to the Protector, 28 January 1549.
12. Ibid. Confession of Katherine Astley, p.99.
13. Ibid, p.89. Letter from Tyrwhitt to Protector, 22 January 1549.
14. Ibid, p.80. Statement by the Marquess of Northampton.
15. LPA, George Carew Earl of Totnes, Collection of Genealogies, MS 318, ff,113–115. See also will of John Pollard, Clerk TNA PROB 11/43/234.
16. Marcus, Mueller and Rose, *Elizabeth I Collected Works*, additional document 24 February: 'The examination of Mistress Ashley' pp.26–27.
17. Marcus, Mueller and Rose, *Elizabeth I Collected Works*, p.27.
18. *Accounts of Princess Elizabeth 1551–1552*, Smythe, P.C.S. (Viscount Strangford) (ed.). This is likely the Elizabeth Slanning mentioned as receiving payment for fabric.
19. Jones, W., *The Slannings of Leye, Bickleigh and Maristow*, p.451.
20. He may be connected to the Eliot family of St Germans in Cornwall.
21. Norton, E., *The Temptation of Elizabeth Tudor*, p.213.
22. Champernowne, C.E., p.93, citing Halsted's *Kent.*
23. Haynes, State Papers, p.95. Confession of Thomas Parry.
24. Ibid.
25. Pollard, A.F., *Biography of William Sharington*, DNB, 1885–1900, Vol. 51.
26. Some accounts suggest that Seymour shot the dog.

Chapter 12

1. If they arrived early in the morning, it is unlikely they had ridden from London overnight.
2. Haynes, State Papers, pp.70–71. Letter from Sir Robert Tyrwhitt to Somerset, 22 January 1549.
3. Ibid.
4. Through her first husband, John Fortescue, Parry's wife was distantly connected to the Boleyns, which may have helped Thomas Parry secure his appointment.
5. Haynes, State Papers, p.70. Tyrwhitt's letter to Somerset 22 February 1549.
6. Von Klarwill, V., *Queen Elizabeth and Some Foreigners,* p.124.
7. Scard. M., *Tudor Survivor: The Life of Sir Anthony Paulet.*
8. Starkey, D., *Elizabeth, The Struggle for the Throne*, p.78.
9. Scard, M., *Tudor Survivor: The Life and Times of William Paulet*, p.130.
10. Haynes, State Papers, pp.63, 67 and 90–93.
11. Mack, P., *Elizabethan Rhetoric, Theory and Practice*, p.104.
12. Marcus, Mueller and Rose, *Elizabeth Collected Works*, additional document: 'The Examination of Kate Ashley', pp.26–27.
13. Norris, *Tudor Costume and Fashion*, p.262.
14. Arnold, J., *Queen Elizabeth's Wardrobe Unlock'd*, pp.7–8.
15. Erondell, P., Hollyband, C., *The Elizabethan Home*, p.38. Quoted by Arnold p.110.
16. Norris, *Tudor Costume and Fashion*, pp.261–262.
17. Mikhaila, M., and Malcolm-Davies, J., *The Tudor Tailor*, p.36.
18. Arnold, J., *Queen Elizabeth's Wardrobe Unlock'd*, 1988, p.361. Black lamb fur, known as budge, used to trim and line gowns of Tudor gentry and royalty.
19. Haynes, State Papers, pp.70–71. Letter from Sir Robert Tyrwhitt to Somerset, 22 January 1549.
20. Wheatley, H.B., *Cunningham, P., London Past and Present: Its History, Associations, and Traditions*, Vol. 3, p.79, (2011) [1891].
21. Marcus, Mueller and Rose, *Elizabeth I, Collected Works*, pp.25–31, additional statement of Katherine Ashley.
22. Haynes, State Papers, pp.99–101, confession of Katherine Ashley.
23. Ibid. p.102. Letter from Sir Robert Tyrwhitt to Somerset 7 February 1549.

Chapter 13

1. Ibid, p.102. The confession of the Lady Elizabeth.
2. Ibid, p.108. Tyrwhitt to Somerset.
3. Tallis, N., *Young Elizabeth*, p.167, citing B.L. Lansdowne MS 1238, f.30r-v.
4. Tallis, N., *Young Elizabeth,* p.167.
5. King Edward VI, King of England, Chronicle, pp.10–11.
6. Tallis, N., *Young Elizabeth*, p.162.
7. Peck, F., *New Memoirs of the Life and Poetical Works of Mr. John Milton,* including *The Legend of Sir Nicholas Throckmorton, and anonymous poem first published 1570/71,* pp.20-22, London, 1740.

8. Harrington, J., Nugae Antiquae, p.330.
9. Leti, G., *Historia overo vita di Elisabetta regina d'Inghliterra (History or Life of Elizabeth, Queen of England)*, cited by Tallis and Norton.
10. Haynes, State Papers, p.108. Robert Tyrwhitt to Somerset, 19 February 1549.
11. Holinshed, R., Chronicles, Vol. III, p.1025.
12. Hooker, alias Vowell, J., *The Antique Description and Account of the City of Exeter,* pp.41–42.
13. Wagner, J., *The Devon Gentleman: A Life of Sir Peter Carew*, p.116.
14. Rose Troup, F.J., *The Western Rebellion*, p.375.
15. Hooker, alias Vowell, J., *The Life and Times of Sir Peter Carew*, p.61.
    Strype, J., *Ecclesiastical Memorials Relating Chiefly to Religion, and the Reformation of It,* Vol. II, pp.173–174. First published Wyatt, London, 1721, Clarendon Press, Oxford, 1822.
16. Britain, Knights of the Realm and Commonwealth Index, accessed via Findmypast.
17. TNA PROB 11/32/514.
18. In 1549 Seymour began building Somerset Place, an opulent palace, on the site of the inns belonging to the Bishops of Chester and Worcester on the Strand, London.
19. Edward VI, Chronicle, p.107.
20. Batley, R., *The Lord Protector and His Wives*, p.156.
21. Robinson, H., original letters relative to the English Reformation, p.277, John Aylmer to Henry Bellinger, cited by Tallis.
22. Garrett, C.H., *The Marian Exiles*. Garrett suggests that Sir Philip Champernowne, who died in 1545, was 'one of the most ardent Protestants of the West'.
23. *Accounts of Princess Elizabeth 1551– 1552,* Smythe, P.C.S. (Viscount Strangford) (ed.) reprinted in the Camden Miscellany LV Camden Old Series, Vol. II, 1853.
24. Edward VI, Chronicle, p33.
25. TNA PROB 11/36/157.
    Joan's will mentions three daughters and four sons and includes many bequests of jewellery. Elizabeth Budockside (Butseyd, Bettiside) was Joan and Kate's niece. Her presence as witness suggests she was spending time with her aunt as part of her education.
26. Some sources suggest that Joan Denny joined her sister Katherine Raleigh in supporting Protestants undergoing persecution on Devon. No evidence supports this claim, and Joan died in 1553, before Queen Mary became queen, while Foxe's *Book of Martyrs* records Katherine Raleigh visiting the Protestant Martyr Agnes Prest in 1557.
27. CSPS, Vol. 11, p.40.
28. Ibid, Vol. 11, p.55.

Chapter 14

1. Marcus, Muller and Rose, *Collected Works,* p.38, letter from Elizabeth to King Edward expressing her distress at being unable to visit him, spring 1553.
2. CSPS, Vol. 11, p.94.
3. Hooker, J., alias Vowell, *The Life and Times of Sir Peter Carew,* p.54.
4. Tallis, N., *Young Elizabeth,* p.197.

5. Machyn, H., *The Diary of Henry Machyn,* p.38.
6. CSPS Vol. 11, p.152.
7. Machyn, H., *The Diary of Henry Machyn,* p.38.
8. Wagner, J., *The Devon Gentleman: A Life of Sir Peter Carew,* p.163.
9. Loades. D., *Two Tudor Conspiracies*, p.15, Citing Renard to emperor, 17 November 1553.
10. Harris Harbison, E., *Rival Ambassadors at the Court of Queen Mary*, pp.79–81.
11. Loades, D., *Two Tudor Conspiracies*, p.18.
12. Hooker, alias Vowell, J., *Life of Sir Peter Carew*, pp.19-21. In 1541 Peter and John had rescued a Spaniard who was being held captive by the Turks in Venice, and paid for new clothes for him. The Spaniard reneged on his promise to repay them.
13. Loades, D., *Two Tudor Conspiracies,* p.16.
14. Tallis, N., *Young Elizabeth,* p.213.
15. Guy, J., *The Children of Henry VIII*, p.155.
16. Loades, D., *Two Tudor Conspiracies*, p.27, citing Report of the Imperial Ambassadors, 29 January 1554, Cal/Span. Vol. XII, p.54. After Kate's death, John married Lord Thomas Grey's illegitimate daughter, Margaret Lenton.
17. CSPS, Vol.11, pp.411, 418, 440.
18. William Brooke was released, partly due to influential connections like William's brother-in-law, Henry Neville, 6th Baron Bergavenny. William's father, George Brooke, 9th Baron Cobham, also paid a substantial bond. Brooke's sister Elizabeth was the wife of William Parr, Marquess of Northampton, Queen Catherine's brother. Nicholas Throckmorton was Catherine Parr's cousin and served in her household from 1544–1548.
19. Loades, D., *Two Tudor Conspiracies*, p.24.
20. Guy, J., *The Children of Henry VIII*, p.155.
21. Wagner, J., *The Devon Gentleman: A Life of Sir Peter Carew,* pp.170-178.
22. Ibid, p.187.
23. Champernowne, C.E., *History of the Champernowne Family,* p.188, citing a letter dated 24 January, from John Ridgeway to Sir Thomas Dennys. See also, Wagner, pp.178 –185.
24. Wagner, J., *The Devon Gentleman: A Life of Sir Peter Carew*, p.183, citing Gawen Carew's deposition of 28 January 1554, TNA SP11/3/34-35.
25. Wagner, J., *The Devon Gentleman: A Life of Sir Peter Carew*, p.190, citing Calendar Spanish Papers, XII, p.55.
26. Loades, D., *Two Tudor Conspiracies*, p.26.
27. Astley Castle transferred from John Astley's ancestors to the Greys in 1420 when Sir William Astley's daughter, Joanna married Reginald Grey, 3rd Baron Grey de Ruthyn.
28. Phillips, W., *The Capture of Lord Thomas Grey at Oswestry, Transactions...*, pp.143–150.
29. Nichols, J.G., *Chronicle of the Grey Friars of London*, p.89.
30. Loades, D., *Two Tudor Conspiracies*, p.97.
31. Ibid, p.80.
32. TNA SP 11/4/2 f.3-3v - The Tide Letter.
33. Dasent, J.R., *Acts of the Privy Council,* Vol. V, p.129.

34. Tallis, N., *Young Elizabeth,* p.243.
35. Dabby, B., *Loyal to the Crown: The Extraordinary Life of Sir Roger Cholmeley*. In 1565 Sir Roger Cholmeley, founded a free school for the education of boys and young men in grammar. None of the original buildings survive, the school having been largely rebuilt in the nineteenth century.
36. Ibid, p.67.
37. Garrett, C.H., *The Marian Exiles: A Study in the Origins of Elizabethan Puritanism*, p.73.
38. Ibid. pp.143–144.
    Henry the eldest, studied in Padua, returning by 1562 when he was admitted to Middle Temple. Anthony was with John Astley in Padua, but returned to England by 1557, when he was admitted to Middle Temple. Charles was also with the others in Padua in 1554, but went on to study in Basle before attending Merton College, Oxford, by 1565. It likely John Astley's brother Thomas remained with the boys who stayed on the Continent. Thomas Astley was seen by Hobey in Frankfurt in 1555. Thomas would marry Mary Denny, Joan's daughter, in 1562, after the death of her first husband, Thomas Crawley.
39. Dasent, J.R., *Acts of the Privy Council*, Vol. V, p.5.
40. Ibid, Vol. V, p.142.
41. Ibid, p.75.
42. Starkey, D., *Elizabeth, The Struggle for The Throne*, p.148.
43. Neale, J.E., *Queen Elizabeth I,* p.46.
44. Starkey, D., *Elizabeth, The Struggle for The Throne*, p.155.
45. George Carew, 1st Earl of Totnes, whose papers are held at Lambeth Palace Library.
46. Fincham, K. and Tyacke, N., *Altars Restored*, p.75.
47. Foxe, J., *Actes and Monuments*, p.294.
48. Guy, J., *The Children of Henry VIII,* p.168.
49. Ryan, L.V., Roger Ascham, p.217.
50. Champernowne, C.E., *The Champernowne Family*, p.102, citing Hooker.
51. CSP Venice, Vol. VI, Part I, p.227.
52. Starkey, D., *Elizabeth, The Struggle for the Throne*, p.194.
53. Tallis, *Young Elizabeth*, p.290, citing the Verney Papers.
54. Dasent, J.R., *Acts of the Privy Council*, Vol. V, Appendix.
55. CSP Venice, Vol. VI, Part I, p.447.
56. Garrett, C.H., *The Marian Exiles*, pp.104–108.
57. CSP, Venice, Vol. VI, Part I, edited by Brown, 1877, p.452.
58. CSP D, Mary I, 1556, 54.
59. Calendar of State Papers, Mary I, Domestic Series 1556, 9 May, p.82.
60. Garrett, C.H., *The Marian Exiles: A Study in the Origins of Elizabethan Puritanism,1938*, p.13.
61. Plowden, A., Elizabeth, p.422, citing CSP Ven, Vol. VI, p.571.
62. CSP, Venice, Vol. VI, Part I, p.718.
63. Latham, A., and Youings, J., The Letters of Sir Walter Raleigh, Letter No. 152.
64. Foxe, J., *Actes and Monuments*, pp.242–44.
65. PROB 11/43/234. Archdeacon John Pollard was the second husband of Kate's sister Elizabeth.
66. Shanette, H., *Elizabeth I's Ladies, Gentlewomen and Maids,* p.12.

Chapter 15

1. Starkey, D., *Elizabeth, The Struggle for the Throne*, p.236.
2. Guy, J., *The Children of Henry VIII*, p.177.
3. Folgerpedia, The Elizabethan Court Day by Day, 18 November 1558.
4. Strype, J., *The Life and Acts of Matthew Parker.* Elizabeth's Archbishop of Canterbury, Matthew Parker was a happily married man and spoke up in favour of married clergy. The right of ministers to marry was reaffirmed in the Articles of Religion in 1563 and 1571.
5. CSP Venice, 1558-1580, p.3. 'The deanery of the late Queen's Chapel, which was held by Monsignor Hutchenson, is given to a priest by name Carey, Doctor in Divinity, late chaplain of her Majesty when she was Lady Elizabeth'.
6. Merton, C., 'The women who served Queen Mary and Queen Elizabeth', p.5.
7. Shanette, H., *Elizabeth's Ladies, Gentlewomen and Maids* gives more details.
8. Mears, M., *Politics in the Elizabethan Privy Chamber: Lady Mary Sidney and Kat Ashley,* cites Wright, P., *A Change in Direction: The Ramifications of a Female Household,* 1558-1603.
9. Merton, C., *The women who served Queen Mary and Queen Elizabeth,* p.6. Mears, M., *Politics in the Elizabethan Privy Chamber: Lady Mary Sidney and Kat Ashley,* pp.67–82.
10. Wagner, J., *The Devon Gentleman: A Life of Sir Peter Carew,* p.219, citing CSP Elizabeth I, pp.16–21.
11. Folger, 1558, p.8.
12. Ibid, 1558, p.14, see also Bowers, R., The Chapel Royal, the First Edwardian Prayer Book, and Elizabeth's Settlement of Religion, The Historical Journal, Volume 43, No.2 (June 2000), pp.317-346.
13. Partlet – a sleeveless garment covering the neck and shoulders, worn by both men and women to fill in low necklines or for added warmth and modesty. Pair of ruffs – intricately folded detachable cuffs, resembling neck ruffs.
14. Lawson, J.A., *The New Year's Gift Exchanges,* 1559–1603.
15. It is unlikely that this was a portrait of Frances together with the queen. Rather, Frances took charge of the gift. The original is lost. Levina Teerlinc (*c.*1510s–1576) was a Flemish Renaissance painter and miniaturist who served as a highly esteemed court painter to four Tudor monarchs: Henry VIII, Edward VI, Mary I, and Elizabeth I.
16. Machyn, T.H., *The Diary of Henry Machyn, Citizen and Merchant-Taylor of London, From A.D. 1550 to A.D. 1563*, p.187.
17. Guy, J., *The Children of Henry VIII,* p.179. See also Fincham, K. and Tyacke, N., Altars restored, and Venables, E., *DNB*, Vol. 42, Owen Oglethorpe. Oglethorpe refused to swear the required Oath of Supremacy and was deprived of his see on 26 June 1559. He died on 31 December 1559.
18. Bowers, R., The Chapel Royal, the First Edwardian Prayer book, and Elizabeth's Settlement of Religion, The Historical Journal, Vol. 43, No.2 (June 2000), pp.317-346.
19. Folger, p.16, citing Tilt and Tourney lists: College of Arms Portfolio.
20. CSP Venice, Vol. 7, 1558–1580, 10.

21. Wagner, J., *The Devon Gentleman: A Life of Sir Peter Carew*, p.244.
22. Somerset, A., *Elizabeth*, p.116.
23. Folger, 1560, p.5.
24. CSP Sim, 1558-1567, p.57.
25. Folger, 1559, p.41.
26. Ibid.
27. Mears, M., *Politics in the Elizabethan Privy Chamber: Lady Mary Sidney and Kat Ashley,* in Daybell, p.69.
    See also Von Klarwill, V., *Queen Elizabeth and Some Foreigners,* p.152. Lady Sidney was 'pusillanimous'.
28. CSP Sim, 1558-1567, p.80, 25 June 1559.
29. Folger, citing Francis Thynne's description of the visit as recorded in Hollinshed Chronicles, 2nd edn, 1587.
30. Von Klarwill, V., *Queen Elizabeth and Some Foreigners,* pp.113–115.
31. Ibid.
32. Neale, J.E., *Queen Elizabeth I,* p.82.
33. Folger, 1559 p.79.
34. Von Klarwill, V., *Queen Elizabeth and Some Foreigners,* p.157.
35. Ibid, p.124.
36. TNA SP.70/22 No. 561.
37. Folger, 1560, p.6. An anonymous account of the marriage celebrations.
38. The figure in red in the foreground may be Mary Dudley, her red dress to show she has survived smallpox; wrapping in red blankets being one of the 'cures' used. If so, that would date the picture after 1562, when Mary suffered and was disfigured by the disease.
39. Wilson, V., *Queen Elizabeth's Maids of Honour and Ladies of the Privy Chamber,* p.52.
40. Ibid. p.21.
41. Folger, 1560, p.68, citing Camden Soc, Misc. 27 (1979), 184.

Chapter 16

1. TNA SP 70/11 f.74.
2. Folger, 1560, p.50. 'In 1561 Dymock went to the new King of Sweden, Eric XIV. He made a statement (6 August 1562), of the events leading up to and during his visit to Sweden.'
3. Ibid, 1561, p.3.
4. CSP Sim, 1558-1567, p.180, 22 January 1561.
5. LHA DU/Vol. I. Correspondence of Lord Robert Dudley, letter 44.
   Transcribed by Jackson, C.E. in *Wiltshire Archaeological and Natural History Magazine*, Vol. Xvii, p.22. The letter is undated. A later secretary erroneously annotated it as 1559.
6. LHA DU/Vol. I. Correspondence of Lord Robert Dudley, letter 44.
   Transcribed by Jackson, C.E. in *Wiltshire Archaeological and Natural History Magazine*, Vol. Xviii p.21. The letter is undated, but the content fits the timeline of John's dismissal from court.

7. No documentary evidence exists for this quote, but it was recorded by Sir Robert Naunton in his work Fragmenta Regalia, published posthumously in 1641.
8. TNA PROB 11/43/234.
9. Folger, 1561, p.16.
10. Katherine Willoughby, Duchess of Suffolk, widow of Charles Brandon, took as her second husband Richard Bertie, who had served as her Master of the Horse (she had done exactly what Elizabeth would have liked to do). The Berties were among the Marian exiles, but returned after Queen Mary's death, and lived at Katherine's Lincolnshire estate and at court.
11. Ascham, R., *The Whole Works of Roger Ascham*, Vol. II,II, p.59.
12. Mears, M., *Politics in the Elizabethan Privy Chamber: Lady Mary Sidney and Kat Ashley,* in Daybell, p.71.
13. Folger, 1562, p.26.
14. Mears, M., *Politics in the Elizabethan Privy Chamber: Lady Mary Sidney and Kat Ashley,* p.71.
15. CSPR Vol. 1, 1558-1571,190, (Newsletter, 26 September, 1562, Louvain.)
16. Folger, 1561, p.39.

Chapter 17

1. Mathews L.G., *The Royal Apothecaries,* Chapter 4, 'The Tudor Period', p.72.
2. Rather oddly Mathews quotes 'oxicrocin' plaster – presumably this is not a misspelling of 'oxytocin', a hormone which induces contractions during childbirth – those properties were unknown until 1906.
3. Folger, 1564, pp.28–36.
4. Ibid, 1564, p.41.
5. TNA E351/2791; Privy Purse, J. Tameworthe, Keeper of the Privy Purse.
6. Lawson, J.A., the Elizabethan New Year's Gift Exchanges 1559–1603.
7. Folger, *The Elizabethan Court Day by Day.*
8. Whitelock, A., *Elizabeth's Bedfellows*, p.100.
9. Ibid, p.16. In May these tensions at court boiled over and Elizabeth 'had a hysterical outburst'.
10. Folger, 1565, p.28.
11. Ibid, p.29.
12. Whitlock, A., *The Queen's Bedfellows*, p.101.
13. Folger, 1565, p.30.
14. Ibid, p.29.
15. Westminster Archives, Westminster, London, England, Church of England Baptisms, Marriages and Baptisms, 1558–1812, St Mary le Strand.
16. Clay, R.M., *The Medieval Hospitals of England*, Methuen and Co., London, 1901, p.12.
17. Richardson, R.E., *Mistress Blanche*, p.133.
18. Loftie, Rev. W.J., *Memorials of the Savoy*, p.131. George Carew's son, George, Earl of Totnes rented a house at the Savoy. He died there in 1629.
19. Loftie, Rev. W.J., *Memorials of the Savoy,* p.222.
20. Strype, J., *Survey of London.*

Chapter 18

1. Folger, *The Elizabethan Court Day by Day,* 24 July 1565.
2. Champernowne, C.E., p.110. Citing a letter from Fitzwilliam to Cecil. Hobey's secretary, Hugh Fitzwilliam, was agent in France until January 1567, when a new ambassador arrived.
3. Merton, C., ODNB, John Astley, *c.*1507–1596, courtier.
4. Folger, *The Elizabethan Court Day by Day,* 1568, p.2.
   John's eldest son, Sir John Astley (1565–1639) became a Gentleman Pensioner, and was Master of the Revels to James I and Charles I. This role involved overseeing royal festivities, the supervision of all kinds of public entertainment, as well as the reading and licensing of plays. Astley was the only Master of the Revels who participated as a performer. He danced as a costumed masquer in Hymenael in January 1606, and Lord Hay's masque in January 1607. He was knighted in 1603 and in 1609 he married Katherine Brydges, daughter of Anthony Brydges of Sudeley Castle.
5. Cooper, T., DNB, *John Astley, Master of the Jewel House*.
6. Griggs, R., *The Dartington Bride* and *Mistress of Dartington Hall*, Troubador Publishing, 2023 and 2024. Two novels in the 'Daughters of Devon' series.
7. Griggs, R., *A Woman of Noble Wit,* Troubador Publishing, 2021, a 'Daughters of Devon' novel.
8. Folger, *The Elizabethan Court Day by Day*, 1566, p.36.
9. Sir Gawen's second wife Mary had died on 17 September 1558.
10. Shanette, H., *Elizabeth's Ladies Gentlewomen and Maids*, citing Howey, C.L., *Busy Bodies: Women, Power and Politics at the Court of Queen Elizabeth 1, 1558-1603,* PhD Thesis, State University of New Jersey, 2007, p.99.
11. Hooker alias Vowel, *The Life and Times of Sir Peter Carew.*
12. Shanette, H., *Elizabeth I's Ladies, Gentlewomen and Maids*, p.126.
13. The *New Year's Gift Exchanges 1565*, Frances received two gilt salt cellars, weighing more than the gilt pots Kate received.
14. William Brooke, 10th Lord Cobham, and his family, by the Master of the Countess of Warwick, showing Frances with her husband, six children, and her sister, 1567.

Conclusion

1. Ascham, R., *The Whole Works of Roger Ascham*, Vol. I, Part I, pp.85–87.
2. Haynes, State Papers, pp.88-89 and 102.
3. CSPR Vol. 1, 1558-1571,190, (Newsletter, 26 September, 1562, Louvain.)

Appendix

1. TNA SP10/6, ff.16-17v.
2. Richardson, R.E., *Mistress Blanche*, p.55.
   Shanette, H., *Elizabeth I's Ladies, Gentlewomen and Maids,* p.30.
   Norton. E., *The Temptation of Elizabeth Tudor*, p.95.
3. His spelling is also very variable; he refers to Kate as both Kayt and Cayt, and as Aschley, Asclhlay, Aschalay.
4. Whitelock, A., *Elizabeth's Bedfellows,* p.7.
5. Haynes, State Papers, p.99.

Select Bibliography

I have consulted a wide range of primary and secondary sources in preparing this book. Many are listed below.

In addition I have read numerous works of historical fiction that highlight Elizabeth's relationship with Katherine Astley, and viewed many on screen portrayals – too many to include here.

Online Resources

Britain, Knights of the Realm and Commonwealth Index, compiled Parry, C.J., from Shaw's *The Knights of England* (1906) and Metcalfe's *Book of Knights* (1885), accessed online https://www.findmypast.co.uk

British History Online: https://www.british-history.ac.uk/

Colthorpe. M.E., 'The Elizabethan Court Day by Day': https://folgerpedia.folger.edu/

JSTOR – a digital library of academic journals, books, and primary sources.

National Archives currency converter: https://www.nationalarchives.gov.uk/currency-converter/

Online Etymological Dictionary: https://www.etymonline.com/

Primary Sources

(More specific references are included in the notes on the text.)

Allegations for marriage licences issued by the Bishop of London, 1520 to [1828], Chester, J.L. Lambeth Palace Archives

Carew Manuscripts, Lambeth Palace Archives

Cecil Papers, Hatfield House Archives

Kressen Kernow (Cornwall Record Office), North East Cornwall records

The National Archives

C: Early Chancery Proceedings, including Inquisitions Post Mortem, Series II, and other Inquisitions, Henry VII to Charles I

DU: Dudley Papers, Correspondence of Robert Dudley (at Longleat House Archive)

E: Records of the Exchequer, and its related bodies, with those of the Office of First Fruits and Tenths, and the Court of Augmentations

PROB: Will and administrations in the Prerogative Court of Canterbury

SP1: State Papers Henry VIII

SP10: State Papers Edward VI

STAC 2 : Star Chamber Proceedings Henry VIII
WARD: Records of the Court of Wards and Liveries
South West Heritage Trust: Devon Archives and Local Studies, Champernowne papers and other documents

Printed Primary Sources

Acts of the Privy Council in England, J.R. Dasent (ed.), 1892
Calendar of Patent Rolls Philip and Mary, Vol. III, 1555–1557, HMSO, (London, 1938)
Calendar of State Papers Domestic: Edward VI, Mary and Elizabeth, 1547–1580, (ed.) Robert Lemon (London, 1856)
Calendar of State Papers Foreign: Elizabeth, Vols. 1-7, 1558–1565, (ed.) Joseph Stevenson, (London, 1863)
Calendar of State Papers, Spain (Simancas), Vol. 1, 1558-1567, (ed.) Martin A.S. Hume (London, 1892)
Calendar Sate Papers, Spain. Papers relating to British diplomacy held in Spanish archives, 1485–1558, (ed.) Royall Tyler (London, 1949)
Calendar of State Papers Relating to English Affairs in the Vatican Archives, 1558–1571, J.M. Rigg (ed.) (London, 1916)
Calendar of State Papers, Venice. Papers relating to British diplomacy held in the archives of Venice, 1202–1675, (ed.) Rawdon Brown, G. Cavendish Bentinck (London, 1873)
Letters and Papers, Foreign and Domestic, Henry VIII, letters and state papers, relating to both foreign and domestic business, from the reign of Henry VIII (1509–1547), J.S. Brewer (ed.) (London, 1920)
The New Year's Gift Exchanges 1559–1603, Lawson, J.A., (ed.) Oxford University Press, 2013

Other Primary Sources

Alumni Oxonienses, members of the University of Oxford from 1500 to 1714, Foster, J., (ed.) 1891
Accounts of Princess Elizabeth 1551–1552, Smythe, P.C.S., (Viscount Strangford) (ed.) reprinted in the Camden Miscellany LV Camden Old Series, Vol. II, 1853
Anonymous, *The Receyt of the Ladie Katerine,* Kipling, G., (ed.) Early Oxford University Press, for the English Text Society, 1990
Ascham, R., *The Scholemaster,* first published 1570, Good Books, [Kindle edn], 2020
The Whole Works of Roger Ascham, Giles, J.A., (ed.) John Russell Smith, 1865
Chronicle of the Grey Friars of London, Nichols, J.G. (ed.) Camden Society, 1852
Edward VI, King of England: The Chronicle of King Edward VI, Jordan (ed.) Cornell University Press, for Folger Shakespeare Library, 1966
Erondell, P. and Hollyband, C., *The Elizabethan Home*, Conversation manuals of two Frenchman who taught language in London in the late sixteenth century, (ed.) St Claire Byrne, M., Methuen, 1949
Foxe, J., *Actes and Monuments of these Latter and Perilous Days, Touching Matters of the Church*, (also known as Foxe's *Book of Martyrs*), 2nd edn, 1570

Gardiner, S., *The Letters of Stephen Gardiner,* Muller, J.A. (ed.) Cambridge University Press, 2013, p.396

Haynes, A., *A Collection of State Papers: From the Year 1542 to 1570*, first published 1740, [Paperback edn], Legare Steet Press, 2023

Holinshead, R., et al, *Chronicles of England, Scotland and Wales,* first published 1587, Johnson, 1807

Hooker, alias Vowell, J., *The Life and Times of Sir Peter Carew, Knight* McClean J., (ed.) (*c*.1527–1601) J. Bell & Daldy, 1857

The Antique Description and Account of the City of Exeter: In Three Parts, first published 1575, published in full by Andrew Brice, Exeter in 1765. Reprinted edn, Gale Ecco Print, 2010

Leland, J., *The Itinerary of John Leland in or About the Years 1535–1543*, (ed.) Smith, L.T., 1838

Leti, G., *La Comediante Politica or La Vie d'Elizabeth Reine d'Angleterre,* Wolfgang, Amsterdam, 1693

Loke, W., *Account of Materials Furnished for the Use of Anne Boleyn and Princess Elizabeth 1535–36.* Edited by Heath, J.B., Philobiblon Society, 1862

Madden, *The Privy Purse Expenses of the Princess Mary,* Pickering, p.831

Machyn, H., *The Diary of Henry Machyn, Citizen and Merchant-Taylor of London, From A.D. 1550 to A.D. 1563*, Nichols, for Camden Society, 1848

Marcus, Mueller and Rose, *Elizabeth Collected Works*, University of Chicago, [Paperback edn], 2000

Metcalfe, W.C., *Compilation of the Heralds' Visitations of the County of Hertfordshire 1572 and 1634, With Additional Hertfordshire Pedigrees From the Harleian Manuscripts*, Harleian Society, 1886

Parker M., *Correspondence of Matthew Parker*, Bruce, J., (ed.) Cambridge University Press, 1853

Pole, William, *Collections Towards a Description of the County of Devon,* first published in 1791

Privy purse expenses of Elizabeth of York: wardrobe accounts of Edward the Fourth, (ed.) Harris, N., Pickering, 1830

Raleigh, W., *The Letters of Sir Walter Raleigh,* Latham, A., and Youings, J., Exeter University Press, 1999

Regia Insignia, *An Account of the King's Honourable Band of Gentlemen pensioners,* Thistleton, W.M. (ed.) Sherwood, 1819

Risdon, T., *A Chorographical Description or Survey of the County of Devon,* (completed *c.*1632), published Rees and Curtis, Plymouth, 1811

St Claire Byrne, M., *Lisle Letters,* University of Chicago Press, 1983

Siddons. M.P., *Visitations by the Heralds in Wales,* New Series, Vol. 14, 297, Harleian Society, 1996

Strype, J., *Ecclesiastical Memorials Relating Chiefly to Religion, and the Reformation of It,* first published Wyat, London, 1721, Clarendon Press, Oxford, 1822

Turpyn, *The Chronicle of Calais* from MS in British Museum, Nichols and son for the Camden Society, 1846

Vivian, Lieutenant Colonell J.L., *The Visitations of the County of Devon, Comprising The Heralds' Visitations of 1531, 1564 & 1620,* compiled and published, Eland, Exeter, 1895

Wotton, *The English Baronetage*, Vol. 3, Woodfall, 1771
Vives, J.L., *The Education (or Instruction) of a Christian Woman,* first published 1539, University of Chicago Press, 2000
Von Klarwill, V., *Queen Elizabeth and Some Foreigners: Being a Series of Hitherto Unpublished Letters From the Archives of the Hapsburg Family.* (Translation by T.H. Nash, Bodley Head, 1928)
Wriothesley, C., *A Chronicle of England During the Age of the Tudors, 1489–1559,* edited by Hamilton W.D., Camden Society, 1874

Secondary Sources

Articles

Bowers, R., 'The Chapel Royal, the First Edwardian Prayer book', and 'Elizabeth's Settlement of Religion', *The Historical Journal*, Vol. 43, No. 2 (June 2000), pp.317–346
Creighton, C., *A History of Epidemics in Britain,* Cambridge University Press, 1891
Cutting, B.M., *She Will Not Be a Mother,* Brief Chronicles, (An annual peer reviewed journal published by Shakespeare Fellowship from 2009–2016), Vol III, 2011
Denny, H., *Biography of the Rt Honourable Sir Anthony Denny,* East Herts Archaeological Society Transactions, Vol. 2, Part 3, 1904
Harrington, J., Nugae Antiquae, a miscellaneous collection of original papers, in prose and verse; written during the reigns of Henry VIII. Edward VI. Queen Mary, Elizabeth, and King James, found amongst the papers of Henry Harrington, London, 1804
Hooker, H., 'A Host of Holborne'. Blog post in Music recommendations by Helen Hooker, recorder player, conductor and educator on 14 March 2024, at https://www.helenhooker.co.uk/blog/2023/3/14/a-host-of-holborne
Jackson, C.E., 'Longleat Papers, 3, Transcription of the letters of Robert Dudley', published in the *Wiltshire Archaeological and Natural History Magazine*, Vol. XVIII, 1878
Jones, W., *The Slannings of Leye, Bickleigh and Maristow*, transactions of the Devonshire Association 1887, Vol. XIX
Mears, N., 'Politics in the Elizabethan Privy Chamber, Lady Mary Sidney and Kat Ashley', in Daybell, J., *Women and Politics in Early Modern England*, Ashgate, 2004
Norton, E., 'The Lost Elsyng Palace', *Tudor Places Magazine*, Issue 18, 2025
Page, W., *Some Notes on Hatfield*, St Albans and Hertfordshire Architectural and Archaeological Society Transitions, Vol1, Part IV, 1901–1902
Peck, F., *New Memoirs of the Life and Poetical Works of Mr. John Milton,* including *The Legend of Sir Nicholas Throckmorton, and anonymous poem first published 1570/71,* London, 1740
Phillips, W., *The Capture of Lord Thomas Grey at Oswestry,* transactions of the Shropshire Archaeological and Natural History Society, Series 3, Vol. 2
Radford, G.H., *Tavistock Abbey,* report and transactions of the Devonshire Association Vol. 46, 1914
Richardson, R.E., 'Lady Troy and Blanche Parry: New Evidence about their Lives at the Tudor Court', *Bulletin of the Society for Renaissance Studies*, October 2009
Sil, N.P., Sir Anthony Denny 'A Tudor Servant in Office', Journal article, *Renaissance and Reformation*, Vol. 20, No. 3, Iter Press, 1984.

Speight, H.M., 'The Politics of Good Governance: Thomas Cromwell and the Government of the Southwest of England', *The Historical Journal*, Vol. 37, No. 3, September 1994, Cambridge University Press

Swenson, P.C., 'Patronage from the Privy Chamber: Sir Anthony Denny and Religious Reform', *Journal of British Studies*, Vol. 27, No. 1, January 1998, pp.25-44, Cambridge University Press

Weir, A., 'Ladies in Waiting', *H for History*, Article, Hodder & Stoughton, for Headline, Little, Brown Book Group and Quercus

Westcott, M.R., 'Katherine Courtenay Countess of Devon', in *Tudor and Stuart Devon: The Common Estate and Government*, Gray, Rowe (ed.) Erskine, Exeter University Press, 1992

Youings, J., 'The South West Rebellion of 1549', *Southern History*, Vol. 1, 1979, pp.99-122

Theses

Hamill, K.A., 'Her mind has no womanly weakness: The Humanist Studies of Princess Elizabeth, 1538-1558', unpublished PhD Thesis, University of Calgary, Alberta, 2017

Maltby, K.E., 'Queen and Scholar: Elizabeth Tudor and Wisdom Imagery', University College London, 2021

Merton, C.I., 'The Women who served Queen Mary and Queen Elizabeth; Gentlewomen and Maids of the Privy Chamber 1553–1603', unpublished PhD Thesis, University of Cambridge, 1991

Other Unpublished Works

Champernowne, C.E., *The Champernowne Family,* unpublished typewritten manuscript, [SWHT 2522Z/1], 1954

Tapley-Soper, H., A collection of typescript abstracts of thirteenth to seventeenth century Inquisitions Post Mortem and wills, prepared in the twentieth century by the City Librarian of Exeter. (Held at SWHT – the original Inquisitions Post Mortem are held at The National Archives)

Williams, J.R., *Summary of the Champernowne Family Records,* unpublished typed manuscript, [SWHT 65/16/1/2a-b], 1914

TV

BBC TV, *Blackadder* – a series of four period comedies which first aired on BBC 1 between 1983 and 1989.

BBC TV, *Yes Minister* – a British political satire written by Anthony Jay and Jonathan Lyn. The series ran from 1986 to 1988. The sequel, *Yes, Prime Minister*, continued with the same cast.

Secondary Sources

Arnold, J., *Queen Elizabeth's Wardrobe Unlock'd,* first published Manuye 1988, Routledge, [Paperback edn], 2018

Ashdown, D.M., *Ladies in Waiting*, Arthur Barker, 1976

Banting, D.R., *An Introduction to the Life and Times of Sir George Carew, Vice Admiral of the Mary Rose,* Gadds, [for Mary Rose Trading Company], 2007

Baring-Gould, Rev. S., *A Book of the West; Being an Introduction to Devon and Cornwall*, Methuen & Co., 1899

Batley, R., *The Lord Protector and His Wives,* Pen and Sword Books, 2025

Bohun, Edmund, *The Character of Queen Elizabeth,* EEB, published 1693

Borman, T., *Anne Boleyn and Elizabeth I,* Hodder and Stoughton, [Kindle edn], 2023

Borman, T., *Elizabeth's Women,* Vintage, 2019

Borman, T., *The Private Lives of the Tudors*, Hodder and Stoughton, [Kindle edn], 2016

Bowle, J.E., *Henry VIII,* Little Brown, 1964

Brewer, J.N., *A Topographical and Historical Description of the County of Oxford*, London, 1819

Bryson, S., *The Brandon Men in the Shadow of Kings,* Amberley, 2021

Carew, R., *The Survey of Cornwall,* first published 1603, Halliday, Adams and Dart, (eds.) 1969

Clay, R.M., *The Medieval Hospitals of England,* Methuen and Co., 1901

Clifford, H., *The Life of Jane Dormer, Duchess of Feria,* first published 1610, reprinted London, Burns and Oates, 1887

Collinson, P., *Elizabeth I (Very Interesting People),* Oxford University Press, [Kindle edn], 2007

Cooper, J.P.D., 'Henry Courtenay. Marquess of Exeter', ODNB, 2008

Cooper, J.P.D., *Propaganda and the Tudor State,* Clarenden Press, 2003

Cooper, T., DNB, *John Astley, Master of the Jewel House,* 1904

Croot, P.E.C., *A History of the County of Middlesex: Volume 12,* Chelsea, (ed.) London, 2004

Cusack, B., *Everyday English, 1500–1700,* Edinburgh University Press, 1998

Dabby, B., *Loyal to the Crown: The Extraordinary Life of Sir Roger Cholmeley,* Sir Roger Cholmeley's School, Highgate, 2015

Emerson, K.L., *A Who's Who of Tudor Women,* independently published, [Kindle edn]

Duffy, E., *The Voices of Morebath - Reformation and rebellion in an English Village,* Yale University Press, 2003

Eales, J., *Women in Early Modern England, 1500–1700*, UCL Press, 1998

Eriksen, C., *The First Elizabeth,* Summit Books, New York, 1983

Everett, M., *The Rise of Thomas Cromwell*, Yale University Press, paperback edn, 2016

Fincham, K., and Tyacke, N., *Altars Restored, The Changing Face of English Religious Worship, 1547–c.1700*, Oxford University Press, 2008

Froude, *A History of England, From the Fall of Wolsey to the Death of Elizabeth,* Vol. VI, Parker, 1860.

Fuller, E., *History of the University of Cambridge and of Waltham Abbey*, University of Cambridge, 1840

Garrett, C.H., *The Marian Exiles,* Cambridge University Press, 1938

Green, M.M.E., *Letters of Royal and Illustrious Ladies of Great Britain, From the Commencement of the Twelfth Century to the Close of the Reign of Queen Mary,* Colburn, 1846

Guy, J., *Children of Henry VIII,* Oxford University Press, 2013

Halsted, E., *The History and Topographical Survey of the County of Kent,* first published 1797, reprinted Canterbury 1817

Hamil, K.A., 'The Humanist Studies of Princess Elizabeth, 1538–1558', MA Thesis, University of Alberta, 1917

Harris Harbison, E., *Rival Ambassadors at the Court of Queen Mary*, Princeton University Press, 1940

Harris, B.J., *English Aristocratic Women, 1450–1550*, Oxford University Press, 2002

Hayward, J., *The Life and Raigne of King Edward the Sixth,* Partridge, 1630

Hodder, S.J., *The York Princesses,* Chronos, 2021

Hoskins, W.G., *Devon,* Phillimore, first published 1954, reprinted 2011

Howell, Bea., *A Galaxy of Governesses,* Verschoyle Ltd., 1954

Hutchinson, R., *The Last Days of Henry VIII*, Weidenfield and Nicolson, [Kindle edn], 2011

James, S.E,. *Catherine Parr: Henry VIII's Last Love,* The History Press, 2008

Jenkins, E., *Elizabeth the Great*, first published Gollancz, 1958, paperback edn, Orion, 2001

Jordan, W.K., *Edward VI: The Young King,* Allen & Unwin,1968

Jones, P., *Elizabeth, Virgin Queen,* New Holland, 2010

Knox-Lawton, J. and Lee, S., *Dictionary of National Biography, 1885–1900*, Vol. 47. Sir Walter Raleigh

Loades, D., *Elizabeth: The Golden Reign of Gloriana,* The National Archives, 2003

Loades, D., *Intrigue and Treason the Tudor Court 1547–1558*, Pearson Longman, 2004

Loades, D., *Two Tudor Conspiracies,* first published Cambridge University Press, 1965

Lobe, M.D., *A History of the County of Oxford: Volume 8, Lewknor and Pyrton Hundreds; 'Parishes: Aston Rowant'*, London, 1964

Loftie, Rev. W.J., *Memorials of the Savoy*, Macmillan, 1878

McElroy, A., *Educating the Tudors,* Pen and Sword Books, 2023

McElroy, A., *Mary Tudor Queen of France,* Pen and Sword Books, 2025

Mack, P., *Elizabethan Rhetoric, Theory and Practice*, Cambridge University Press, 2002

McIntosh, J.L., *From Heads of Household to Heads of State,* Columbia University Press, 2008

Mackay, L., *Inside the Tudor Court,* Amberley, [Kindle edn]

Macleane, D., *A History of Pembroke College Oxford, Anciently Broadgates Hall*, Clarendon Press, 1897

Martienssen, A., *Queen Katherine Parr,* Sapere, 1973

Mathews L.G., *The Royal Apothecaries,* Welcome, 1967

Merton, C.I., *Katherine Champernowne/Ashley,* ODNB, 2004

Merton, C.I., *John Astley,* ODNB, 2004

Mikhaila, M., and Malcolm-Davies, J., *The Tudor Tailor,* Batsford, 2006

Miller, H., *Henry VIII and the English Nobility*, Blackwell, 1986

Mueller, J.M., *Katherine Parr: Complete Works and Correspondence,* Chicago University Press, 2011

Mumby, F.A., *The Girlhood of Queen Elizabeth* Constable, 1909

Neale, J.E., *Elizabeth I,* Chaucer Press, 1967

Neame, A., *The Holy Maid of Kent,* Hodder and Stoughton, 1971

Norris, H., *Tudor Costume and Fashion,* first published 1938, Dover edn, New York, 1997

Norton, E., *Catherine Parr,* Amberley, 2010

Norton, E., *Jane Seymour, Henry VIII's True Love,* Amberley, 2009

Norton, E., *The Temptation of Elizabeth Tudor*, Head of Zeus, 2015

Oliver, G., *Ecclesiastical Antiquities of Devon,* Harvard University, 1828

Perry, M., *The Word of a Prince, Life of Elizabeth I*, Boydell Press, 1990

Pierce, H., *Edward I's Fatal Legacy,* Pen and Sword Books, 2025

Plowden, A., *Elizabeth I,* Sutton, 2004

Plowden, A., *The Young Elizabeth,* The History Press, 2013

Prince, *Danmonii orientales illustres: or, The Worthies of Devon,* first published 1701, Rees & Curtis, 1810

Quinn, D.B., *The Voyages and Colonising Enterprises of Sir Humphrey Gilbert*, first published 1940, Hakluyt Society, Second Series, 2010

Richardson, R.E., *Mistress Blanche, Queen Elizabeth I's Confidante,* Logaston Press, 2007

Rogers, W.H., Hamilton, *The Ancient Sepulchral Effigies and Monumental and Memorial Sculpture of Devon,* Pollard, 1877

Robinson, H., original letters relative to the English Reformation, (chiefly from the archives of Zurich), Cambridge University Press, 1846

Rose Troup, F., *The Western Rebellion of 1549,* University of Toronto, 1913

Ryan, L.V., *Life of Roger Ascham,* Stanford University Press, 1963

Scaid, M., *Tudor Survivor: The Life of Sir William Paulet,* The History Press, 2011

Shanette, H., *Elizabeth's Ladies Maids and Gentlewomen,* Pen and Sword Books, 2025

Sil, N.P., *Denny, Anthony (1501–1549) Courtier*, ODNB, 2004

Simon, J., *Education and Society in Tudor England,* first published Cambridge University Press, 1966, paperback edn, 1979

Sitwell, Dame E., *Fanfare for Elizabeth,* first published Macmillan, 1946, [Kindle edn], Bloomsbury, 2011

Snell, L.S., *The Suppression of the Religious Houses of Devon and Cornwall*, Wordens of Cornwall, 1967

Soberton, S.B., *The Forgotten Tudor Women: Gertrude Courtenay: Wife and Mother of the Last Plantagenets,* independently published, [Kindle edn], 2021

Somerset, A., *Elizabeth 1,* Orion, 1997

Starkey, D., *Elizabeth, The Struggle for the Throne,* Harper, 2007

Stebbing, W., *Sir Walter Raleigh A Biography,* Clarenden Press, 1889

Stone, I., *The Crisis of the Aristocracy* 1558–1641, Abridged edn, Oxford University Press, 1965

Strickland, A., *The Life of Queen Elizabeth*, one of twelve volumes entitled *Lives of the Queens of England From the Norman Conquest*, first published between 1840–1848, [Kindle edn], Hard Press, 2018

Strype, J., *Survey of London,* first published 1720, London County Council, 1900

Strype, J., *The Life of the Learned John Cheke*, Clarenden, 1821

Tallis, Nicola, *Young Elizabeth,* O'Mara, 2024

Wagner, J., *The Devon Gentleman: A Life of Sir Peter Carew*, The University of Hull Press, 1998

Weir, A., *Henry VIII, King and Court*, Random House, 2001

Weisener, L., edited from the French by Yonge, C.M., *The Youth of Queen Elizabeth,* Oxford University Press, 1879

Westcott, M.R., *Katherine, Countess of Devon, (1479–1527) princess,* ODNB, 2004

Wheatley, H.B. and Cunningham, P., *London Past and Present; Its History, Associations and Traditions*, Murray, 1891

Whitelock, A., *Elizabeth's Bedfellows*, Bloomsbury, 2013

Whiting, R., *The Blind Devotion of the People,* University of Cambridge, 1989

Wilson, V., *Queen Elizabeth's Maids of Honour and Ladies of the Privy Chamber,* Lane, 1922

Youings, J., *The Dissolution of the Monasteries*, Allen and Unwin, 1971

Index